The Green Corporation

The Green Corporation

The Next Competitive Advantage

Vasanthakumar N. Bhat

Q

QUORUM BOOKS
Westport, Connecticut • London

Library of Congress Cataloging-in-Publication Data

Bhat, Vasanthakumar N.
   The green corporation : the next competitive advantage /
Vasanthakumar N. Bhat.
      p.   cm.
   Includes bibliographical references and index.
   ISBN 0–89930–979–8 (alk. paper)
      1. Industrial management—Environmental aspects. 2. Environmental
auditing. 3. Competition—Environmental aspects. I. Title.
   HD30.255.B49   1996
   658.4'08—dc20   95–41389

British Library Cataloguing in Publication Data is available.

Library of Congress Catalog Card Number: 95–41389
ISBN: 0–89930–979–8

First published in 1996

Quorum Books, 88 Post Road West, Westport, CT 06881
An imprint of Greenwood Publishing Group, Inc.

Printed in the United States of America

♾™

The paper used in this book complies with the
Permanent Paper Standard issued by the National
Information Standards Organization (Z39.48–1984).

10 9 8 7 6 5 4 3 2 1

Copyright Acknowledgments

The author and publisher gratefully acknowledge permission to use extracts from
the following.

Sixteen Principles of the Business Charter for Sustainable Development are reprinted
with permission of the International Chamber of Commerce.

IoPP Packaging Reduction, Recycling, and Disposal Guidelines, 1990, are reprinted
with permission of the Institute of Packaging Professionals.

CERES Principles, September 7, 1989, Revised April 18, 1992, are reprinted with
permission of the Coalition for Environmentally Responsible Economies.

Responsible Care®: Guiding Principles, 1988, are reprinted with permission of the
Chemical Manufacturers Association.

Environmental Reporting in a Total Quality Management Framework: A Primer,
1994, is reprinted with permission of Global Environmental Management Initiative.

HD
30,255
.B49
1996

Contents

Illustrations

Preface

Over the last 25 years, the United States has made great strides in eliminating most of the harmful effects of pollution and waste. The air most Americans breathe is clean, more than 60 percent of rivers and streams are suitable for fishing and swimming, and many dangerous hazardous waste sites have been identified and are being cleaned. However, a clean environment is not free. Americans pay about $115 billion a year to reduce pollution and environmental degradation. U.S. companies spend less than 1 percent of their sales revenue on environmental capital and operating expenditures. Studies show that environmental regulations reduce productivity. Employee layoffs are blamed on environmental regulations. Company executives argue that environmental regulations are putting them at a severe competitive disadvantage with foreign firms that are not subject to such restrictions. They claim that stringent environmental regulations are driving new plants and jobs abroad.

This book emphasizes that green does not mean inefficiency, lower productivity, increased layoffs, migration of new plants to other countries, smaller paychecks, and depressed profits. A preliminary analysis of some 250 companies indicates that lower emissions do mean higher profits and higher market values. Lower emissions also mean lower penalties and fewer spills. This book describes various techniques to prevent and reduce pollution and wastes.

While U.S. companies invest little sales revenue on environmental capital and operating expenditures, studies show that as much as 20 percent of their operating expenditures is environmentally related costs. In other words, U.S. companies spend a lot of money on raw materials, labor, and other resources to produce wastes and then clean them up. In the process, many people get sick, many die, and many lawyers get rich. Companies must prevent generation of wastes in the first place, and an emphasis must be placed on pollution prevention rather than pollution control.

The pollution is not reduced when waste discharges into one medium are shifted into another medium. Therefore, reducing emissions into the atmosphere is not pollution reduction if it increases discharges into water or onto land. Similarly, if waste is reduced during manufacturing while waste generation increases during other phases of production, this does not constitute waste reduction. Waste is reduced only if the effects of all wastes generated during the life of a product are reduced. In short, pollution-elimination efforts should be directed toward all phases of a product's life, not just any singular phase.

Current accounting systems fail to consider total environmental costs and instead aggregate many environmental costs under the category of overhead. This results in the selection of wrong product mix, inaccurate pricing of products, and inappropriate choice or rejection of pollution-reduction alternatives. Full accounting is a prerequisite for both understanding the total costs of environmental degradations and achieving a green corporation.

Pollution control was the primary strategy of the 1970s. The passage and enforcement of many new regulations made compliance the predominant strategy of the 1980s. Companies are now learning that pollution prevention is the method for the 1990s. However, a polluting plant cannot be replaced overnight, and changing product specifications will take time. Companies must go through a slow learning process that involves a reordering of priorities. Pollution prevention is a long-term process that requires long-term planning. Pollution-prevention strategy must begin with strategic planning.

Decisions made during different phases of a product's development have a significant impact on pollution generation. For example, a decision made during design may lock a company into using a polluting manufacturing process during production. Greening is a start-to-finish process encompassing design, concurrent engineering, and product stewardship.

Greening also requires involvement of employees, suppliers, and consumers. Companies have developed experience in encouraging such participation through total quality management. Green auditing, benchmarking, and continuous improvement can help companies to reduce pollution continuously until it is eliminated.

To sum up, pollution prevention, full accounting, green strategic planning, green design, concurrent engineering, product stewardship, total green management, green auditing, and benchmarking are the tools for greening. This book explains how these tools can be used to the maximum advantage.

This book consists of 15 chapters divided into three parts. Part I deals with essential topics. Chapter 1 describes major environmental concerns. These concerns form the basis for goal setting. Chapter 2 deals with a systematic methodology for strategic planning. Chapter 3 provides an overview of federal environmental laws. Chapter 4 describes the life-cycle assessment process.

Part II deals with the greening of functional areas. Chapter 5 describes design strategies and evaluation methods for developing green products. Chapter 6 concerns green manufacturing and Chapter 7, green packaging. Chapter 8 explains green marketing including a product-stewardship program. Chapter 9 deals with in-plant, off-plant, and postconsumer recycling. Chapter 10 explains green communication techniques, particularly disclosure guidelines.

Part III contains a description of the tools needed for greening a company. Total green management is explained in Chapter 12. Chapter 13 outlines a system of green auditing and contains the U.S. Environmental Protection Agency's guidelines for green auditing. Chapter 14 describes green benchmarking. Chapter 15 discusses green markets and careers.

There are two appendixes. In Appendix I the effects of environmental capital expenditure on profit margins are explored. Appendix II presents an analysis on the relationships among market values, profit margins, and companies with low emissions.

While this book is geared primarily toward an audience comprising practicing managers and students of business and engineering, others interested in green management should find it an accessible and useful starting point with many references for further studies contained within. I welcome your comments about this book.

I

INTRODUCTION

1

The Green Corporation

Growing population, rising deficits, public opinion, strict enforcement of environmental laws, increasing tort liabilities, and effects of the environment on competitiveness are forcing companies to be green. Loss of market share to green products is forcing companies to operate differently. The insight that prevention of waste is less expensive than its safe disposal is causing companies to reevaluate their environmental strategies. The gut feeling among the managers that greenness is tantamount to efficiency is inducing managers to consider the environment as an additional dimension on which to evaluate their day-to-day decisions. Love Canal, Bhopal, Three-Mile Island, Prince William Sound, and other disasters have compelled people around the globe to demand corporate responsibility. U.S. businesses are inundated with environmental challenges.

GREEN CHALLENGES

The Population Time Bomb

The world population is increasing exponentially. In 1991 the population growth rate was about 1.7 percent. At this rate the world's population can double every 40 years. Along with a population growth rate comes a rise in human activities and demand for products. Figure 1.1 displays worldwide increases in various human activities from 1950 to 1990. Though population only doubled from 1950 to 1990, the number of registered automobiles increased 7.25-fold, the world gross domestic product grew almost five times, and energy consumption increased about four times. Metal consumption rose by six times and aluminum consumption skyrocketed by 1,000 percent.[1]

Improving health care and a sluggish adoption of family-planning methods are increasing the population of developing countries at a faster rate than that of the developed countries. Consequently, 90 to 95

FIGURE 1.1
World Growth in Human Activities, 1950–90

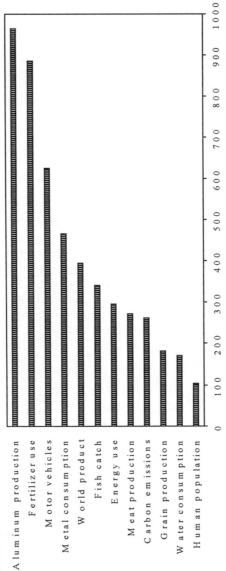

Source: Walter H. Corson and Henry R. Norman, "Global Environmental Issues and Sustainable Resource Management," in *Environmental Strategies Handbook*, ed. Rao V. Kolluru (New York: McGraw-Hill, 1994), p. 930.

percent of the population increase is found in developing countries. Increasing population will put dramatic pressures on the environment. Forests are generally the first casualty as more wood will be cut for fuel needs. Land degradation that usually accompanies increased population will reduce food production and cause famine in several parts of the world. When food production cannot keep up with population growth, malnourishment and poor health will result. According to Thomas Homer-Dixon, Jeffrey Boutwell, and George Rathjens, the population is likely to skyrocket to 9 billion within the next 50 years.[2] Global output of goods and services will rise fivefold. Fertile farm areas will diminish. The forests and species inhabiting them will vanish. Resource shortages will result in violent conflicts.

Stratospheric Ozone Depletion

The ozone layer in the stratosphere protects the earth from harmful solar ultraviolet radiations. However, the ozone layer is being destroyed by chemicals. The growing population and rising standards of living across the globe are dramatically changing the global atmospheric composition. Chlorofluorocarbons (CFCs) are the major culprits. CFCs are found in refrigeration, aerosols, and foams and are used for sterilization, food freezing, heat detecting, and fire fighting. CFCs are stable, nontoxic compounds. They do not corrode materials and they are excellent insulators. Their boiling points make them excellent coolants for refrigerators. They are good cleaning agents. As a result production of CFCs rose 500 percent from 1960 to 1985.[3] Despite their usefulness, the harmful effects of CFCs outweigh their benefits. Increased ultraviolet radiations because of ozone depletion can cause skin cancer, eye damage, and immune response system suppression. Wheat, rice, corn, and soybeans can be adversely affected by increased ultraviolet radiations, which can also harm aquatic and terrestrial ecosystems. Excess concentrations of ozone at ground levels are a major health concern. In 1993 about 51.3 million people in the United States lived in counties with ozone levels above those considered safe by the U.S. Environmental Protection Agency (EPA).[4] International boundaries cannot protect a country from the effects of ozone depletions. The U.S. EPA banned CFCs in aerosols in 1978 and there are international agreements to phase out CFCs by the year 2000.

The Greenhouse Effect

The greenhouse effect represents the warming of the atmosphere by pollutants. The atmosphere has become a major dumping ground for emissions. U.S. industries released 1,845 million pounds of wastes into the atmosphere in 1992 alone.[5] That is about 58 percent of all emissions by industries in the United States. Such a dramatic dumping of wastes into the atmosphere is changing its composition. The atmosphere is unable to cope with the plethora of gases emitted into it. These gases, such as carbon dioxide, methane, nitrous oxide, and CFCs, block infrared radiations. Gases in the atmosphere stabilize global climate by regulating the earth's absorption of heat from the sun and the radiation of heat back into the atmosphere. Concentration of these gases in the lower atmosphere and troposphere can significantly reduce the radiation from the earth's surface. This increases the temperature of the earth's surface and its atmosphere. Deforestation, combustion of fossil fuels, rice cultivation, and mining have steadily contributed to the concentration of greenhouse gases. Carbon dioxide accounts for about 50 percent of the greenhouse effect. The United States produces about one-fifth of the world's 5.7 billion tons of carbon dioxide. The per capita generation of carbon dioxide by the United States grew from 4.57 million metric tons in 1950 to 5.33 million metric tons in 1991.[6] There is general consensus that the rising concentrations of these gases will ultimately increase earth's temperature and will result in worldwide changes in the global climate. Sea levels will rise due to thermal expansions and melting of ice. Rising temperatures will destroy crops. Famine will increase in arid regions such as those in Africa and Asia.

Acid Rain

Coal-burning power stations and ore smelters emit enormous amounts of sulfur dioxide. Automobiles and power plants produce nitrous oxides. These gases are converted into sulfuric acid, nitric acid, ammonium sulfate, and ozone. The United States produced 21.9 million short tons of sulfur dioxide and 23.4 million short tons of nitrous oxide in 1993.[7] Deposition of sulfur dioxide and nitrogen oxides causes acidification of lakes and streams. Acidic deposition, called acid rain, contaminates lakes, kills fish, damages trees, and destroys forests. About half of the acid rain in Canada is caused by the U.S. emissions. Figure 1.2 presents U.S. emissions of sulfur dioxide, nitrogen oxide, volatile organic compounds, and carbon monoxide during the 1984–93 period.[8] About 1.4 million people in the United States live in counties with sulfur dioxide levels above that which is considered safe by the U.S. EPA.

Vanishing Forests

Two billion hectares of forests disappeared from the surface of the earth from the time humans invented agriculture. One billion hectares of forests disappeared during the last 40 years alone. Out of 4 billion hectares of forests that currently exist only 1.5 billion hectares are undisturbed primary forest. About 85 percent of primary forests have vanished in the United States, and very little remains in Europe.[9]

FIGURE 1.2
U.S. Emissions of Air Pollutants, 1984–93 (in million short tons)

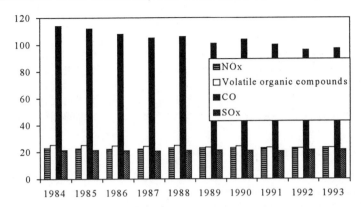

Source: Council on Environmental Quality, *Environmental Quality, Twenty-fourth Annual Report* (Washington, D.C.: Government Printing Office, 1995), pp. 435–440.

Rain forests play a vital role in the well-being of the earth by converting carbon dioxide into oxygen. Rain forests, which cover one-fourteenth of the earth's land surface, reduce soil erosion, prevent desertification, and provide a habitat for thousands of species. However, logging for timber and clearing for cultivation, cattle ranching, and resource development are depleting rain forests on such a massive scale as to threaten the earth's ecosystems. Increasing carbon dioxide in the atmosphere can accelerate global warming and endanger the habitats for half to two-thirds of all living species on the planet. Several crops we currently consume originally came from tropical rain forests. The cutting of trees from rain forests not only hastens desertification but also causes flooding and soil erosion.

Widening Income Disparities

Poverty in the developing countries is one of the most pressing environmental problems. According to the World Commission on Environment and Development, also known as the Brundtland Commission, acute poverty generally accompanies environmental degradation.[10] The richest 20 percent enjoyed about 83 percent of GNP in 1989 as compared with only 1.4 percent enjoyed by the poorest 20 percent. The disparities in trade, commercial bank lending, domestic investment, domestic savings, and foreign private investments are very significant.[11]

Rising Garbage

The United States generated about 13 billion tons of nonhazardous solid waste including 200 million tons of municipal solid waste in 1992. The generation of municipal solid waste on a per capita and overall basis is rising. The per capita generation of solid waste in the United States rose from 2.7 pounds per person per day in 1960 to 4.4 pounds per person per day in 1993. About 62.4 percent of all municipal solid waste generated in the United States is placed in landfills. Increased garbage disposal destroys both renewable and nonrenewable materials.

Hazardous and Toxic Wastes

Industries currently use about 100,000 chemicals worldwide and thousands of chemicals are being introduced every year. Extensive testing of these chemicals needs to be done before they can be introduced for commercial use. However, toxicity information about many chemicals is very scanty. The world produces 1 million tons of hazardous waste every day. Ninety percent of this waste is produced in the developed countries. According to the 1992 Toxic Release Inventory Public Data Release,[12] U.S. industries produced about 37.3 billion pounds of toxic chemicals and emitted about 3.182 billion pounds of toxic chemicals into the land, waters, and air. Each day, on average, five industrial accidents involving hazardous wastes occur in the United States.

Water Quality

About 70 percent of the earth's surface is covered by seawater. About six-tenths of the world's population lives within 60 miles of the coasts. More than 75 percent of fresh water is found in glaciers and icecaps. Another 22 percent of fresh water is in the ground. About 3,000 cubic kilometers of water are consumed every year. The total runoff of all the streams and rivers of the world is about 41,000 cubic kilometers. This means that only about 7 percent of this runoff is being consumed every year. However, because most runoff is seasonal, the total potential of runoff cannot be exploited. It is almost impossible to store 41,000 cubic kilometers of water. As a result, 28,000 cubic kilometers of water per year flow into the sea. Mismatches of water supply with demand and high transportation costs make water scarce in several parts of the world. Countries dependent on water supplies whose rivers originate in other countries have fought wars for water. India and Pakistan; Chile and Bolivia; Jordan and Syria; and Syria, Iraq, and Turkey have all engaged in water-related conflicts. In such countries as Ethiopia some women travel miles to find water and carry it home. By 2025, such countries as Algeria, Cyprus, Egypt, Haiti, Iran, South Africa, and Tanzania will have less than 1,000 cubic meters of water per person per year, the minimum considered necessary per year in a developed country. Such countries as Libya, Saudi Arabia, and Jordan will have far less than 100 cubic meters per person per year.[13] Though the Clean Water Act and Safe Drinking Water Act have been passed in the United States to ensure water quality, a lack of resources has impeded effective enforcements of these two acts.

Green Organizations

About one in seven Americans is actively involved with green organizations.[14] Green organizations are using their muscle to develop tough regulations. Alar would not have been withdrawn promptly without the involvement of green organizations. Memberships in green organizations are rising. Between 1980 and 1989, the membership in green organizations rose between 40 and 670 percent. The Wilderness Society had its membership rolls increase from 45,000 in 1980 to 317,000 in 1989.[15] Environmental groups can only apply pressure; it is up to the company to take actions to be green. Provisions in most of the federal environmental laws for citizens' suits have dramatically increased the clout of green organizations. Any citizen can to go federal court to prevent a company from violating the relevant federal laws or the permit terms and force compliance with the laws. Environmental and citizen groups filed 78 lawsuits under the National Environmental Policy Act to force various federal agencies to comply with the act's requirements in 1991 alone.[16]

Green Laws

Green laws are exploding. The U.S. Congress, states, and localities are enacting many laws and regulations with which companies must comply. Rising threats of lawsuits are forcing companies to change operations to reduce consequences of legal actions rather than take advantage of the benefits of environmental planning. During the 1980s an average of 100 companies were indicted for environmental crimes per year; seven in ten involved in criminal indictments were individuals; 12 percent of firms prosecuted were publicly traded stock companies; the median criminal fine for an organization was $50,000 and rising; and about one in three individuals convicted along with their corporate employers were to serve seven months of jail time, and more than one in two individuals convicted without a corporate defendant was to serve 18 months of jail time.[17] The U.S. government and industry are spending about $115 billion a year to comply with the environmental laws enacted over the last 20 years. By the end of the 1990s this amount will rise to $160 billion a year.[18] As a result, meeting compliance challenges of coming years will be one of the most pressing concerns of all companies.

Workplace Accidents

About 13 people die in the U.S. workplace each day and about 460 people are injured each hour. The economic consequences of such an astounding number of deaths and injuries were about $83 billion in 1989 alone, not counting economic losses from occupational illnesses.[19] Death and injuries also involve emotional costs and lower morale. Therefore, workplace accidents are of serious concern to corporate executives.

Environmental Equity

Considerable differences in death rates, life expectancy, and disease rates exist among whites, African Americans, and Hispanic Americans. Though African Americans and Hispanic Americans are generally poorer, less educated, and more likely to be unemployed than whites, the factors that create these disparities are not clear. However, more African Americans and Hispanic Americans than whites live in EPA-designated air quality nonattainment areas.[20] Other studies indicate that ethnic minorities and the poor are likely to reside in the vicinity of incinerators and hazardous waste sites. In response to a study conducted in 1987 by the United Church of Christ,[21] which found an insidious form of racism in the locations of hazardous waste dumps, the term *environmental racism* was introduced. According to Ben Goldman, racial and ethnic minorities face far greater exposure to environmental risks than nonminority populations.[22] According to the *National Law Journal*,[23] penalties for crimes committed in white communities are higher than those in nonwhite neighborhoods, and the time it takes to clean up sites in minority communities is longer than the cleanup time of white neighborhoods.

Summary of Green Challenges

Green challenges include: the population bomb, rising consumption, soil degradation, wildlife management, energy efficiency, stratospheric ozone depletion, the greenhouse effect, air pollution and its globalization, acid rain, indoor radon, radiation, water pollution, deterioration of the wetlands, drinking water pollution, groundwater contamination, scarcity of landfills, accidental release of toxic gases, oil spills, pesticide residues in food, new toxic substances, workplace accidents, deforestation, toxic waste generation, waste treatment and disposal, recycling and recovery, urbanization, global transportation of pollutants, climate changes, the explosion of environmental knowledge, information and knowledge transfer, green laws, green groups, and green equity.

THE GREEN CORPORATION:
THE NEXT COMPETITIVE ADVANTAGE

Pollution is expensive. It increases compliance costs. A company generating a significant quantity of waste can be subject to fines and cleanup and litigation costs. Pollution reduces efficiency and increases costs because wastes discharged contain expensive materials, labor, and overhead. Wastes also contain energy inputs for which a company has paid. In addition, wastes generated need to be transported and disposed of, which costs additional money. New community right-to-know laws require companies to inform the public of the quantities of wastes discharged. These disclosures are public relations nightmares. A polluting image can turn away customers, investors, and suppliers. Banks and financial institutions may be afraid to extend loans to a polluting company. Insurance premiums for various kinds of risks will be higher. Employees may prefer not to work for a company with poor environmental records. Health and environment are closely related. Severe air pollution is generally associated with illness and increased mortality rates. Smog and other types of air pollution can worsen respiratory, heart, and other health problems. Four out of five cancers are directly or indirectly attributed to environmental pollutants. Hazardous substances such as benzene can cause cancer, leukemia, and nausea; cadmium can damage the liver and kidneys; lead can cause mental impairment in children; and mercury can damage the brain. Water pollutants can cause cancer, and trihalomethane can damage kidneys. Airborne pollutants such as carbon monoxide can cause unconsciousness and death; CFCs can increase ultraviolet radiations, in turn causing cancer and eye disorders; ground-level ozone can aggravate lung and heart disease; and sulfur dioxide can cause eye irritation. A rough analysis presented in Appendix II indicates that investors are likely to value a polluting company less than a green company. If the world looks at the polluting companies with a jaundiced eye, then why do companies continue to pollute? According to a provocative article in the *Harvard Business Review*, "It's Not Easy Being Green," Noah Walley and Bradley Whitehead argue that tackling green problems is a no-win situation for managers.[24] U.S. companies are spending too much money on the environment with no economic return. Therefore, they challenge the company's green strategies on the assumption of win-win situations.

It is true that the U.S. companies spend too much money on pollution abatement. However, capital and operating expenses of the U.S. manufacturers for pollution abatement and control as a percentage of sales were only about 0.9 percent of sales in 1991.[25] Those who consider these costs to be high should examine a company's overall environmentally driven costs. According to the World Resources Institute case studies, environmental costs can be as high as 20 percent of the total operating costs. The costs of materials, labor, and overhead contained in disposed wastes, compliance costs, additional power and water consumed, costs of packaging, and costs of record keeping, for example, are recorded under categories *other than* environmentally related costs, thus magnifying costs of compliance. In addition, many costs such as increased mortality rates and illness among employees and community residents surrounding plants are borne by society. These cost distortions force companies to choose wrong product mix and waste reduction options, use inappropriate inputs, and price products wrongly. An example of road salt usage will illustrate this problem. Road salt is used to reduce driving risks on icy roads. A ton of road salt costs about $40 but causes about $1,400 in damages. However, calcium magnesium acetate can reduce many harms caused by the road salt. However, it costs about $650. So a person who needs to decide what product he should use to reduce icing problems is likely to choose road salt rather than calcium magnesium acetate because he is looking for the most cost-effective solution from his point of view, not from society's point of view.[26] Until we have accounting systems that capture all costs, wrong decisions will continue to be made and industries will continue to be apprehensive about turning green.

Currently environmental strategies in many companies are driven by regulations. As a result, companies are retrofitting existing equipment with pollution-reduction accessories rather than working to eliminate pollution. Companies then blame regulations for increased costs and reduced competitiveness. Recent studies indicate that superior environmental performance is not associated with reduced profits.[27]

A preliminary analysis presented in Appendix II indicates that investors assign higher valuations to companies with lower emission levels. A life-cycle perspective can increase options and reduce pollution significantly. Total green management can encourage employee involvement. The notion that companies have employed simple measures to reduce pollution and that further pollution reduction would be too difficult is wrong. Continuous improvement is the name of the game. Figure 1.3 presents the efficacy of lightbulbs in lumens per watt along with their lifetimes. During the last 100 years, the efficacy has gone up from 1 lm/watt to 150 lm/watt, and lifetime hours have risen to more than 7,500 hours in 1975.[28] Anyone who thinks that only simple measures have been employed should look at efficiency increases gained by technological means of meeting the lighting demand.

When computers were first introduced in the 1950s, opponents argued that computers would make certain jobs obsolete. At first companies simply computerized existing manual systems, with the result of more jobs being created. After three to four decades, companies learned how to look at their operations as a whole rather than as individual departments. The total quality management revolutionized employee involvement. In recent years, more companies have learned

FIGURE 1.3

Efficacy in Lumen/Watt and Lifetime Hours of Technological Means of Meeting the Lighting Demand (for White Light)

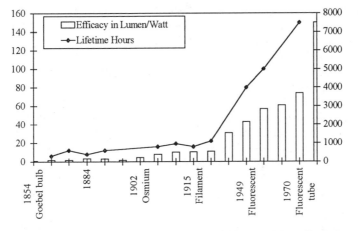

Source: Heinz-Dieter Haustein, *Innovation and Efficiency* (New York: Pergamon Press, 1985), pp. 225–231.

how best to use computers and maximize productivity. Understandably, it will take several decades for companies to learn and exploit pollution elimination strategy.

In the 1980s West Germany had some of the toughest environmental standards. Yet according to recent environmental damage accounting, pollution caused damage of over 104 billion DM ($58 billion) in 1984 alone. This represents approximately 6 percent of the West German Gross National Product.[29] According to the Organization for Economic Cooperation and Development, it is possible for West Germany to reduce waste by 50–60 percent using low-level technologies.[30]

According to a survey of senior executives, companies are finding green opportunities in their core business. Various opportunities and their percentages are as follows:[31]

Reduced waste-disposal costs	73%
Improved reputation for greenness	69%
Reduced costs	61%
Effective operations	55%
Green packaging	42%
Green marketing of existing products	33%
New green product opportunities	32%
Pollution-control equipment	20%
Compliance consulting	6%

After all, environmental management is not about costs alone.

Based on the environmental performance, companies can be categorized into red, yellow, and green (Table 1.1). Red companies, because of recent negative experiences such as permit violations, accidental releases, waste disposal liabilities, explosions in the plant, and so on, have decided to end the "business as usual" posture and support improved compliance of laws and regulations. Such companies solve environmental problems in a "fire-fighting" mode. Their planning horizon is typically a week or month. Emphasis for pollution reduction is unit operation. Approach is piecemeal. Compliance is achieved through either waste treatment or incineration. Red companies try to lobby legislatures to relax environmental laws. Environmental departments of such companies are typically headed by people from legal departments. The process of waste reduction is subject to inspection and corrective maintenance; it has no public relations agenda and it follows reactive strategy. All company decisions are based solely on cost. Employees receive little training in environmental matters. Management style is paternal and communication is top-down only. Management involvement is virtually nonexistent. Rules and regulations drive red companies' environmental programs. The company typically blames its employees and suppliers for its environmental mishaps.

Companies typically go from red to yellow by some initiatives that force top management to take action. Passage of a regulation that significantly increases the pollution control cost may be one reason for such a transition. Accidents such as those at Bhopal, *Valdez*, and Rhine River can cause panic among board members to demand improved environmental performance from their managers. Community right-to-know legislations and investors' actions could be events that trigger a company's desire to become a yellow company. Yellow companies have moved beyond a fire-fighting mode. Their goal is zero violations. Management is oriented to preventing environmental problems. The planning timeframe is usually about a year and the planning process typically involves identification of actions to prevent mishaps. The pollution-reduction programs have moved up to plant level. Frequently used pollution-reduction techniques include recycling and improved housekeeping. Cooperation is evident between the legal and operations departments. Yellow companies try to prevent environmental problems by engaging in preventive activities.

The color green represents the ultimate stage in environmental responsibility. Companies become green not only because they want to comply with laws, improve their image, and reduce costs but also because they believe that it is the right thing to do. It is this green consciousness that drives these companies to be green. Improved compliance, reduced costs, increased sales, better image, and reduction of liability risks are secondary motivators. The company management has clearly articulated its environmental policies and whole

TABLE 1.1
Red, Yellow, and Green Corporations

Features	Red Corporation	Yellow Corporation	Green Corporation
Management approach	Problem solving	Problem preventing	Opportunity seeking
Time horizon	Short term	Medium term	Long term
Top management involvement	Nonexistent	Not wholehearted	Intense and continuous involvement
Organization	Unit operation	Plant	Companywide
Manager responsible for environment	Legal department	Plant or legal department	Chief executive officer
Company policy	Nonexistent	Not well written	Comprehensive
Driving force	Laws and regulations	Costs of compliance	Opportunities
Strategy	Cure	Prevention	Prevention
Pollution-reduction techniques	Treatment, landfilling, and incineration	Recycling and better housekeeping	Source reduction and housekeeping
Public relations	Responds to accidents	Responds to accidents	Systematic and well-organized
Supplier selection	Only price	Price and selected green factors	Price and selected green factors
Training	Nonexistent	Not well organized	Lifelong and systematic
Management style	Paternal	Somewhat paternal	Egalitarian
R&D	Nonexistent	Compliance-oriented	Focused on new opportunities
Use of resources	Ineffective	Somewhat effective	Efficient and effective
Communication	Top-down	Mostly top-down	Two way
Green performance	Violations, permit denials, discharges, spills	Amount of waste reduced, disposal costs	Cradle to grave, audits, life-cycle assessment, benchmarking
Reward system	Blame for violations and accidents	Blame for violations and small reward for compliance	Green performance major factor
Technology	Compliance oriented	Reduced compliance costs in products and services	Continuous integration

commitment and support for green programs. The person responsible for environmental management reports to the board of directors or the chairperson. She allocates adequate resources for green programs. The corporation has effective training programs developed for various levels of employees. The purpose of environmental planning is to seek out opportunities for profit improvements and cost reductions. Long-term planning is emphasized. Environmental programs are companywide and a systems approach is used to identify green opportunities. Managers responsible for environmental planning try to anticipate future regulatory changes and take steps to reduce the costs of future regulatory changes. Rules and regulations are not viewed as constraints. Rather, they are considered cost-reduction and profit-improvement measures. Tough rules and regulations are exploited to build competitive advantages. Source reduction is the primary waste-reduction technique. Life-cycle assessment, benchmarking, and environmental auditing are well-established practices in the company. Green corporations have well-developed green marketing programs, and two-way communication is apparent. A green corporation discloses risks to employees, communities, and the public at large. Employees are evaluated and rewarded based on green performance in an egalitarian work setting. Top management's involvement in environmental affairs is intense and continuous. Suppliers are chosen based on cost and environmental performance. Top management is also accountable for any violations, accidents, or defects, and it is guided by a belief that green performance can always be improved.

CONCLUSION

Green corporations, by sheer exploitation of environmental opportunities, have created a competitive advantage that only another green corporation can overcome. This book presents a blueprint for such a corporation.

NOTES

1. Walter H. Corson and Henry R. Norman, "Global Environmental Issues and Sustainable Resource Management," in *Environmental Strategies Handbook*, ed. Rao V. Kolluru (New York: McGraw-Hill, 1994), p. 930.

2. Thomas F. Homer-Dixon, Jeffrey H. Boutwell, and George W. Rathjens, "Environmental Change and Violent Conflict," *Scientific American*, February 1993, pp. 38–45.

3. Joseph P. Glas, "Protecting the Ozone Layer: A Perspective from Industry," in *Technology and Environment*, ed. Jesse H. Ausubel and Hedy E. Sladovich (Washington, D.C.: National Academy Press, 1989), p. 144.

4. Council on Environmental Quality, *Environmental Quality, Twenty-fourth Annual Report* (Washington, D.C.: Government Printing Office, 1995), p. 447.

5. U.S. Environmental Protection Agency, *1992 Toxics Release Inventory: Public Data Release*, EPA 745-R-94-001 (Washington, D.C.: Government Printing Office, 1994), p. 4.

6. Council on Environmental Quality, *Environmental Quality, Twenty-fourth Annual Report*, p. 442.

7. Ibid., pp. 435–436.

8. Ibid., pp. 435–440.

9. Donella H. Meadows, Dennis L. Meadows, and Jorgen Randers, *Beyond the Limits: Confronting Global Collapse, Envisioning a Sustainable Future* (Post Mills, Vt.: Chelsea Green, 1992), p. 57.

10. World Commission on Environment and Development, *Our Common Future* (Oxford: Oxford University Press, 1987), p. 8.

11. Neil Middleton, Phil O'Keefe, and Sam Moyo, *The Tears of the Crocodile* (London: Pluto Press, 1993), p. 18.

12. U.S. Environmental Protection Agency, *1992 Toxics Release Inventory*, p. 3.

13. Homer-Dixon, Boutwell, and Rathjens, "Environmental Change and Violent Conflict," pp. 38–45.

14. "Seeing the Green Light," *The Economist*, October 20, 1990, p. 88.

15. Matthew Alan Cahn, *Environmental Deceptions: The Tension between Liberalism and Environmental Policymaking in the United States* (Albany: State University of New York Press, 1995), p. 152.

16. Council on Environmental Quality, *Environmental Quality, Twenty-third Annual Report* (Washington, D.C.: Government Printing Office, 1993), p. 167.

17. T. H. Tietenberg, "Introduction and Overview," in *Innovation in Environmental Policy*, ed. T. H. Tietenberg (Brookfield, Vt.: Edward Elgar, 1991), pp. 9–10.

18. U.S. General Accounting Office, *Environmental Protection Issues*, GAO/OCG-93-16TR (Washington, D.C.: Government Printing Office, 1993), p. 4.

19. U.S. General Accounting Office, *Occupation Safety and Health*, GAO/HRD-92-68 (Washington, D.C.: Government Printing Office, 1992), p. 1.

20. U.S. Environmental Protection Agency, *Environmental Equity, Reducing Risk for All Communities*, vols. 1 and 2, EPA 230-R-92-008 and EPA 230-R-92-008A (Washington, D.C.: Government Printing Office, 1992), p. 14.

21. C. Lee, *Toxic Wastes and Race in the United States: A National Report on the Racial and Socio-economic Characteristics of Communities with Hazardous Waste Sites* (New York: United Church of Christ, Commission for Racial Justice, 1987).

22. B. A. Goldman, *The Truth about Where You Live: An Atlas for Action on Toxins and Mortality* (New York: Times Books, 1991).

23. Marianne Lavelle and Macia Coyle, "Unequal Protection: The Racial Divide in Environmental Law," *National Law Journal*, 15(3) (September 21, 1992): p. S2..

24. Noah Walley and Bradley Whitehead, "It's Not Easy Being Green," *Harvard Business Review* 72 (May–June 1994): 46–52.

25. Daryl Ditz, Janet Ranganathan, and R. Darryl Banks, *Green Ledgers: Case Studies in Corporate Environmental Accounting* (Washington, D.C.: World Resources Institute, May 1995), p. 7.

26. Carl L. Henn and James A. Fava, "Life-cycle Analysis and Resource Management," in *Environmental Strategies Management*, ed. Rao V. Kolluru (New York: McGraw-Hill, 1994), p. 575.

27. Robert Repetto, *Jobs, Competitiveness, and Environmental Regulation: What Are the Real Issues?* (Washington, D.C.: World Resources Institute, 1995), p. 18.

28. Heinz-Dieter Haustein, *Innovation and Efficiency* (New York: Pergamon Press, 1985), pp. 225–231.

29.   Ernest Callenbach, Fritjof Capra, Lenore Goldman, Rudiger Lutz, and Sandra Marburg, *Ecomanagement* (San Francisco: Barrett-Koehler Publishers, 1993), p. 4.

30.   Organization for Economic Cooperation and Development, *The State of the Environment, Annual Report, 1991* (Paris: Organization for Economic Cooperation and Development, 1991), p. 197.

31.   John C. Newman and Kay M. Breeden, "Managing in the Environmental Era: Lessons from Environmental Leaders," *Columbia Journal of World Business* 27 (Fall and Winter 1992): 210–221.

2

Green Management Begins with Strategic Planning

In no other field is the old saying "an ounce of prevention is worth a pound of cure" more appropriate than in pollution reduction. Growing public concern and legislative actions are forcing corporate executives to do more than pay lip service to the goal of pollution abatement. Multimillion-dollar liability suits, stricter civil and criminal enforcement of environmental regulations, community pressures, and skyrocketing cleanup costs have driven pollution issues into corporate boardrooms. Board members are demanding definitive actions against pollution from their operations managers. As regulations become more stringent and state-of-the-art pollution-disposal technologies are installed, the pollution-disposal costs will escalate dramatically in the industrialized world. Pollution-reduction costs in the United States alone soared to $174 billion in 1995 from $56 billion in 1989. In addition, the U.S. Environmental Protection Agency estimates $450 billion will be needed just to upgrade and construct water- and sewage-treatment plants over the next decade.[1] As environmental regulations become more severe all over the world, pollution elimination becomes an appealing alternative compared with environmentally compatible waste disposal. Pollution reduction, to be effective, requires careful planning and implementation. Pollution-reduction programs should not be isolated from other functions of a firm but should support a firm's overall strategic plan. Pollution reduction should not be viewed as a public relations ploy but rather as a shrewd competitive weapon. Moreover, pollution minimization can result in significant benefits for a firm. It can dramatically reduce costs through better use of resources and by eliminating the need for pollution treatment and disposal technologies. According to a conservative estimate, U.S. companies can dramatically increase profits and enhance global competitiveness through pollution reduction, as they presently generate five times the pollution per dollar of revenue compared with Japanese companies and more than twice that of German companies.[2]

Smart companies, such as DuPont, Monsanto, Dow Chemical, Minnesota Mining and Manufacturing (3M), and several other blue-chip firms, have already developed plans to reduce and eliminate wastes. However, planning for pollution reduction has not yet become widespread among smaller companies. In the meantime, the problems of pollution are so great that planning for pollution abatement must be done along with the firm's strategic planning. While every firm's pollution problems are different, it is possible to outline a general planning procedure to develop strategies for pollution reduction in a wide range of companies. The following nine steps are essential to formulating plans for pollution reduction.

1. Present a business strategy summary.
2. Assess company situations and circumstances.
3. Audit and analyze existing company facilities and operations.
4. Forecast future changes in regulations and operations.
5. Develop objectives.
6. Generate alternatives to achieve objectives and compliances.
7. Perform quantitative and financial analysis of alternatives.
8. Develop and implement action plans.
9. Audit and review the actual results.

These nine steps should be used to develop pollution-reduction programs and to decrease the likelihood of major alternatives being overlooked.

PRESENTING A BUSINESS STRATEGY SUMMARY

A business strategy summary, the output of a firm's strategic planning exercise, is the starting document for the pollution-reduction plan. This summary describes a firm's objectives and priorities, the products that will be developed over the next few years, life-cycle plans for existing products, new markets that will be penetrated, new manufacturing facilities that will be built, and so forth. A business strategy summary will help planners anticipate potential pollutants and formulate plans to either eliminate or mitigate them.

ASSESSING COMPANY SITUATIONS AND CIRCUMSTANCES

A second step in the development of plans for pollution reduction is to assess company situations and circumstances. The aim of this step is to collect information on a firm's products, processes, consumers, personnel, research and development, capital-raising ability, procedures, management and organization, and applicable environmental statutes that affect the company. It is important to note as well how the company responds to the regulations. The goal is to identify strengths and weaknesses of each functional area. Table 2.1 summarizes strengths and weaknesses of various factors.

TABLE 2.1
Assessing a Company's Strengths and Weaknesses

Strengths	*Weaknesses*
Products	
Do not endanger the environment	Do endanger the environment
Use recyclable materials	Use nonrenewable materials
Consume little energy	Consume too much energy
Generate little waste	Generate considerable waste
Do not use polluting materials	Use materials that threaten environment or endangered species
Processes	
Do not generate pollution	Generate pollution
Consume little energy	Consume a significant amount of energy
Very efficient	Very inefficient
No health hazards to employees and community	Health hazards to employees and community
Consumers	
Educated and concerned about the environment	Not concerned about the environment
Management	
Committed to environment	Not committed to environment
Demands beyond compliance	Does not demand compliance
Achieves whatever goals are set	Poor prior performance
Credible management	Ambivalent management
Senior management consists of environmental experts	No environmental leader among the senior management
Well drawn up environmental policies	No comprehensive policy on the environment
Line managers accountable for environmental performance	No environmental performance goals for line managers
Team work encouraged	Team work not encouraged
Reward system in place	No reward system in place
Personnel	
High skill level	Low skill level
Periodic training programs	No training programs
Employees sensitive to the environment	Lack of sensitivity to the environment
Research & Development	
History of innovations	No innovations
Time between innovations short	Long time between innovations

Every company must have an explicit written policy statement endorsed by its board demonstrating environmental commitment in every functional area. Typically, these policy statements emphasize integrated approaches to pollution reduction; environmental leadership goals; preference for prevention over cure; responsibility toward stakeholders, including employees, customers, stockholders, and the general public; and the importance of compliance and safety. Products should be evaluated for energy consumption, generation of wastes, and use of inputs that threaten the environment, endangered species, and so on. Typically, manufacturing generates the greatest quantities of wastes. Therefore, manufacturing processes should be examined for both inputs and outputs. The amounts of water consumed and discharged should be estimated. Energy consumption should also be determined.

Consumers play a significant role in the success or failure of a company. If consumers who use a company's products are environmentally sensitive, a company should take immediate action to improve the greenness of its products. These consumers generally include women and better-educated and upper-income individuals.

A well-trained staff is essential for any company to meet environmental challenges successfully. New regulations call for innovative methods, high technology equipment, improved process controls, and new materials. Therefore, any company trying to improve its environmental performance must have well-trained personnel at all levels.

Research and development is another essential area of expertise. Environmental regulations have made many products obsolete. Chlorofluorocarbons used in spray cans, refrigerators, air conditioners, and the electronics industry; daminozide (alar) used to preserve apples; and dichloro-diphenyl-trichloroethane are some products that have been withdrawn from markets because of their effects on the environment and human health. To come up with substitutes for these and other products, a company needs to employ new technologies. In addition, developing products that can easily be recycled, use less packaging, and do not contain harmful chemicals requires a company to have well-developed expertise in these areas.

Top management's ability to achieve performance goals should be evaluated. An organizational culture committed to environmental regulatory compliance is important for any pollution-reduction plan to succeed. Credibility of management, internal procedures, and teamwork are all factors that should be analyzed and evaluated to see how the organization fares.

Public relations plays a vital role in forming a favorable image about a company. Therefore, companies should provide clear instructions to managers about communications relating to employees, customers, shareholders, suppliers, the local community, and the public at large. Companies should evaluate steps they have taken to protect employees and surrounding communities from accidents and inadvertent release of chemical substances.

The status of the environmental department also affects environmental performance. If management treats the environmental department as an outsider, then this attitude needs to be changed. The environmental department should be involved in all decision making relating to production, marketing, and finance. The environmental department should not be viewed simply as another cost of doing business; rather, it should be seen as an opportunity-identifying resource. In addition, the environmental department should be an integral part of the management. Management should install effective management systems to hold line managers accountable for environmental performance. Environmental training and education should be a continuous process in the organization. Adequate resources should be allocated to the environmental department. Management should set measurable environmental goals for line managers. The organizational culture should encourage problem finding rather than problem hiding.

Assessing existing conditions and circumstances will provide a snapshot of a firm's total pollution-management system at any given time. Planners should be prepared to identify the incentives and barriers that will help guide the planning process through organizational mine fields. Common barriers include capital shortage, scarcity of technical personnel, competing priorities, and lack of management support. The report developed during this step describes how a firm is complying with various permits, guidelines, and regulatory requirements.

AUDITING AND ANALYZING EXISTING
FACILITIES AND OPERATIONS

The purpose of this step is to generate more detailed information about products, processes, types and quantities of wastes generated, existing treatment and disposal procedures, and so forth. Specifically, information regarding quantities of pollution generated, amounts of hazardous waste in the total waste produced, treatment and disposal costs, operating and management practices, compliance with environmental laws, employees' understanding of the environmental consequences of their actions, worker's compensation claims by plant workers, and so on are collected. The information gathered during this step will be of tremendous help not only in avoiding criminal, regulatory, and common law tort liabilities but also in uncovering opportunities for cost reduction and developing a system of policies and procedures to ensure compliance.

To formulate objectives for the quantity of pollution reduction possible, a firm needs an accurate estimate of the pollution generated at each stage of production. For this purpose, a firm should define pollutants and processing stages. This is the hardest thing to do as many processes must be examined in detail. One way to collect information about them is to construct flow diagrams. These diagrams indicate inputs, outputs, and wastes generated at each processing stage. The flow diagrams also describe quantities of raw materials that go into the final products; those transformed in the process; those released as solid, liquid, and vapor wastes; those parts of products that end as waste; any by-products produced; and so on. The material balance principle, based on the conservation of mass, may be used to get more accurate estimates of waste outputs than those that can be obtained from direct measurements. This principle, based on the conservation of mass, is particularly helpful when waste is produced in small quantities. The material balance principle will also assist in estimating the size and cost of additional equipment, piping, instrumentation, and economic performance. During this step, specific statistics regarding product and process, technology employed and its effects, facilities and equipment, accidents and injuries on the job, input materials, wastes generated, and other factors at each stage of production are to be collected and reviewed. The information collected from each process helps a firm to uncover opportunities and formulate targets for pollution abatement. Performing this step will allow a firm to have better information about its operations, strengths and weaknesses in complying, and a database for its strategic planning process.

FORECASTING FUTURE CHANGES IN REGULATIONS AND OPERATIONS

This is one of the most important steps in the planning for waste reduction. More than 70 percent of a product's costs are decided during product and process design stages, and the decisions are very difficult to reverse once they have been made. Consequently, if a product or process is found to have any pollution-related problems due either to the changes in the law or other circumstances, it will be very hard for a firm to salvage its investment. Increasing public pressures force legislatures to enact tougher pollution abatement statutes. As a result, conforming to pollution-control laws becomes exorbitantly expensive and future costs become more uncertain. Consider the chemical waste dump used by Hooker Chemical and Plastics Corporation in Love Canal, New York. Even though, according to Hooker, chemical wastes were disposed of by burying them in landfills (an acceptable method at the time), Hooker was forced to dig up the same waste and dispose of it again in a manner deemed safer a few years later.[3]

A firm must also identify wastes that are not yet restricted and take actions to cut them so that it can continue to maintain its competitive position. Instead of waiting for government deadlines, many firms are going ahead with their own plans to reduce wastes. For example, 3M replaced underground storage tanks for liquids and gases by 1992 instead of 1998 as required by federal regulations.[4] Besides identifying operations that do not conform to existing rules, a firm must forecast how future changes in the statutes will affect its operations.

A firm should systematically collect information regarding new products, equipment, and technologies used for pollution reduction. Innovative changes are taking place in manufacturing equipment and pollution-reduction equipment. A firm may find itself at a competitive disadvantage if it has not taken advantage of technological improvements.

DEVELOPING OBJECTIVES

Objectives should indicate the performance measures that a firm must achieve concerning pollutants generated. They should be expressed in quantitative terms. Environmental challenges discussed in Chapter 1 are some areas for the development of objectives. Reducing water consumption; increasing energy efficiency; conserving non-renewable resources; improving worker health and safety; preventing accidents; preparing for emergencies; reducing emissions into water, air, and land; increasing recycling initiatives; and reducing ozone-depleting emissions are some examples of objectives to respond to green challenges. Because compliance with laws and regulations is essential for the survival of any company, objectives relating to compliance must be set by top management. Objectives could also be established for measures that benefit stakeholders. Developing green products, improving greenness of suppliers, reducing inadvertent release of chemical substances, and reducing storage of toxic materials are some examples of corporate goals that will be looked upon favorably by stakeholders. The goal of compliance should not be just conformance with laws and regulations; compliance must reduce accidents and improve working conditions and safety. Therefore, objectives must be set for workplace safety. In short, objectives should be set for energy, health, and safety concerns; discharges into air, water, and land; compliance with laws and regulations; public relations; and research and development. At this stage, it is a good idea to look through various principles developed by business and industry groups. The 16 principles of the Business Charter for Sustainable Development given below could also be used to develop objectives.

1. *Corporate priority*. To recognize environmental management as among the highest corporate priorities and as a key determinant to sustainable development to establish policies, programs and practices for conducting operations in an environmentally sound manner.
2. *Integrated management*. To integrate these policies, programs and practices fully into each business as an essential element of management

in all its functions.

3. *Process of improvement.* To continue to improve corporate policies, programs and environmental performance, taking into account technical developments, scientific understanding, consumer needs and community expectations, with legal regulations as a starting point; and to apply the same environmental criteria internationally.

4. *Employee education.* To educate, train and motivate employees to conduct their activities in an environmentally responsible manner.

5. *Prior assessment.* To assess environmental impacts before starting a new activity or project and before decommissioning a facility or leaving a site.

6. *Products and services.* To develop and provide products or services that have no undue environmental impact and are safe in their intended use, that are efficient in their consumption of energy and natural resources, and that can be recycled, reused, or disposed of safely.

7. *Customer advice.* To advise, and where relevant educate, customers, distributors and the public in the safe use, transportation, storage and disposal of products provided and to apply similar considerations to the provision of services.

8. *Facilities and operations.* To develop, design and operate facilities and conduct activities taking into consideration the efficient use of energy and materials, the sustainable use of renewable resources, the minimization of adverse environmental impact and waste generation, and the safe and responsible disposal of residual wastes.

9. *Research.* To conduct or support research on the environmental impacts of raw materials, products, processes, emissions and wastes associated with the enterprise and on the means of minimizing such adverse impacts.

10. *Precautionary approach.* To modify the manufacture, marketing or use of products or services or the conduct of activities, consistent with scientific and technical understanding, to prevent serious or irreversible environmental degradation.

11. *Contractors and supplier.* To promote the adoption of these principles by contractors acting on behalf of the enterprise, encouraging and, where appropriate, requiring improvements in their practices to make them consistent with those of the enterprise; and to encourage the wider adoption of these principles by suppliers.

12. *Emergency preparedness.* To develop and maintain, where significant hazards exist, emergency preparedness plans in conjunction with the emergency services, relevant authorities and the local community, recognizing potential transboundary impacts.

13. *Transfer of technology.* To contribute to the transfer of environmentally sound technology and management methods throughout the industrial and public sectors.

14. *Contributing to the common effort.* To contribute to the development of public policy and to business, governmental and intergovernmental

programs and educational initiatives that will enhance environmental awareness and protection.

15. *Openness to concerns*. To foster openness and dialogue with employees and the public, anticipating and responding to their concerns about the potential hazards and impacts of operations, products, wastes or services, including those of transboundary or global significance.

16. *Compliance and reporting*. To measure environmental performance; to conduct regular environmental audits and assessments of compliance with company requirements, legal requirements and these principles and periodically to provide appropriate information to the Board of directors, shareholders, employees, the authorities and the public.

The Coalition for Environmentally Responsible Economies principles are another set of relevant guidelines that could be used to develop objectives. The Coalition for Environmentally Responsible Economies principles include "protection of the biosphere, sustainable use of natural resources, reduction and disposal of wastes, energy conservation, risk reduction, safe products and services, environmental restoration, informing the public, management commitment, and audits and reports."[5] Planning is most effective when it focuses on areas with the greatest risks and liabilities. Goals should be aggressive and quantitative with a feasible timeframe. Sample objectives might include:

pollution-reduction costs as a percent of sales and/or unit cost not exceeding x percent,

reportable pollutants reduced by x percent annually,

corporatewide waste reduced by 5 percent per year,

hazardous waste discharge eliminated from facilities by the end of 1995,

CFC emissions eliminated from manufacturing by 1995,

60 percent of the paper recycled by 1995, and

energy consumption reduced by x percent annually.

For example, DuPont reached its objective to reduce waste by 35 percent by 1990 compared with 1982 values. Objectives should be stated annually for several years in the future and should be consistent with the financial results stated in the business plan. In other words, investments in pollution abatement should be consistent with returns on capital, profitability, and other performance targets for the firm. Objectives should be formulated by external market factors rather than internal manufacturing and technological factors.

The objectives should also clearly define what pollutants a firm is trying to reduce so that pollution-elimination programs can be appropriately focused. One way to define pollutants is to examine state and federal statutes. Some companies consider only wastes regulated by the Resource Conservation and Recovery Act. DuPont, for example, defines wastes more broadly than Resource Conservation and Recovery Act and in accordance with the manner in which they are produced or managed.

GENERATING ALTERNATIVES TO ACHIEVE OBJECTIVES AND COMPLIANCES

The purpose of this step is to uncover problems and generate alternatives to remedy these problems. A variety of alternatives exist from housekeeping changes to the installation of the most modern equipment. Pollution strategies should be developed by considering the entire life cycle of a product including its raw and packing materials, manufacturing processes, and final disposal or reuse. Though traditional thinking suggests that pollution reduction would increase costs and escalate prices of finished products, manufacturers are actually experiencing some decline in costs from new manufacturing techniques. Some samples of methods of waste reduction are given below:

Housekeeping
    Inventory control
Product redesign
Process modification
    Substitution of polluting materials
    Redesign of processes
    New equipment
    Elimination of intermediate processes
Recovery and reuse
    On-site recovery
    Off-site recovery
Volume reduction
Treatment and disposal

Companies usually use the most effective combination of strategies to reduce pollution. The procedures to reduce pollution should be based on their effectiveness and costs.

PERFORMING QUALITATIVE, TECHNICAL, AND FINANCIAL ANALYSES OF ALTERNATIVES

Every alternative should be evaluated for technical feasibility, financial soundness, and other qualitative factors. For example, 3M evaluated alternatives in terms of current and potential waste reductions, resources conserved, technological improvements, and savings.[6]

The purpose of technical analysis is to ascertain whether the proposed alternatives are technically feasible for a specific application. During this process, a review will be made determining whether necessary technologies are currently available and, if not, whether development efforts will be successful. In addition, the time required to implement the alternative, effects of the process on quality control, capacity, and other factors will be considered. If the alternative does not involve capital expenditure, then the feasibility can be verified by experimenting with the alternative. Technical feasibility can be evaluated for safety, output quality, productivity, installation costs, and any new pollution created by the alternative.

Alternatives involving large capital expenditures can be assessed using economic analysis techniques such as payback period, return on investments, or net present value. A capital expenditure proposal for pollution reduction, unlike that for production equipment, may not necessarily generate revenues. Therefore, to get better evaluations of capital expenditure proposals for pollution reduction, benefits from cost avoidance, improved productivity, reduced liability risks, better regulatory compliance, waste and safety hazard reduction, and so forth should be considered. When a company generates waste, it incurs cost due to the waste handling, record keeping, disposal, liability, and underutilization of resources. Financial evaluation should also incorporate benefits from federal and state governments for making investments in pollution abatement.

DEVELOPING AND IMPLEMENTING ACTION PLANS

Action plans indicate various activities to be undertaken, persons responsible, and target dates. The plan should be monitored on a periodic basis. In addition, team members should act as catalysts to maintain the momentum of the program.

Once the alternatives are chosen, top management reviews and approves them along with an allocation of funds for implementation. The report prepared in the previous steps should be sufficient to facilitate the approval of funds. Implementation should be monitored closely to ensure that the alternative does what it is intended to do. Even the best laid plans can go awry for unanticipated reasons. If something does go wrong, the chosen alternative can always be modified to accomplish the original goal.

Educating the public should be a major part of implementation. According to a *New York Times*/CBS News poll conducted in June 1989, 79 percent of the people surveyed agreed that "protecting the environment is so important that requirements and standards cannot be too high, and continuing environmental improvements must be made regardless of cost." Although Exxon has spent more than $1 billion to clean up an oil spill in Prince William Sound, the oil giant's reputation has suffered greatly. Welcoming environmental audits by outside organizations can be a useful step toward educating the public and maintaining a positive corporate image. Polaroid keeps "community right-to-know" basis emission statistics with a view to educating the community.[7]

Employee training is particularly important during implementation. Without trained labor, the implementation will be sluggish and ineffective at best and may even lead to disastrous results. Three-Mile Island, Bhopal, and Chernobyl all serve as examples.

AUDITING AND REVIEWING RESULTS

A firm must have a system to audit the pollution-reduction program. Since one major objective of pollution reduction is legal compliance, auditing is essential to confirm that the plan has indeed achieved targeted goals. Such audits can also help the firm to improve its plans. Those options that do not measure up to their objectives should be reworked.

PLANNING PROCESS

Any pollution-reduction strategy must have the commitment of top management if it is to be effective. The chief executive officer must be the chief environmental planning and control executive of the company. The strategy must be developed by the chief executive officer and all personnel must understand that their company takes a pollution-reduction plan seriously. Putting the policy in writing, designating a waste-elimination "czar" at the highest management level to coordinate the program, introducing incentive systems, and training employees are some ways to demonstrate top management support of the plan. To inform its employees about its "Pollution Prevention Pays" program, 3M showed a 12-minute videotape and distributed an 8-page pamphlet. Management was thus able to show its support for the program while at the same time articulating its expectations of employees.

Pollution liabilities have driven many companies into bankruptcy in the United States. Planning for pollution reduction is therefore an important part of overall strategic planning. Because diverse skills are needed for plan developing, strategies for waste reduction are best set forth by a planning team. This team should consist of top executives from the environmental, manufacturing, plant, maintenance, engineering, laboratory, marketing, accounting, purchasing, and legal departments. The team should be a permanent one that will follow and track the performance and progress of the program. An outside consulting firm may also be engaged to help the team. Outside consultants can contribute significantly as a result of their exposure to a wide variety of processes and regulations in other similar companies. Since a consultant may not have a clear understanding of a company's internal processes, however, he or she should work closely with inside technical staff. Whenever problems of nonconformance are identified, a consultant can help the in-house technical staff to generate ideas to eliminate the problem or reduce pollution generation. An effective accounting system for waste generation is an important requirement for meaningful reviews and audits.

CONCLUSION

Pollution reduction may be the most formidable challenge confronting corporations in the 1990s. Many trend spotters and forward thinkers are labeling the 1990s the decade of the environment. Therefore, any company that wishes to achieve and maintain an advantage over its competitors must seriously consider strategic planning for pollution reduction. It should also evaluate all its new raw and packaging materials, processes, equipment, and finished products from an environmental perspective. The nine-step process for drafting a strategic plan that was presented in this chapter will not only formalize the process but also ensure that no worthwhile opportunities are left unexamined.

NOTES

This chapter is a revision reprinted from *Long Range Planning*, Volume 25, Number 4, Vasanthakumar N. Bhat, Strategic Planning for Pollution Reduction, pages 54–61, Copyright 1992, with kind permission from Elsevier Science Ltd., The Boulevard, Langford Lane, Kidlington OX5 1GB, UK.

1. Emily T. Smith, "Cleaning Up on the Coming Cleanup," *Businessweek*, October 16, 1989, p. 98.
2. Amal Kumar Naj, "Some Companies Cut Pollution by Altering Production Methods," *Wall Street Journal*, December 24, 1990, p. A1.
3. Samuel S. Epstein, Lester O. Brown, and Carl Pope, *Hazardous Waste in America* (San Francisco: Sierra Club Books, 1982), p. 119.
4. David Kirkpatrick, "Environmentalism: The New Crusade," *Fortune*, February 12, 1990, pp. 44–52.
5. The Coalition for Environmentally Responsible Economies, *CERES Principles*, September 7, 1989, Revised April 18, 1992.
6. Joseph Ling, "3M Company: Creating Incentives within the Individual Firm," in *Corporations and the Environment: How Should Decisions Be Made*, ed. David L. Brunner, Will Miller, Nan Stockholm (Stanford, Calif.: Stanford University, Graduate School of Business, Committee on Corporate Responsibility, 1980), p. 99.
7. Therese R. Welter, "A Farewell to Arms," *Industry Week*, August 20, 1990, pp. 37–44.

3

Complying with Green Laws

Environmental laws embody people's will to preserve nature, protect public health, and prevent environmental degradations. The purpose of early environmental laws in the United States was to protect natural resources such as forests and water. The initial basis for environmental litigation is found in the principles of common tort law. The establishment of the U.S. Environmental Protection Agency (EPA) and the enactment of comprehensive sets of environmental laws created a new legal framework in which to arbitrate environmental disputes. Environmental laws try to satisfy various interest groups. Engineers, administrators, lawyers, economists, corporate managers, and politicians are all involved in making laws. Environmental regulations are formulated in two stages in the United States. Congress makes laws indicating broad objectives and intent and directs the EPA to enact model programs. The actual laws that need to be obeyed by the people are typically made by the EPA in consultation with interested parties and the executive branch. Working groups of career civil servants draft the regulations. They prepare a list of pollutants, industries, and users and then establish standards for each one of them. The management team consisting of top EPA officials reviews proposals and suggests changes. When the new rules are approved, they are published in the *Federal Register* asking interested parties to submit detailed comments on the regulations. EPA administrators evaluate the comments and suggestions of the working group and send them to the president for approval. The president either approves or disapproves the regulations after considering comments from various federal agencies. If the president approves new regulations, they are promulgated and have the force of law. Otherwise, the president sends them back to the EPA for revisions. The regulations and standards may be applicable to existing sources, new or significantly modified sources, or sources of a certain size. States, towns, and private parties can challenge the environmental regulations in the federal courts. The administration and implementation of federal laws are delegated to the states. Therefore, state laws are typically at least as stringent as federal laws.

Environmental laws are enforced broadly and strongly, but increased regulations are creating uncertainty among corporate executives concerning legal compliance. Penalties for violations of the environmental laws are rising. A corporation was recently fined $18.5 million for Resource Conservation and Recovery Act and Clean Water Act felonies. Currently, corporate executives can be held responsible for environmental violations. New federal sentencing guidelines have removed flexibility in enforcement. Enforcement, therefore, is changing the way companies conduct their manufacturing operations. According to a survey of business leaders conducted by McKinsey & Company[1] compliance with regulations is their top environmental concern. The database linkages among the EPA, Securities and Exchange Commission, Occupational Safety and Health Administration, and other agencies provide a broader information base for enforcement actions. Incentive-based penalties, tax subsidies for money spent for environmental compliance, and pressure from communities are forcing companies to review their compliance critically. Government contracts are not being awarded to companies with compliance problems.

There are three categories of environmental laws. One mandates a cradle-to-grave management system and cleanup of hazardous wastes. The second set of statutes is media specific and regulates the quantities of wastes that can be emitted into the air, water, and landfills. The third category of statutes regulates production and products that may generate wastes. In addition, states and localities can pass their own laws and regulations. This chapter provides a broad perspective of the major federal environmental laws. Readers are advised to contact a competent attorney and refer to acts and regulations to understand the full impacts of these regulations.

OVERVIEW OF MAJOR FEDERAL ENVIRONMENTAL LAWS

National Environmental Policy Act of 1969

According to the Council on Environmental Quality, the National Environmental Policy Act (NEPA) is the "nation's environmental magna carta."[2] By promulgating this act, the United States declared the encouragement of "productive and enjoyable harmony between man and his environment" as its national policy. NEPA, besides establishing the Council on Environmental Quality to advise the president on environmental matters, requires federal agencies to take into consideration the environmental consequences in any activity "significantly affecting the quality of the human environment." NEPA has had powerful influence on federal plans. Between 1974 and 1991, 1,871 cases were filed by citizens against federal agencies demanding compliance with NEPA. In addition, federal agencies have prepared thousands of environmental impact statements that describe the probable and possible effects of projects on the environment, resources, and whole ecosystem before projects were started.

Clean Air Act

Every living creature has a stake in the quality of our air. Air pollution causes health problems including eye, nose, and throat irritations, bronchitis, emphysema, and other serious problems. Air pollution can impair visibility and destroy crops, forests, and lakes. Automobiles, manufacturing plants, power plants, and businesses are major contributors to air pollution. The purpose of the Clean Air Act is to protect human health and the environment from air pollution. Before the passage of the Air Pollution Control Act in 1955, air pollution was primarily the responsibility of states and towns. The Air Pollution Control Act therefore marked the beginning of a dramatic shift in air pollution policy in the United States. Since the enactment of the clean air legislation in 1955, the act has been amended 16 times. The Clean Air Act amendments of 1990, which contain more than 800 pages, require the EPA to promulgate several regulations. The Clean Air Act assigns to states the responsibility of ensuring suitable air quality. For this purpose, the act requires actions to reduce air pollution in areas not in compliance with mandated minimum air quality standards. The act also mandates air quality research and deals with ozone nonattainment, mobile sources, air toxins, acid rain problems, ozone depleting chemicals, enforcement, training, and other issues. This act consists of six titles: Air Pollution Prevention and Control, Emission Standards for Moving Sources, General, Acid Deposition Control, Permits, and Stratosphere Ozone Protection.

The Clean Air Act requires the EPA to issue nationwide ambient air quality standards (NAAQS) periodically for several air pollutants. Currently, the EPA has promulgated NAAQS for sulfur dioxide, nitrogen dioxides, carbon monoxide, particulate matter, ozone, and lead. The primary standards are designed to protect human health, the secondary standards to prevent environmental and property damages. If the air contains pollutants in amounts in excess of the air quality standards, it is considered to be unhealthy and regulatory actions must be taken to reduce them.

While the EPA establishes criteria for ambient air quality standards, the states develop state implementation plans to achieve quality standards in the areas within their jurisdiction. The states are expected to ensure air quality through a variety of permits. The Clean Air Act establishes standards to control automobile emissions such as carbon monoxide, hydrocarbons, and nitrogen oxides. These standards were written into the statute itself rather than delegated to the EPA, making it hard for the powerful automobile industry to weaken them. They require, for example, the use of "reformulated" gasoline in the worst ozone nonattainment areas. For hazardous pollutants, the act requires the EPA to come up with technology-based emission standards for targeted chemicals. The EPA is also required to develop performance standards for solid waste incinerators. Another major development in the 1990 Clean Air Act amendments is the requirement of health-based standards for air pollutants and the development of and appropriate use of risk assessment and risk management. The EPA is also required to establish standards for stationary "area sources" such as gas stations and dry cleaners. To prevent accidental releases of hazardous chemicals, an independent chemical safety and hazard investigation board has been established to study, investigate, and recommend measures to reduce the risk of such accidents.

New source performance standards are another feature of the clean air legislation. These standards establish amounts of air pollution allowed to new facilities in different industrial sectors. Such national standards help to prevent states from using lenient pollution standards to attract polluting industries. The act also divides areas into three classes for the purpose of attainment of air quality standards and stipulates pollutants allowed in each. Class I areas such as national parks and wilderness regions should have very little deterioration of air quality. In Class II areas, those not belonging to Class I and areas where NAAQS have been attained, the allowable increase in the new pollution is moderate. Large increments in air pollution are allowed in Class III areas designated by states primarily for development. Most areas are designated as Class II, a notable exception being the national parks. The Clean Air Act amendments of 1990 introduced a permit program for large polluters and for small polluters in nonattainment areas. To set up a new facility in an area with air quality exceeding NAAQS, an applicant must show that the facility's emissions will not exceed NAAQS or violate the Clean Air Act. In addition, the facility must be equipped with best available control technology for all pollutants. For nonattainment areas that exceed NAAQS for one or more contaminants, permits are issued only if total pollutants are reduced, even though a new facility is added. The 1990 amendments tightened penalties by changing violations from misdemeanors to felonies. These amendments also accelerate the phaseout of ozone-depleting substances.

The Clean Air Act also addresses problems of acid rain. It sets goals for sulfur dioxide and nitrogen dioxide reductions. It introduces a new regulatory approach to cut down emissions by allowing electric utilities to trade allowances to emit sulfur dioxide. Each utility is awarded a fixed number of allowances to emit sulfur dioxide based on a formula in the law. The utilities are allowed to emit one ton of sulfur dioxide for each allowance they hold. They can either reduce their emissions of sulfur dioxide or buy allowances from other utilities if their emissions are more than the amount allowed by the number of allowances they hold. Therefore, utilities can comply with the law by either reducing their emissions using various means or buying allowances from other utilities, whichever is less expensive.

Every company should ensure that it is in compliance with the Clean Air Act and that pollution emitted to the air is consistent with the requirements of the state implementation plans. It should verify that it has all permits required under the act. Monitoring, record keeping, and reporting requirements should be reviewed periodically.

Clean Water Act

Even though water covers most of the earth's surfaces, only 3 percent of it is fresh water. The purpose of the Clean Water Act is "to restore and maintain chemical, physical, and biological integrity of the Nation's waters." This act, originally enacted in 1948, was completely revised in 1972 and has been revised another three times since then. The purpose of the Clean Water Act is to prevent discharges of pollutants into navigable waters, ensure sufficient water quality for the protection and procreation of fish and wildlife, and ban the discharge of pollutants. This act consists of six titles: Research and Related Programs, Grants for Construction of Treatment Works, Standards and Enforcement, Permits and Licenses, General Provisions, and State Water Pollution Control Revolving Fund.

By requiring the use of the best practicable wastewater treatment to clean up waste discharges, the Clean Water Act forces industries to achieve higher levels of pollution reduction and requires states to develop water quality standards based on their designated use. States also should develop pollution-control strategies for waters labeled *toxic hot spots*, which remain polluted even after industries have cleaned up their discharges using best practicable control technologies.

The EPA regulates discharges into the surface waters through issuance of permits. This act requires permits for the discharge of conventional pollutants — bacteria and oxygen-consuming materials, for example — and toxic pollutants — heavy metals, pesticides, other organic chemicals, and so on. Industries are only allowed to discharge into water either directly or through publicly owned treatment works. The act mandates maintenance of records and monitoring of discharges. National Pollutant Discharge Elimination System permits, typically granted on a case-by-case basis, regulate concentrations of pollutants in effluents discharged into waters. The effluents sent to publicly owned treatment works must satisfy pretreatment standards. Willful and negligent violations can lead to imprisonment. Companies should ensure compliance of this act by analyzing wastewater discharges into waters and publicly owned treatment works, storm water runoff to surface waters, wastewater discharges from ships, and storage of petroleum products.

Safe Drinking Water Act

The Safe Drinking Water Act seeks to protect public drinking water supplies from harmful contaminants. This act, originally promulgated in 1974, was amended in 1977, 1979, 1980, 1986, and 1988. This act consists of four sections: Definitions, Public Water Systems, Protection of Underground Sources of Drinking Water, and Emergency Powers. This act requires the EPA to develop guidelines for the treatment and monitoring of drinking water and protect underground sources of drinking water by regulating underground injection. This act is applicable only to public and private systems that serve a minimum of 25 people for at least 60 days in a year.

Resource Conservation and Recovery Act

Originally enacted as the Solid Waste Disposal Act of 1965, the Resource Conservation and Recovery Act (RCRA) seeks to regulate solid and hazardous wastes. It gives the EPA broad authority to establish standards for generators and transporters of hazardous waste, and permit programs for hazardous waste treatment, storage, and disposal facilities. It establishes the elimination and reduction of hazardous waste as the national policy of the United States. The RCRA states that "wherever feasible, the generation of hazardous waste is to be reduced or eliminated as expeditiously as possible. Waste that is nevertheless generated should be treated, stored, or disposed of so as to minimize the present and future threat to human health and the environment."

Since its enactment in 1965, the Solid Waste Disposal Act has been revised several times. The Resource Recovery Act of 1970 shifted emphasis from efficiency of disposal to recovery of energy and materials. It also expanded the definition of solid waste to include solid, semisolid, liquid, and contained gas. A waste is hazardous if it is ignitable, corrosive, reactive, or toxic or if it is one of the wastes in the list published by EPA. This list is organized into three categories of wastes: source specific, generic, and commercial chemical products. Source-specific wastes include wastes from specific industries such as petroleum refining. Common manufacturing and industrial process wastes belong to the category of generic wastes. Products such as creosote and pesticides make up the commercial chemical products. This list, continuously updated, contains approximately 100 industrial process waste streams and more than 500 discarded commercial products and chemicals.

Subtitle C of RCRA describes the hazardous waste management program. It requires generators; transporters; and treatment, storage, and disposal facilities to comply with guidelines regarding record keeping and reporting, the labeling of wastes, the use of suitable containers, the use of manifest systems, the need for permits, the compliance with operating standards, and the satisfaction of insurance requirements in the event of an accident.

The solid waste provisions in RCRA prohibit open dumps and establish criteria for landfills such as liners, leachate collection, and groundwater monitoring. The provisions relating to underground storage tanks establish financial responsibility requirements for tank owners, lead detection and prevention, detection and cleanup programs, technical standards for tank design and operation, and reporting corrective action.

Comprehensive Environmental Response, Compensation, and Liability Act

Unlike most environmental laws that are intended to prevent future pollution, the Comprehensive Environmental Response, Compensation, and Liability Act (CERCLA), also known as the Superfund, seeks to clean up highly contaminated hazardous waste sites. This act gives the EPA the authority either to do the cleanup or force parties responsible for the hazardous wastes to help in the cleanup. This act consists of four sections: Hazardous Substances Releases, Liability, Compensation; Hazardous Substance Response Trust Fund; Miscellaneous Provisions; and Pollution Insurance. This act also authorizes the EPA to take action to control spills and releases of hazardous substances. There are two types of responses under this law. When emergency actions are required, the EPA must respond immediately. However, short-term removals should cost less than $2 million and last less than one year. Long-term actions typically are expensive and require extensive engineering at the sites. The EPA investigates potential hazardous waste sites and notes the most severely contaminated in the national priorities list (NPL) for cleanups. The ranking system calculates a numerical score for each site based on criteria such as the toxicity of waste; the likelihood of contamination of groundwater, surface water, and air; and the risk of human exposure. As of September 30, 1992, there were 1,275 sites nationwide in the NPL. The EPA either forces those responsible for polluting the site to clean it up or does the cleaning up itself using Superfund money and then takes court action to have the expenses reimbursed. If more than one party is responsible for the waste, the EPA can recover all cleanup costs from one party, leaving that party to recover its costs from others. One unique feature of the Superfund is that if a party denies responsibility in court and loses the case, it is subjected to treble damages.

Cleanups of federal hazardous waste sites should be done using federally appropriated funds, not Superfund money. States should bear 10 to 50 percent of the cleanup costs for sites within their jurisdiction and are also responsible for operation and maintenance costs when the cleanup job is done. The major sources of revenue for the Superfund include taxes on petroleum, chemical feedstock, corporate income, general revenue, imported chemical derivatives, interest income, and money reclaimed from companies responsible for the cleanup. According to a survey conducted in 1995 by the U.S. General Accounting Office, Fortune 500 companies spent a median amount of $1.5 million since January 1, 1987, on 17 sites on average per company.[3] One-third of this amount was spent on legal expenses.

Emergency Planning and Community Right-to-Know Act

To demonstrate that tragedies like Bhopal and Chernobyl will not be tolerated, the U.S. Congress in 1986 added three new titles to CERCLA. One of these, the Emergency Planning and Community Right-to-Know Act (EPCRA), also known as Title III, requires a chemical emergency response plan and ensures that planning officials are provided with required information by local facilities dealing in hazardous chemicals. It further extends right-to-know provisions to communities. This act consists of three chapters: Emergency Planning and Notification, Reporting Requirements, and General Provisions. Under this act, the governor of each state must appoint a state emergency response commission that in turn creates emergency planning districts and appoints local emergency planning committees. These planning committees should consist of elected state and local officials, law enforcement personnel, media personnel, community groups, and owners of facilities subject to EPCRA. Each committee prepares plans that are reviewed annually for likely chemical emergencies in the planning districts. The emergency plans should identify facilities, specify methods and procedures to be followed in case of a chemical release, describe emergency equipment and facilities available, explain evacuation plans, indicate training programs, and designate community emergency coordinators and facility emergency coordinators for facilities subject to EPCRA.

A facility is subject to the notification requirements of EPCRA only if the facility has a substance specified on the EPA's list of some 400 extremely hazardous substances in an amount equal to or greater than the threshold planning quantity. The governor or state commission can designate additional facilities subject to these requirements. Similarly, after public notice, the governor or state commission can designate facilities to be covered outside these guidelines.

Under EPCRA, every covered facility must report immediately to the community coordinator of its local emergency committee any accidental releases of extremely hazardous substances or substances defined under the CERCLA. Follow-up notices with information regarding response taken, health risks, and advice about medical attention for individuals exposed to the chemicals are required.

Another major feature of EPCRA is the community right-to-know program. EPCRA requires businesses to submit two sets of annual reports containing hazardous chemical inventory and toxic chemicals release inventories. For the hazardous chemical inventory, each facility must submit material safety data sheets or related information to the local committee, state committee, and local fire department. Owners of facilities with ten or more full-time employees falling in standard industrial classification codes 20–39 are required to file annual toxic chemicals release inventory reports if they manufactured, processed, or used a listed toxic chemical in excess of threshold level. The requirements related to toxic release are governed by section 313 of the act. The report should indicate the quantities of releases into the air, land, and water or transferred off-site, the maximum quantities of the chemical present at the facility, and the treatment and disposal methods used during the preceding year. Both sets of reports are available to the public through various publications.

Toxic Substances Control Act

According to the U.S. General Accounting Office, traces of toxic chemicals can be found in almost every American's body because of exposure to chemicals released into air, water, or land and absorbed by skin contact.[4] Though several substances including asbestos, chlorofluorocarbons, kepone, mercury, and polychlorinated biphenyls are found to cause significant health and environmental problems, they were not always regulated. Existing environmental laws regulated substances only when they were released. In addition, thousands of new substances are being developed every year. Therefore, in 1976 the U.S. Congress enacted the Toxic Substances Control Act to study health and environmental effects of existing and new chemicals used in manufacturing and commerce and to take appropriate regulatory actions. This act consists of three chapters: Control of Toxic Substances, Asbestos, and Hazardous Response and Indoor Air Pollutants. Since its enactment in 1976, the act has undergone five major revisions.

Only a few chemicals in use have been tested for their likely health and environmental effects. This act requires the EPA to collect data about adverse effects of chemical materials, evaluate their risk, and take action if the chemical may present "an unreasonable risk of injury to health or the environment" or if it will be produced in such large quantities to result in significant human exposure. If existing data are insufficient or no data exist, then the EPA must issue a rule to require tests.

Every manufacturer or importer is required to give notice 90 days before producing or introducing a new chemical product into the United States. The notice should describe test data concerning likely adverse effects on human health or the environment. The EPA should also be notified if an existing chemical is going to be produced, processed, or used in a significantly different way. The purpose of this notification is to identify likely hazards of chemicals and control them before their use becomes extensive. The EPA can impose such restrictions as stringent quality control procedures, distribution restrictions, warning labels on the containers, regulation of disposal methods, and outright bans. Currently, some substances subjected to regulations include chlorofluorocarbons, asbestos, metalworking fluids, and polychlorinated biphenyls.

This act requires the EPA to compile and maintain an inventory of chemical substances and all chemicals not on the inventory list are considered "new" and are subject to premanufacture notification. In addition, this act requires strict reporting and record keeping of manufacturers and processors of the regulated chemicals. These records should include data on environmental and health effects.

Federal Insecticide, Fungicide, and Rodenticide Act

The Federal Insecticide, Fungicide, and Rodenticide Act was enacted in 1947 primarily to regulate pesticides, those substances used to prevent, kill, repel, or control pests. Since 1947, this act has been amended and revised eight times. The act mandates the registration of a pesticide before it can be marketed. The decision to register a pesticide hinges on the condition that the pesticide perform its intended function without "unreasonable adverse effects on the environment." Registration is usually for a five-year period but it can be renewed. All pesticides must contain a label indicating approved uses and restrictions. Pesticides cannot be used inconsistently with the label instructions. In order to control their use, pesticides are divided into general and restricted categories. Restricted pesticides can only be used by a certified applicator who is trained in the use and handling of such pesticides.

Pollution Prevention Act of 1990

The Pollution Prevention Act is a major milestone in the efforts to reduce pollution in the United States. This act shifts emphasis from reduction of environmental degradations to prevention of pollution itself. This act sets forth the policy that "pollution should be prevented or reduced at the source whenever feasible." It defines source reduction as any practice that

(i) reduces the amount of any hazardous substance, pollutant, or contaminant entering any waste stream or otherwise released into the environment (including fugitive emissions) prior to recycling, treatment, or disposal; and

(ii) reduces the hazards to public health and the environment associated with the release of such substances, pollutants, and contaminants.

This act also establishes the Office of Pollution Prevention, which reviews and advises on promotion of multimedia approaches to source reduction. This act requires collection of information about source reduction and recycling activities from manufacturing plants.

The national pollution prevention strategy document prepared by the EPA emphasizes voluntary private initiatives as an approach for pollution prevention. The strategy documentation suggests incorporation of pollution prevention into regulations and enforcement. The industrial toxics project, developed as a result of this strategy, allows private-sector companies to choose the most cost-effective pollution-prevention options to achieve environmental goals. The "33/50 program" allows companies up to six additional years to comply with the regulations of the 1990 Clean Air Act amendments if they voluntarily reduce emissions of 17 targeted chemicals significantly before the regulations are expected to take effect.

Noise Control Act

The purpose of the Noise Control Act is to establish noise emission standards for transportation and construction equipment, regulate aircraft noise emissions, mandate labeling of products emitting high levels of noise, and develop state and local programs to control noise. This act was initially enacted in 1972 and was amended in 1976, 1978, and 1987. This act requires the EPA to develop noise standards for new products including portable air compressors, earth-moving equipment, buses, jackhammers, and lawn mowers. Performance standards for construction equipment, transportation equipment, and electrical or electronic equipment are also mandated by this act.

Other Environmental Laws

There are several other laws relating to the environment. The National Historic Preservation Act establishes the National Register of Historic Places to develop a list of properties for protection. Federal agencies are required to consider effects of their projects on properties listed in the register. The Wild and Scenic Rivers Act requires the consideration of scenic values of rivers when planning the utilization of water and land resources. The Endangered Species Act mandates the preparation of a list of animal and plant species whose survival is in danger and their protection from activities that may adversely affect their survival. This act relies on a combination of criteria for determining endangerment. These include: threatened destruction of the species' habitat, overexploitation of the species, diseases, deficient current regulations, and other factors making species' continued existence in danger. The Occupational Safety and Health Administration seeks to reduce injuries in the workplace by establishing standards for safe and healthy working conditions. The act strives "to assure so far as possible every working man and woman in the nation safe and healthful working conditions and to preserve our human resources." The Ocean Dumping Act regulates intentional dumping of materials into the ocean and establishes a permit program to control dumping of dredged materials into the ocean. The Federal Food, Drug, and Cosmetic Act seeks, besides other goals, "to keep interstate channels from deleterious, adulterated and misbranded articles of specified types to the end that public health and safety might be advanced." The Hazardous Materials Transportation Act strives "to improve the regulatory and enforcement authority of the Secretary of Transportation to protect the Nation adequately against the risks to life and property that is inherent in the transportation of hazardous materials in commerce." It also establishes record keeping, labeling, packaging, training, and other requirements. Besides federal laws, states and localities have also enacted environmental laws.

KEEPING ABREAST OF ENVIRONMENTAL REGULATIONS

Environmental laws are growing exponentially. Table 3.1 lists various environmental laws since 1862 and Figure 3.1 presents the exponential growth in the number of environmental laws. New amendments to these laws are continually being proposed by the U.S. Congress and regulations are enacted by federal agencies. It is therefore essential to monitor these developments closely to stay ahead of the regulations.

The *Federal Register*, published daily except on Saturdays, Sundays, and official holidays, is the publication that should be studied for upcoming changes in laws and regulations. It includes executive orders, regulatory plans, proposed changes in the regulations, and announcements required to be published by various acts. Regulatory plans provide details about various regulations and their revisions. The *Environment Reporter*, published weekly by the Bureau of National Affairs, contains environmental current events. *Inside EPA's Superfund Report*, *Inside EPA Weekly Report*, and *Inside EPA's Environmental Policy Alert* provide up-to-date information about environmental laws, regulations, and litigations. There are on-line systems that can provide

TABLE 3.1
Environmental Laws in the United States, 1862–1992

1862 Homestead Act	1972 Marine Mammal Protection Act
1872 Mining Law	1972 Ports and Safe Waterway Act
1891 Forest Reserve Act	1973 Endangered Species Act
1899 Refuse Act	1974 Deep Water Port Act
1899 Home and Harbors Act	1974 Safe Drinking Water Act
1900 Lacey Act	1974 Energy Supply and Environmental
1902 Reclamation Act	Coordination Act
1910 Insecticide Act	1974 Federal Non-Nuclear Research and Develop-
1911 Weeks Law	ment Act
1916 National Parks Service Act	1974 Forest and Rangeland Renewable Resources
1918 Migratory Bird Treaty Act	Planning Act
1920 Mineral Leasing Act	1974 Solar Energy Research, Development and
1934 Migratory Bird Hunting Stamp Act	Demonstration Act
1934 Taylor Graring Act	1975 Eastern Wilderness Act
1935 Soil Conservation Act	1975 Hazardous Materials Transportation Act
1937 Flood Control Act	1976 Toxic Substances Control Act
1937 Wildlife Restoration Act	1976 Federal Land Policy and Management Act
1938 Food, Drug and Cosmetics Act	1976 Resource Conservation and Recovery Act
1938 Natural Gas Act	1976 Energy Policy and Conservation Act
1948 Water Pollution Control Act	1976 National Forest Management Act
1954 Atomic Energy Act	1977 Clean Air Act Amendments
1955 Air Pollution Control Act	1977 Clean Water Act
1956 Federal Water Pollution Control Act	1977 Surface Mining Control and Reclamation Act
1957 Price-Anderson Act	1977 Soil and Water Resources Conservation Act
1958 Fish and Wildlife Coordination Act	1978 Endangered Species Act Amendments
1960 Hazardous Substances Act	1978 Environmental Education Act
1960 Multiple Use-Sustained Yield Act	1978 Energy Tax Act
1963 Clean Air Act	1978 Public Utilities Regulatory Policy Act
1964 Classification and Multiple Use Act	1980 Comprehensive Environmental Response
1964 Public Land Law Review Commission	Compensation and Liability Act
Act	1980 Alaska National Interest Lands Conservation
1964 Wilderness Act	Act
1965 Solid Waste Disposal Act	1980 Low-Level Radioactive Waste Policy Act
1965 Water Resources Planning Act	1980 Nongame Wildlife Act
1966 National Historic Preservation Act	1982 Nuclear Waste Policy Act
1966 Animal Welfare Act	1984 Resource Conservation and Recovery Act
1966 Laboratory Animal Welfare Act	Amendments
1968 Wild and Scenic Rivers Act	1984 Environmental Programs and Assistance Act
1969 National Environmental Policy Act	1986 Safe Drinking Water Act Amendments
1969 Coal Mine Health and Safety Act	1986 Emergency Planning and Community Right-to-
1970 National Mining and Minerals Act	Know Act
1970 Clean Air Act	1987 Superfund Amendments and Reorganization
1970 Occupational Safety and Health Act	Act
1970 Resource Recovery Act	1987 Marine Plastic Pollution Research and Control
1972 Water Pollution Control Act	Act
1972 Marine Protect., Res. & Sanctuaries Act	1988 National Appliance Energy Conservation Act
1972 Coastal Zone Management Act	1988 Alternative Motor Fuels Act
1972 Home Control Act	1988 Medical Waste Tracking Act
1972 Federal Insecticide, Fungicide and	1990 Oil Pollution Act
Rodenticide Act	1990 Pollution Prevention Act
1972 Parks and Waterways Safety Act	1992 Federal Facility Compliance Act

Sources: Richard E. Balzhiser, "Meeting the Near-term Challenge for Power Plants," in *Technology and the Environment*, ed. Jesse H. Ausubel and Hedy E. Saldovich (Washington, D.C.: National Academy Press, 1989), p. 101; William P. Cunningham et al., *Environmental Encyclopedia* (Detroit, Mich.: Gale Research, 1994), pp. 939–42.

FIGURE 3.1
Growth in the Number of Green Laws

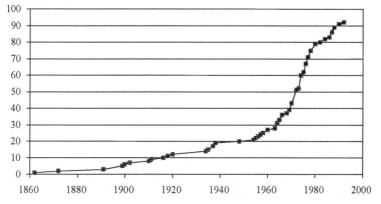

Sources: Richard E. Balzhiser, "Meeting the Near-term Challenge for Power Plants," in *Technology and Environment*, ed. Jesse H. Ausubel and Hedy E. Sladovichy (Washington, D.C.: National Academy Press, 1989), p. 101; William P. Cunningham et al., *Environmental Encyclopedia* (Detroit, Mich.: Gale Research, 1994), pp. 939–42.

access to the full text of environmental laws and regulations. Justice Retrieval and Inquiry System is the computer-based storage and retrieval system operated by the U.S. Department of Justice. It is a full-text system designed primarily for use by federal lawyers. LEXIS, operated by Mead Data Central, can provide information on U.S. codes, *Code of Federal Regulations*, the *Federal Register* (from July 1980), Supreme Court decisions (from 1960), and state court decisions. Westlaw, like LEXIS, is a full-text retrieval system that can display full texts of U.S. codes, *Code of Federal Regulations*, the *Federal Register*, Supreme Court and state court decisions, and *Shepard's Citations*.

IMPLEMENTATION AND ENFORCEMENT

Environmental enforcement has been intense in recent years. It is primarily the environmental regulations written by the federal agencies, not environmental laws enacted by the Congress, that determine legally enforceable environmental requirements. Therefore, statutory language in itself does not indicate the severity of any law. Consequently, the enforcement and implementation of various laws are affected by the political party in power and who is in charge at the EPA and other federal agencies. Though each statute regulates different media, they share many commonalities. Most laws allow the EPA to choose similar enforcement strategies. Most statutes require facilities to self-monitor compliance, prepare their own findings, and maintain records. The EPA has the authority to enter any regulated facility.

However, according to a report by the U.S. General Accounting Office, the self-reported compliance monitoring data for the hazardous waste program authorized by the RCRA and National Pollutant Discharge Elimination System program authorized by the Clean Water Act cannot be relied on.[7]

Enforcement actions increased during the 1980s. According to the U.S. Department of Justice, criminal indictments rose from about 40 in 1983 to 174 in 1992. Federal fines collected exceeded $163 million in 1992. The value of federal environmental actions for the first time approached $2 billion in 1992.

Figure 3.2A displays federal administrative enforcement actions taken under the Clean Air Act, the Clean Water Act/Safe Drinking Water Act, and RCRA during 1972–92. The number of actions under the Clean Air Act increased from 21 in 1982 to 404 in 1989. The number of actions under the Clean Water Act/Safe Drinking Water Act reached a high of 2,177 in 1991 up from 329 in 1982. RCRA actions involving management of wastes from cradle-to-grave peaked in 1984 with 554 actions and then started falling.

FIGURE 3.2A
Federal Administrative Enforcement Actions by
Environmental Laws, 1972–92

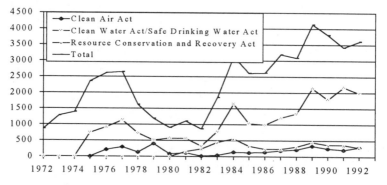

Source: Council on Environmental Quality, *Environmental Quality, The Twenty-third Annual Report* (Washington, D.C.: Government Printing Office, 1993), pp. 81–90.

Figure 3.2B presents federal administrative enforcement actions taken under the Federal Insecticide, Fungicide, and Rodenticide Act, the Toxic Substances Control Act, and the Emergency Planning and Community Right-to-Know Act. Actions taken under the Federal Insecticide, Fungicide, and Rodenticide Act were high from 1973 through 1977 and then stabilized. Toxic Substances Control Act actions peaked in 1987 at 1,051 and then started declining. As new statutes were added, total enforcement actions increased and peaked sometime in 1989.

FIGURE 3.2B
Federal Administrative Enforcement Actions by
Environmental Laws, 1972–92

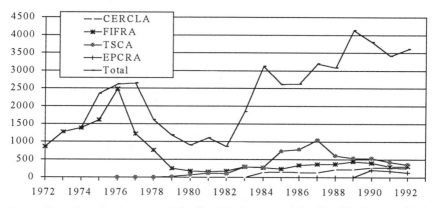

Source: Council on Environmental Quality, *Environmental Quality, The Twenty-third Annual Report* (Washington, D.C.: Government Printing Office, 1993), pp. 81–90.

Industrywide analysis of penalties and emissions indicates that steel and containers (metal and glass) top the industries with the highest penalties per $1 million revenue. The chemicals and machine tools are at the top among industries with maximum emissions per revenue. Figure 3.3 presents an industrywide analysis of environmental law violations. The chemical industry has the maximum violations with the largest number of Superfund sites per revenue. Permits for building materials received the highest number of denials per revenue under the RCRA.

In Table 3.2, an analysis of companywide environmental compliance parameters is presented. The NPL site index represents the ratio of sites in which a company has been listed as a responsible party by the EPA as of July 24, 1992, to the total company revenue in years from 1988 to 1990 expressed in ten billions of dollars. The RCRA Corrective Actions Index is the ratio of the number of facilities at which a company was financially responsible for RCRA corrective actions to the revenue from 1988 to 1990 in ten billions of dollars. The Investor Responsibility Research Center (IRRC) calls these cleanup indices. The RCRA permit denials index is calculated by dividing the number of RCRA permit denials by the EPA from 1986 to 1990 into the revenue from 1988 to 1990 in hundreds of billions of dollars. The Minerals Management Service Shut-ins Index is computed by dividing the number of Minerals

FIGURE 3.3
Industrywide Analysis of Environmental Law Violations

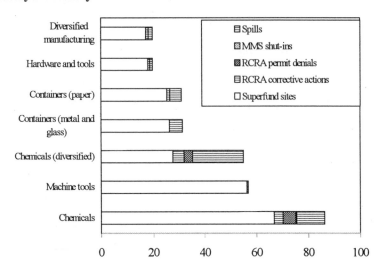

Source: Investor Responsibility Research Center, *Corporate Environmental Profiles Directory* (Washington, D.C.: Investor Responsibility Research Center, 1993).

Management Service Shut-ins from 1986 to 1990 into the revenue from 1988 to 1990 in billions of dollars. The IRRC Emission Efficiency Index® is the ratio of emissions in pounds to the company's domestic revenue. The Spill Index is obtained by dividing the number of oil and chemical spills into the revenue expressed in tens of billions of dollars. The IRRC Compliance Index is calculated by dividing the sum of penalties by revenue. The penalties under the various acts described above are summed to compute a Compliance Index.

The Spearman Rank Correlations are used to identify the statistical relationships. The data of 255 companies belonging to the Standard and Poor Index are used. Out of 21 relationships, 11 relationships are statistically significant as indicated by asterisks. The Emission Efficiency Index has statistically significant positive relationships with the NPL Site Index, RCRA Corrective Actions Index, Spill Index, and IRRC Compliance Index. These positive relationships indicate that companies with high emissions per revenue are likely to have many NPL sites, spills, and compliance problems. This points to the need for reducing pollution to cut down compliance problems. Positive relationships between the Emission Efficiency Index and the penalty index indicate that companies emitting a disproportionate amount of wastes are likely to be subjected to disproportionately large amounts of penalties. Other relationships can easily be gleaned from Table 3.2.

TABLE 3.2
Spearman Rank Correlations between Various Environmental
Compliance Parameters of 255 Companies

Variable	B	C	D	E	F	G
A	0.35*	0.14	0.04	0.50*	0.22	0.35*
B		0.33*	0.29	0.44*	0.48*	0.43*
C			0.36*	0.12	0.34*	0.23
D				0.04	0.37*	0.25
E					0.47*	0.56*
F						0.51*

A = NPL Sites Index
B = RCRA Corrective Actions Index
C = RCRA Permit Denials Index
D = Minerals Management Service Facility Shut-ins Index
E = IRRC Emission Efficiency Index
F = Spill Index
G = IRRC Compliance Index

*Associations are statistically significant at the probability level of 0.05 if the Spearman Rank Correlations in the above table are greater than 0.305.

Source: Compiled by the author.

IMPROVING COMPLIANCE

Environmental laws significantly affect the free-market economy. However, without environmental laws polluters will not be paying for market degradation. According to the theory known as the tragedy of the commons, individuals will maximize their gains by destroying collectively owned resources such as the environment. In other words, individuals have incentives to pollute to maximize their gains because they do not pay for it. In the economic literature, this is known as the free-rider problem. This insight provides theoretical justification for environmental laws.[8]

Federal sentencing guidelines have provided for strict penalties for environmental violations.[9] The federal guidelines typically increase fines, and managers' actions have significant impact on the fine levels.[10] There are actions a company can take to improve compliance. These include: establishing a management system to ensure compliance; designating a high-level person to oversee compliance; never entrusting discretionary authority to those likely to act unlawfully; organizing a system to anticipate emerging environmental trends and issues; instituting environmental auditing to identify and avoid environmental problems; monitoring regulatory changes; developing a system to act on environmental trends, issues, and regulatory changes; installing an information system to bring plant problems to the attention of the headquarters; promoting a team approach to avoid departmental infighting; integrating environmental compliance in strategic planning; incorporating environmental compliance in capital budgeting; preparing a corporate environmental compliance program indicating responsibilities for environmental compliance; improving record keeping; cooperating with legislators, regulators, and environmental groups in making laws and regulations; instituting product-stewardship programs; communicating compliance requirements; providing periodic training programs for various levels of employees; installing a system for employees to communicate criminal acts without fear of retribution; acting swiftly when criminal acts are detected; taking steps to prevent the repeat occurrence of similar offences; identifying chemicals likely to invite mega-lawsuits and taking corrective actions; and emphasizing environmental integrity rather than just compliance.

The goal should be to go beyond compliance and emphasis should be on environmental integrity. Compliance should guide organizational decision making. The program should not be driven by lawyers, rather, it should involve everyone. Training, leadership, accountability, auditing, and penalties are the means to achieving environmental integrity. Company leaders should be committed to environmental integrity and this commitment should be reflected in all major activities.

CONCLUSION

Rising federal deficits, falling productivity, skyrocketing cleanup costs, and increasing job losses are likely to result in the relaxing of environmental laws. The role of states in administration and enforcement of environmental regulations is likely to expand. Though public support for stringent environmental laws is likely to continue, rising unemployment and falling living standards are likely to force the use of risk analysis and economic cost-benefit analysis in environmental decision making. Because of inefficiencies generated by command-and-control legislation, market-based approaches to pollution reduction will be preferred. More voluntary approaches such as Responsible Care, principles set forth by the Coalition for Environmentally Responsible Economies, and ISO 14000 are likely to form a basis for green corporations. Green corporations, by embracing environmental integrity, are likely to gain worldwide acceptance.

NOTES

1. McKinsey & Company, "The Corporate Response to the Environmental Challenge," in *Transactional Environmental Law and Its Impact on Corporate Behavior*, ed. Eric J. Urbani, Conrad P. Rubin, and Monica Katzman (Irvington-on-Hudson, N.Y.: Transnational Juris Publications, 1994), pp. 217–262.

2.   Council on Environmental Quality, *Environmental Quality, Twenty-third Annual Report* (Washington, D.C.: Government Printing Office, 1993), p. 151.

3.   U.S. General Accounting Office, *Superfund: Legal Expenses for Cleanup-related Activities of Major U.S. Corporations*, GAO/RCED-95-46 (Washington, D.C.: General Accounting Office, 1995), p. 1.

4.   U.S. General Accounting Office, *EPA Toxic Substances Program*, GAO/AIMD-94-25 (Washington, D.C.: General Accounting Office, 1994), p. 2.

5.   Richard E. Balzhiser, "Meeting the Near-term Challenge for Power Plants," in *Technology and Environment*, ed. Jesse H. Ausubel and Hedy E. Sladovich (Washington, D.C.: National Academy Press, 1989), p. 101.

6.   Russ Hoyle, ed., *Gale Environmental Almanac* (Detroit: Gale Research, 1993), pp. 939–942.

7.   U.S. General Accounting Office, *Environmental Enforcement*, GAO/RCED-93-21 (Washington, D.C.: General Accounting Office, 1993), pp. 4–5.

8.   Garret Hardin, "The Tragedy of the Commons," *Science* 162 (1968): 1243.

9.   Gary E. Marchant, "Environmental Legal Liabilities: Prevention and Control," in *Environmental Strategies Handbook*, ed. Rao V. Kolluru (New York: McGraw-Hill, 1994), pp. 289–324.

10.   Lynn Sharp Paine, "Managing for Organizational Integrity," *Harvard Business Review* 72 (March–April 1994): 107–117.

4

Life-cycle Assessment: Measuring Greenness

The green objective of the 1970s was compliance with regulations. Pollution prevention became the goal in the 1980s. Cradle-to-grave pollution prevention is the name of the game in the 1990s. Life-cycle assessment is the measuring tool. Companies trying to ascertain whether cloth diapers are greener than disposable diapers or whether paper cups are more environmentally friendly than polystyrene cups must consider the total environmental effects of their products over the course of their entire life, not simply during the product manufacturing stage. Life-cycle assessment objectively evaluates the many environmental impacts of products. It is based on the principle that most materials will ultimately end as waste. Life-cycle assessment examines energy and material flows during the extraction and processing of raw materials, production, transportation, distribution, use, and final disposal. Such an assessment provides an objective evaluation of the overall greenness of a product and helps to optimize all stages of a product. Individuals, industries, and governments have used life-cycle assessment for various purposes; life-cycle costing, for example, focuses on capital and operating costs. However, life-cycle assessment is still a relatively new concept and it requires new tools to provide better gauges and interpretations of the greenness of a product.

As yet, there are no well-defined approaches for life-cycle assessment. We know that it involves the development of inventory of all inputs and outputs in terms of materials and energy during the entire life cycle of a product and the expression of effects of this inventory on the environment. Life-cycle assessment has been defined as an attitude through which manufacturers accept responsibility for the pollution caused by their products from design to disposal. This is contrary to conventional belief that the responsibility begins with the raw material acquisition and ends with the dispatch of finished products. Life-cycle assessment is considered a quantitative tool that ensures real pollution reduction.

As a useful tool for developing decisions involving environmental criteria, life-cycle assessment has been used by environmental consumer groups to help consumers to decide what to buy, by manufacturers to identify areas for improvement, and by legislators to develop criteria for environmental labeling schemes. Life-cycle assessment should not be confused with risk assessment. While life-cycle assessment deals with environmental quality, risk assessment deals with environmental safety by identifying and evaluating risks. Risk assessment tries to predict potential harm whereas life-cycle assessment sums up environmental degradation. Risk assessment deals with potential accidents, inadvertent releases of hazardous chemicals, and fires whereas life-cycle assessment deals with energy and material inputs and emissions. Finally, risk assessment is typically site and time specific whereas life-cycle assessment is for a specific geographic area and length of time.

LIFE-CYCLE ASSESSMENT: A LITERATURE REVIEW

Life-cycle assessment is labor intensive, data intensive, and complex. Technological changes make life-cycle assessment obsolete within a short time of its preparation. The results of life-cycle assessments are dependent on data that are often inaccessible to nonindustry researchers. Therefore, life-cycle assessments are very costly and only a few products have been evaluated using this method. Since most of these studies were privately funded, the public does not have access to them. An excellent review of the history of life-cycle assessment can be found in the work of Robert Ayres.[1] "Net energy analysis" was an important 1970s forerunner of life-cycle assessment. Many studies examine energy consumption by packaging alternatives.[2] The book edited by J.A.G. Thomas contains some significant contributions of the net energy analysis.[3] Use of input-output models for energy analysis can be found in works by R. A. Herendeen; Robert Ayres, Thomas Betlach, and Christofer Decker; and C. W. Bullard, P. S. Penner, and D. A. Pilati.[4] One of the earliest studies comparing glass, polyethylene, and polyvinyl chloride bottles based on the waste emissions during production was done by Robert Ayres, James Cummings-Saxton, and Martin O. Stern.[5] Mary Ann Curran summarizes the life-cycle assessment studies that are publicly accessible for various products.[6] A list of life-cycle assessments of products cited in the literature include: beer containers,[7] beverage containers,[8] cloth and disposable diapers,[9] foamed polystyrene and bleached paperboard,[10] grocery sacks,[11] hard surface cleaners,[12] laundry detergent packaging,[13] packaging,[14] plastics,[15] soft drink containers,[16] soft drink delivery systems,[17] and vinyl packaging.[18]

LIFE-CYCLE ASSESSMENT PROCESS

Life-cycle assessment is a holistic approach toward examining the environmental effects of a product. Companies use life-cycle assessment to identify waste-reduction opportunities. Government regulations typically focus on one aspect of the pollution. For example, the Clean Air Act deals with air pollution, the Clean Water Act addresses water pollution, and so on. Consequently, pollution-reduction activities also address pollution problems of a given medium. Such approaches frequently reduce pollution in one area but increase it in another. However, the life-cycle assessment approach can eliminate such narrowly focused decision making by concentrating instead on the sum total of pollution generated by a product.

One major benefit of life-cycle assessment is that it focuses evaluation on products rather than processes. By widening the evaluation process, evaluations are performed both up and down the supply chain. Because little pollution is generated during the design phase of a product, most analyses are focused on the production, distribution, use, and disposal stages. Green tools such as green auditing, total green management, and so on rarely examine the greenness of design decisions even though significant decisions that influence pollution during production and subsequent stages are made during design stages. Therefore, the systems approach adopted by the life-cycle assessment begins analysis with the design.

Life-cycle assessments mean different things to different people. Life-cycle assessments performed by Franklin Associates, called the resource and environmental profile analysis, identify consumption of energy and materials at each physical stage of a product. The Society of Logistics Engineers' life-cycle costing program estimates ownership costs over a complete life span of a product. The Association of the Dutch Chemical Industry's integrated substance chain management system shows areas for reducing environmental impact through life-cycle, full-cost systems. Based on a review of more than 6.6 million references on life-cycle assessments, the Danish Packaging and Transportation Research Institute and the Swedish Packaging Research Institute conclude that most models consider consumption of raw materials, energy, and water.[19] Only a few models consider energy recovery, work environment, resource consumption, and environmental emissions. The resource and environmental profile analysis model of the Midwest Research Institute deals with energy balances and pollutants of products from raw material extraction to waste disposal. The detailed personal computer-based life-cycle assessment model developed by Sundstrom begins with the raw material extraction from mines, forests, and wells and ends with the final waste management by incineration and disposal. The Boustead model used by the Industry Council for Packaging and the Environment incorporates raw material consumption and energy during various phases of a product's life cycle and has background data from several European countries. Some life-cycle assessments consist of two stages. In the first stage, an inventory of all inputs and outputs in terms of energy and materials during the life cycle of a product is generated. In the second stage, the environmental effects of this inventory are identified. The data generated during the second stage can be used to develop improvements; this is called life-cycle management. According to the 1990 Society of Environmental Toxicology and Chemistry conference, the complete life-cycle assessment should consist of three separate but interrelated stages, namely an inventory stage, an impact analysis stage, and an improvement stage.[20] The Canadian Standards Association suggests four phases: the initiation phase, consisting of the problem and objective definition; the inventory phase, defining raw materials and energy inputs and solid, liquid, and gaseous wastes; the impact analysis, connecting inputs and outputs to real-world environmental problems; and the improvement phase, focusing on the overall green performance. Life-cycle assessment is not carried out in sequential steps. Information from any stage can be used in other stages.

Life-cycle Scoping

The first step in performing a life-cycle assessment is to identify the purpose of analysis. The assessment may be done to compare materials, products, or processes; compare resource use; train employees in waste reduction; develop policy; or educate the public. The studies could be generic or product specific. The next step is to define the system boundaries. The system definition should include where the "cradle" begins and where the "grave" ends. It should begin with material extraction and end with final disposal of the product. The system definition should also take into account the depth of analysis. For example, should oil discarded from manufacturing equipment used to drill a hole be included? The system boundaries can affect the outcomes of a life-cycle assessment study. Therefore, when comparisons between two products are made, it is essential to ensure that the same system boundaries are used in both studies. One major difficulty during this step is the lack of a consensus about what should form the system boundaries and what phases should be covered.

Life-cycle Inventory Analysis

The purpose of life-cycle inventory analysis is to develop a model to account for all inputs and outputs during each stage in the life cycle. Typically, the system is broken down into various stages such as raw material extraction, raw material processing, manufacture, product fabrication, filling and packaging, assembly, distribution, use, reuse, maintenance, and recycle and waste disposal. The material and energy flows are indicated for each process (see Figure 4.1). Raw material acquisition includes extraction of raw materials from the earth, harvesting trees, and their transportation. The manufacturing stage includes a transformation process consisting of manufacture, fabrication, assembly, filling, and packaging. Use, reuse, and maintenance include energy consumption, storage, and consumption of a finished product. A recycle–waste-management stage includes energy consumption and environmental wastes produced during recycling and waste disposal. Energy requirements at each stage include energy consumed during process as well as transportation. Environmental wastes are typically categorized into discharges into air, water, and land. A variety of waste-disposal alternatives including land filling, incineration, recycling, and composting are considered.

FIGURE 4.1
Life-cycle Analysis

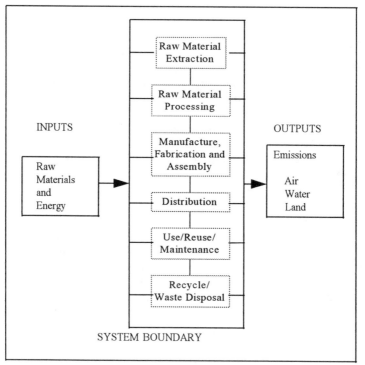

The focus of this step is data collection. Precisely measuring material and energy inputs at various stages is tedious and time consuming. The data can be collected from various sources. Government and industrial databases, government reports, life-cycle analysis reports, and laboratory test data and facilities are some sources for data. Consultants are also a valuable source for data. The amount of materials and energy expended may vary among different geographical regions. Therefore, caution is suggested while using such data. One way to overcome errors is to express results of life-cycle assessment as ranges (maximums and minimums). Life-cycle assessment output suffers from the garbage in, garbage out phenomenon. Accuracy will be directly affected by the data used. Therefore, it is essential to use reliable, comprehensive, and up-to-date data.

Life-cycle Impact Analysis

The life-cycle impact analysis evaluates the effects of resources and emissions identified in the life-cycle inventory analysis. One major problem during this step is deciding how to account for recycling and by-products. Once the data are collected and inventory of inputs and outputs prepared, the next step is to quantify the effect of the inventory on the environment. Impact analysis is still in the early stages of development. It should take into account, however, environmental and human health impacts, resource depletion, and social welfare. Impact analysis typically consists of classification, characterization, and valuation. The first step in impact analysis is to assign an item from inventory analysis to categories of environmental stressors. Stressors represent conditions that may lead to an impact. Stressor categories for each impact area have been identified. Impact categories typically include resource depletion, ecological degradation, and human health. However, quantifying these effects involves two serious problems: translating the effect and determining its aggregation. Currently, most impact-analysis methods involve some kind of scoring system. The ecological-scarcity method uses ratios of actual to maximum accepted environmental loading; the environmental theme method uses "affect categories" in relation to environmental policy objectives; and the environmental priority strategies in a product design method uses ecological scores. The Danish Technological Institute uses a panel of experts to develop impacts.[21]

Life-cycle Improvement Analysis

The purpose of improvement analysis is to identify opportunities to reduce energy and raw material consumption and emissions. The emphasis of the improvement analysis is on the entire life cycle of a product.

PROBLEMS

As the burgeoning literature on life-cycle assessment indicates, there is no one correct approach to employing this method of analysis. Energy requirements typically include the inherent energy of raw materials because life-cycle assessment is based on the thermodynamic principles. However, some models only include inherent energy in materials used as fuels. The second problem relates to the allocation of energy and wastes generated in processes producing several products. The most common allocation method is based on the mass ratios of products. The third problem relates to the allocation of energy savings from recycling. If energy savings are attributed to the process generating the wastes, such allocations will promote processes with wastes that can be recycled. However, if the energy savings are attributed to the processes that are using the recycled products, then such computations will encourage use of recycled products. Another fundamental problem of the life-cycle assessment relates to definitions of boundaries for analysis. The definition of boundaries, the quality of data, and the assumptions can significantly affect results. In the case of paper production, should analysis include fertilizer used to foster tree growth? While the life-cycle assessment approach has been used to compare such products as disposable and cloth diapers, groundwood and polystyrene hamburger containers, and returnable and reusable glass bottles, it has failed to provide clear-cut answers about the greenness of these products. The major problem with life-cycle assessment relates to comparison of data. Energy consumption can be aggregated in megajoules. However, combining energy consumption during transportation with the inherent energy in the inputs can be misleading. Solid wastes can be combined in terms of their volume or weight. Different impacts of emissions make it difficult to aggregate emissions into air although emissions are expressed in terms of parts per million. For instance, the impact of one part of sodium chloride on humans is different from the impact of one part of potassium cyanide. Aside from problems relating to aggregating data, life-cycle assessment is also problematic in evaluating environmental impacts. Some environmental impacts are local and others are global. Emissions into air and water typically have significant impacts on the local level. The local impacts of emissions depend on time, site, and factors such as the concentration of emissions. For example, impacts of emissions in urban areas are more serious than impacts of emissions in rural areas because urban emissions are typically more concentrated. Often, a combination of chemicals can have a more serious impact than individual chemicals on humans. Therefore, adding pollution may not represent actual impacts. Another problem relating to impact assessment is the differences in long- and short-term impacts. Life-cycle assessment considers only environmental factors. However, socioeconomic and political factors may affect the interpretation of these environmental factors. For example, durability of a product should be considered in the evaluation. In short, life-cycle assessment suffers from serious problems of aggregation of emissions and energy consumptions, and their conversion to environmental impacts.

USES OF LIFE-CYCLE ASSESSMENTS

Life-cycle assessment can be used for a variety of purposes. Anyone who wants to evaluate the greenness of a product can start with life-cycle assessment. Such an analysis can provide valuable information about environmental burdens of a product to its manufacturer and can also provide information about how to improve the greenness of a product. Since life-cycle assessment provides valuable information about wastes generated at different phases, a manufacturer can develop effective design and production changes to reduce waste. Life-cycle assessment can help a product or process designer by directing her through appropriate development work. Outputs of the life-cycle assessment are an objective basis for eco-labeling schemes and informing consumers about environmentally friendly products.

Manufacturers generally advertise their products as eco-friendly based on a single criterion such as recycling potential or the amount of waste generated during one or two stages of a product's life. Life-cycle assessment helps to prevent such claims with a comprehensive analysis of wastes generated. It considers every stage of a product's life and analyzes all inputs and outputs generated at all stages of a product. Traditionally, manufacturers took responsibility for wastes generated from the time the raw material enters the production stage and to the time the finished product left the factory. However, life-cycle assessment now includes stages from the extraction of raw materials to the final disposal of a product. It considers the entire life cycle of a product. In short, life-cycle assessment represents an integrated approach.

Life-cycle assessment goes beyond factory walls to examine a product's environmental impact. By evaluating both the upstream and downstream activities of a product, life-cycle assessment provides more data on which informed decisions can be made. Although this method advocates a systems approach, it can also be used to select a process, material, product, or policy. For instance, the battery-powered electric vehicles are wrongly called zero-emission vehicles, because they do not generate air emissions during a use stage. Since gasoline vehicles emit hydrocarbons, carbon monoxide, and nitrogen oxides during a use stage, electric vehicles are considered greener than gasoline vehicles. However, power plants that generate the electricity used to charge these batteries do emit sulfur dioxides and particulate matters. Life-cycle assessments can be extremely useful in analyzing these types of situations.

EXTENSIONS OF LIFE-CYCLE ASSESSMENTS

Value:impact Assessment

We should not evaluate products solely on life-cycle assessments. While some products may generate more waste than others, at the same time they may provide a better value to the consumer. Products should be judged in terms of both waste generated and their value, which may be measured in terms of performance, condition of the product, and consumer satisfaction.[22]

One reason for a low market share of several green products may be that they are not delivering performance. The goal should be to provide maximum performance while minimizing waste. The strategy is to incorporate performance measurements while performing life-cycle assessments. The value represents how well a product performs compared with what the consumer wants and is willing to pay. In other words, the value measures fitness for use. The fitness for use of a product will vary from consumer to consumer. It will depend on how well a product satisfies a customer's needs. These needs are identified by asking customers for input by means of questionnaires, group discussions, and focus groups. Once needs are identified, products advance to the research and development phase. The product is then tested in laboratories and homes. Based on the responses received from the testing, the product is improved. Other aspects of products that need to be evaluated include the cost and total risk (see Figure 4.2).

Environmental Option Assessment

One major drawback of life-cycle assessment is the need for technical experts to make environmental tradeoffs. In addition, life-cycle assessment fails to provide a comprehensive analysis of environmental effects and economic costs and benefits. The objective of the environmental option assessment is to help decision makers evaluate options to diminish the environmental impact of a product during its life cycle.[23] Environment option assessment begins with the estimation of volume flows and identification of environmental issues involved. This step consists of drawing volume flow diagrams, identifying major environmental issues, defining options, and selecting options for detailed evaluation. Major environmental concerns can be pollution issues (e.g., global warming, ozone depletion, acidification, and disposal of waste), conservation issues (e.g., depletion of mineral and energy resources, soil degradation, and depletion of biological resources), and diversity issues (e.g., decrease of biological diversity). Priorities are set in the next phase, which consists of collecting data, determining the economic profile, and positioning options. Both hard and soft data must be gathered concerning the environmental impacts

FIGURE 4.2
Value:impact Analysis

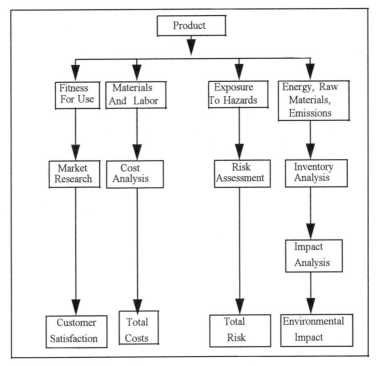

of each option. Economic data concerning annual costs and the operating and capital costs of the options are also collected. Once both environmental and economic data are collected, the next step is to estimate the environmental yields and economic impacts of each option. This estimation is calculated by decision makers rather than environmental experts. Economic impacts and environmental yields are then plotted on an option map. Using option maps, policy makers establish goals, allocate resources, and assign responsibilities.

Impact Analysis Matrix

An impact analysis matrix is a valuable tool with which to make decisions on pollution prevention options.[24] An impact analysis matrix comprises columns of inputs and outputs and rows of environmental impacts. Inputs may be raw materials and energy; outputs may be atmospheric emissions, liquid wastes, and solid wastes. Impact areas may include global warming, ozone depletion, acidification, waste disposal, depletion of energy resources, soil degradation, and a decrease in biological diversity. The columns and rows are application dependent. Once inputs, outputs, and impact areas are established, the next step is to assign unweighted scores. A score of +1 or greater typically represents a larger environmental impact than the base option; −1 or less signifies lesser impact; and 0 represents no significant difference in impact. This matrix can be improved by using weighted scores.

THE BENEFITS OF LIFE-CYCLE ASSESSMENT

By providing comparisons of environmental burdens of similar systems, the life-cycle assessment approach proves to be an objective evaluation method. Life-cycle assessment can also be used to compare different products, but interpretation will require more care. Life-cycle assessment is an integrated approach that includes all components; inputs and emissions from the system; inputs and emissions over the entire life cycle of a product; facilities, raw material acquisition methods; distribution and disposal methods; and issues including recycle, reuse, and so on. It expresses environmental degradation in terms of multiple criteria rather than a single criterion. Life-cycle assessment provides a framework for communication between scientists and engineers, purchasers and suppliers, and regulators and polluters. It helps the industry to understand the global effects of its decisions. It encourages companies to realize pollution-prevention activities that need to be initiated. Life-cycle assessments improve green audits by providing an inventory of emissions. By supplying data on the effects of various pollutants, life-cycle impact analysis also helps management rank pollution-reduction activities. Life-cycle assessment highlights the seriousness of various pollutants and can thus help policy makers to develop "green taxes."

EXAMPLES OF ENVIRONMENTAL IMPACTS

When environmental impacts of a product are considered, the focus is typically on manufacturing operations. However, many environmental impacts are not necessarily the result of manufacturing operations. For example, according to the American Fiber Manufacturers Association, an "average" polyester blouse consumes more resources during washing and drying than during its manufacture.[25]

Steel is one of the primary materials used in the manufacture of combustion engine vehicles. Using steel as a basis, consider some examples of the environmental impacts that occur during the various stages of the life cycle of a combustion engine vehicle. Steel is made out of iron, which is extracted through surface operations. The ore is concentrated using separation techniques. Extraction degrades landscapes, flora and fauna, and surrounding water systems because of the storm-water runoffs it causes. The concentration operation produces dusts, liquid wastes, and tailing. Extraction of one ton of iron ore produces five tons of wastes. Steel is produced by purifying iron. This energy-intensive process releases significant quantities of off-gases in addition to producing slags. The scrubbers used to clean the off-gases generate wastewaters that need to be disposed of.

Car manufacturing also produces a variety of hazardous wastes. Manufacturing operations generate dirty water that contains metals, dirt, oils, and grease. The assembly steps involve cleaning, sanding, and painting, a process that generates metal scraps and packaging wastes. Painting can release significant quantities of volatile organic compounds into the atmosphere. Shrink-wrap plastic coating used to protect finished surfaces during transportation ends up in a landfill as solid waste.

Vehicles with internal combustion engines generate most of their wastes during use and maintenance. They pollute the air by generating carbon monoxides, nitrogen oxides, and particulates. Road building can contaminate surface water and groundwater by surface runoff. Steel found in cars is typically recycled, but many other car products, including upholstery, foam, plastics, fiberglass, and rubber, will end up in a landfill. This is increasingly problematic as steel parts are now often replaced with hard-to-recycle plastics.

IMPLEMENTATION

Life-cycle assessment emphasizes a systems approach to company problem solving and offers a new perspective for company decision makers. Life-cycle assessment is best performed by a team consisting of personnel from manufacturing, design, engineering, marketing, and accounting. The team should formulate objectives of the life-cycle assessments and then define system boundaries and develop assumptions. The team should also decide timeframes over which environmental impacts will be studied, taking into account the sensitivity of the timeframe on the environmental impacts. The team must develop an inventory checklist, which should include decisions about various aspects of life-cycle assessment such as purpose, system boundaries, geographic scope, data categories, data collection procedures, data quality indicators, model development, and presentation of the results. Since life-cycle assessment involves several subjective decisions, it is essential to have a peer group to review the process. The peer group should examine system boundaries, data collection, and key assumptions and interpretations of the study. Data collection is the next major step. For data collection, the whole system may be broken down into subsystems. For each subsystem, input materials, energy consumption, transportation, outputs of products and by-products, emissions into air, discharges into water, solid wastes generated, and other releases should be identified. Industrial and government electronic databases, government reports, and laboratory test data are some sources of data for life-cycle inventory analysis. The material balance analysis is one approach to develop data. The next step is to construct a model. Computer spreadsheets are extremely useful for calculating inventory. The final step is to present the results of the analysis. The full report should present original data; details of the model including system boundaries, assumptions, and sources of data; sensitivity analysis of various assumptions; inventory of inputs and outputs; and the basis for impact analysis.

CONCLUSION

Life-cycle assessment is an important tool for green management. By measuring greenness from cradle to grave, it provides an objective basis for comparison and improvement. As more life-cycle assessments are performed, systems definition, methodology, and databases will become standardized. Consensuses about converting life-cycle inventories into environmental burdens will emerge. As more life-cycle assessments are published, public debates about a variety of environmental issues will follow. Peer reviews will significantly improve the quality of life-cycle assessments. The next few years should prove an exciting period for the development of life-cycle assessments. By providing objective measuring tools, life-cycle assessments are likely to improve the quality of our environment.

NOTES

1. Robert U. Ayres, "Life Cycle Analysis: A Critique," working paper 94/33, The Centre for the Management of Environmental Resources, INSEAD, Fontainebleau, France, July 15, 1994.

2. Bruce Hannon, *Systems Energy and Recycling: A Study of the Beverage Industry* (Urbana: University of Illinois, Center for Advanced Computation, 1972; Ian Boustead, *The Milk Bottle* (Milton Keynes, U.K.: Open University Press, 1972).

3. J.A.G. Thomas, ed., *Energy Analysis* (Boulder, Colo.: Westview Press, 1977).

4. R. A. Herendeen, *Energy Costs of Goods and Services, 1963 and 1967*, CAC Documents 69 (Urbana: University of Illinois, Center for Advanced Computation, 1974); Robert U. Ayres, Thomas Betlach, and Christofer Decker, "The Potential for Energy Conservation with Particular Application to Personal Transportation and Space Heating," research report (IRT-404-R) prepared for Energy, Mines and Resource, Canada, International Research and Technology Corporation, Washington, D.C., October 1975; C. W. Bullard, P. S. Penner, and D. A. Pilati, "Net Energy Analysis: Handbook for Combining Process and Input-Output Analysis," *Resources and Energy* 1 (1978): 267–313.

5. Robert U. Ayres, James Cummings-Saxton, and Martin O. Stern, "Materials-Process-Product Model — A Feasibility Demonstration Based on the Bottle Manufacturing Industry," technical report (IRT-305-FR) prepared for the National Science Foundation, International Research and Technology Corporation, Washington, D.C., July 1974.

6. Mary Ann Curran, "Broad-based Environmental Life Cycle Assessment," *Environmental Science and Technology* 27(3) (1993):430–436.

7. R. G. Hunt and W. E. Franklin, "Resource and Environmental Profile Analysis," *Chemtech* 5(8) (1975): 474–480.

8. Council on Plastics and Packaging in the Environment, *COPPE Quarterly*, 5(1) (Spring 1991): 2–4; Midwest Research Institute, "Resource and Environmental Profile Analysis of Nine Beverage Container Alternatives," report prepared for the U.S. Environmental Protection Agency, Washington, D.C., 1974, EPA 530-SW-91C.

9. Franklin Associates, Inc., "Energy and Environmental Profile Analysis of Children's Disposable and Cloth Diapers," report prepared for the American Paper Institute, Washington, D.C., June 1990; Arthur D. Little, Inc., "Disposable versus Reusable Diapers — Health, Environmental and Economic Comparisons," report prepared for Procter & Gamble, Cincinnati, Ohio, 1990; C. Lehburger, J. Mullen, and C. V. Jones, "Diapers: Environmental Impacts and Life Cycle Analysis," report prepared for the National Association of Diaper Services, Philadelphia, Pennsylvania, January 1991.

10. Franklin Associates, Inc., "Resource and Environmental Profile Analysis of Foamed Polystyrene and Bleached Paperboard Containers," report prepared for the Council for Solid Waste Solutions, Washington, D.C., 1990.

11. Franklin Associates, Inc., "Resources and Environmental Profile Analysis of Polyethylene and Unbleached Paper Grocery Sacks," report prepared for the Council for Solid Waste Solutions, Washington, D.C., June 1990.

12. Franklin Associates, Inc., "Project Synopsis: Resource and Environmental Profile Analysis of Hard Surface Cleaners and Home Remedy Cleaning Systems," report prepared for Procter & Gamble, Cincinnati, Ohio, April 14, 1992.

13. D. G. Koch and C. C. Kuta, *Inside Environment*, 3(12) (1991): 8–20.

14. The Tellus Institute, "Packaging Study (Project Summary)," report prepared for the Council of State Governments, Lexington, Kentucky, November 1991; The Tellus Institute, "Impacts of Production and Disposal of Packaging Materials — Methods and Case Studies," report prepared for the Council of State Governments, Lexington, Kentucky, November 1991.

15. Midwest Research Institute, "Resource and Environmental Profile Analysis of Plastics and Competitive Materials," report prepared for the Society of the Plastic Industry, Kansas City, Missouri, 1974.

16. Franklin Associates, Inc., "Family-size Soft Drink Container — A Comparative Energy and Environmental Impact Analysis, Volume I — Summary," report prepared for the Goodyear Tire and Rubber Company, Akron, Ohio, 1978.

17. Franklin Associates, Inc., "Comparative Energy and Environmental Impacts for the Delivery of Soft Drinks in Nine Containers," report prepared for the National Association for Plastic Container Recovery, Charlotte, North Carolina, 1989.

18. Chem Systems, "Vinyl Products Life Cycle Assessment," report prepared for the Vinyl Institute, Washington, D.C., March 1992.

19. Sven-Olof Ryding, *Environmental Management Handbook* (Amsterdam: IOS Press, 1992), pp. 439–441.

20. Society for Environmental Toxicology and Chemistry, *A Technical Framework for Life-cycle Assessments* (Washington, D.C.: Society for Environmental Toxicology and Chemistry, 1991).

21. Ryding, *Environmental Management Handbook*, pp. 444–445.

22. Peter Hindle, Peter White, and Kate Minion, "Achieving Real Environmental Improvements Using Value:impact Assessment," *Long Range Planning* 26(3) (1993): 36–48.

23.   Pieter Winsemius and Walter Hahn, "Environmental Option Assessment," *Columbia Journal of World Business* 27 (Fall and Winter 1992):248–266.

24.   Bruce Vigon, "Life-cycle Assessment," in *Industrial Pollution Prevention Handbook*, ed. Harry M. Freeman (New York: McGraw-Hill, 1995), pp. 305–307.

25.   Jennifer Nash and Mark D. Stoughton, "Learning to Live with Life Cycle Assessment," *Environmental Science and Technology* 28(5) (1994): 236A–237A.

II

GREEN FUNCTIONAL MANAGEMENT

5

Green Design

Product design determines input materials, manufacturing processes, packaging, distribution, and disposal methods. Therefore, an effective design can improve quality, reduce costs, and develop green products. For green products to withstand public scrutiny, product development must begin with green design. Product design is the ideal stage to address environmental concerns. Products can obtain environmental labeling only if they are designed to achieve labeling requirements. Even though design activity consumes only a very small fraction of the corporate budget, the decisions that determine more than 70 percent of total product costs are made during the design stage. In addition, product design decisions have significant impact on the quantity of wastes generated at different stages of a product's life cycle. According to a conservative estimate, only 6 percent of the 20,000 pounds of materials extracted per person from U.S. territories each year are incorporated in durable goods and the other 94 percent are discarded as waste within months of extraction.[1] Even a small reduction in the raw material consumption can significantly reduce landfills and the depletion of the earth's mineral riches. Therefore, companies recognize that green design is the strategy to follow to remain competitive and receptive to consumers. Companies also support green design because of their desire to be good corporate citizens. Impending regulations are also spurring green design efforts. In Germany, manufacturers are responsible for product packaging. Many countries in Europe require companies to take back products they manufacture after use by consumers. Therefore, companies that wish to sell globally must make their products compatible with the green dictates of international markets. Computer and auto manufacturers in the United States are developing plans to reuse their products.

However, green design is easier said than accomplished. New varieties of available materials have made design a complex process. There has been a dramatic shift from the use of agricultural and forestry materials to materials derived from minerals and petroleum. High labor costs have made buying newer products cheaper than repairing existing ones. Product liability concerns have encouraged companies to produce nonreparable products. These disincentives suggest that a company will support green design only if compelled by government regulations. Consequently, many designers view environmental considerations as constraints rather than objectives. Smart companies, however, recognize that green design is consistent with competitive product design. Fewer materials in products reduce manufacturing and inventory costs. Reduction of hazardous materials in products makes workplaces safer, disposal of wastes easier, and threats of potential liability lower. In addition, total quality, global sourcing, concurrent engineering, and design for manufacture are consistent with the goals of green design. For example, Siemens Nixdorf's green model PC41 has only 29 assembly pieces, takes only 7 minutes to assemble, and 4 minutes to disassemble. However, the previous model, PCD-2, took 33 minutes to assemble, 18 minutes to disassemble, and had 87 assembly pieces.[2] This chapter presents various design strategies to reduce pollution, methods to evaluate alternative designs, and ways to promote green designs.

GREEN DESIGN STRATEGIES

A product design conceived by a designer must satisfy a variety of goals. It must be functional; it must be in compliance with federal, state, and local regulations; it should lend itself to easy manufacture and assembly. A designer can improve greenness by modifying either a product or whole product system including the manufacturing process, distribution, use, and disposal. Overhauling whole systems can achieve maximum reduction in pollution for the time spent, but bringing changes to the product system is an ambitious task that is usually not within the realm of designers.

Source reduction and better waste management are two broad types of green design strategies. Source-reduction strategies eliminate pollution at the source itself by using less material to perform the same job. Weight reduction, material substitution, and product-life extensions are all goals of source reduction. Better waste-management techniques promote recycling, reuse, and reclamation of materials. Waste-management techniques include design for disassembly, design for recyclability, design for remanufacturing, and design for composting and incineration (see Figure 5.1).

Source-reduction Strategies

Materials are major contributors of environmental degradation. Even though extraction, processing, and manufacturing add value to

FIGURE 5.1
Green Design Strategies

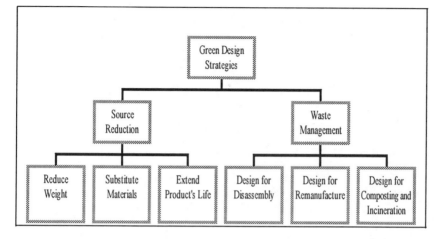

products, these processes also damage the environment. Therefore, any reduction in material consumption can save energy and prevent environmental damage. World demand for materials is rising. During the 1970–1991 period, total world consumption of raw materials grew by 40 percent. During the same time, demand for agricultural products rose by 40 percent, forestry products by 44 percent, metals by 26 percent, and organic chemicals by 69 percent.[3] Falling prices of commodities, in constant U.S. dollars, is one of the reasons for such a dramatic increase in consumption (see Figure 5.2).[4] Economic growth in developing countries is another reason. An average person in a developed country uses as much as ten times the amount of metals as that used by a person in a developing country. If every person on this earth used materials at the rate of developed countries, then the world would require a staggering sevenfold increase in steel production, elevenfold increase in copper production, and twelvefold increase in aluminum production.[5]

Materials are wasted when they are used nonproductively or excessively. Generally more material is wasted in use and disposal than in extraction, processing, or manufacturing. Weight-reduction strategies involve reducing material content required to perform a given function. By using high-strength materials and reducing the thickness of components, for example, it is possible to cut down on the quantities of waste generated. However, weight reduction by itself will not be beneficial for society as a whole. For example, every 250-pound reduction in body weight of an automobile reduces fuel consumption by increasing by one the mileage for each gallon of the fuel. If a design uses only a small quantity of a material, then waste discharges, emissions,

FIGURE 5.2
Percentage Changes in the World Price for Metals, 1980–92 (in U.S. dollars)

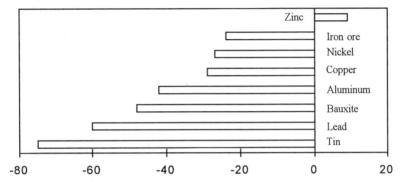

Source: John E. Young and Aaron Sachs, *The Next Efficiency Revolution: Creating a Sustainable Materials Economy* (Washington, D.C.: Worldwatch Institute, 1994), p. 17.

and energy consumed by that material are also reduced.[6] Automobile weights were significantly reduced during the 1976–1988 period.[7] The term *dematerialization* is used to describe the reduction over time in weight of the materials used in several products. According to Figure 5.3, there was a significant reduction in material used in cars between 1978 and 1988. There was also a change in the composition of materials used.[8] However, according to L. Evans, the likelihood of the unbelted driver dying in a 2,000-pound car is 2.6 times the likelihood of a similar driver dying in a 4,000-pound car. The likelihood of a serious or fatal injury resulting from two-car crashes involving two 2,000-pound cars is twice the likelihood of a similar occurrence in two-car crashes involving two 4,000-pound cars.[9] Therefore, weight reduction by itself may not be a sufficient reason for choosing a product design.

There has been impressive lightweighting in packaging. Glass bottles now contain 30 to 50 percent fewer materials and beverage cans contain 60 percent less aluminum than they did in the 1950s. Lightweighting, in addition to reducing material, minimizes energy use during transportation. However, less material consumption by itself does not lead to greenness. If smaller and lighter products are of inferior quality, then their frequent replacement will result in more waste from production as well as consumption. Consumer products such as toasters, irons, and television sets have been produced with reduced weights. However, if they break down easily, then more of them will be discarded, causing increased demand for them. In the United States, consumption of nonrubber shoes, which are difficult to repair, has risen from 3.9 per person in 1970 to 4.6 per person in 1985.[10] However, tire consumption per unit mile traveled has been falling because of improved tire

FIGURE 5.3
Automobile Weight Category Distribution Percentages, 1976–78 and 1986–88

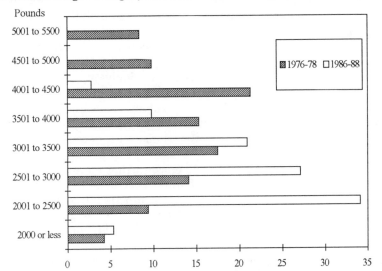

Source: U.S. General Accounting Office, *Highway Safety*, GAO/PEMD-92-1 (Washington, D.C.: General Accounting Office, 1992), p. 15.

quality.[11] The effect of lightweighting in manufacturing should also be considered. For example, the shift from mainframe to personal computers has increased the number of personal computers used, causing more material usage and waste. Similarly, economies of scale in production may make it possible to have few large plants rather than many small plants. Few large plants may be environmentally more benign than many small plants. To sum up, quality, manufacturing process, production costs, ease of repair, size, and complexity of product are just some of the factors that can affect the amounts of materials used by a product. Lightweighting strategy should be evaluated in terms of effects of other factors before implementation.

Companies focusing on packaging redesign and concentration strategies can reduce waste. Since packaging materials constitute about one-third of municipal solid waste, it makes sense to redesign packaging. Elimination, reduction, and recyclable packaging are some approaches to packaging redesign. Colgate, for example, redesigned its toothpaste tube to stand on its head and eliminated the cardboard box. Procter & Gamble eliminated the outer cartons on its Sure and Secret antiperspirants, which reduced production costs by 20 percent. Concentration strategy used by detergent manufacturers, in addition to minimizing shipping costs, considerably reduces packaging waste. Bulk packaging is another strategy to reduce wastes. Products serving multiple purposes can significantly reduce wastes and be convenient for consumers. Shampoos, conditioners, and detergents with bleach are some examples of multipurpose products. Reusable or refillable packaging can also reduce waste.

If a consumer has to make a choice between a polluting and a nonpolluting product, he is likely to choose a nonpolluting one. Hence a manufacturer of a polluting product is likely to lose its market share in the long run. Therefore, substitution of polluting materials with less polluting ones is a sensible strategy to reduce pollution and remain competitive. However, material substitution is not easy as it may change final product specifications and necessitate careful implementation.

A product's service life can be increased using more durable materials or through modular designs. Modular designs build products from a combination of components of definable functionality. The modular design expands product options. Modular products are easy to manufacture and design and their components can be serviced, upgraded, or replaced without affecting other components. By replacing affected components, product performance can be maintained over several years. However, products with longer service lives are typically more expensive to purchase and because consumers tend to consider only initial costs rather than lifetime costs, this reduces a manufacturer's incentive to produce durable products. Therefore, to reap maximum advantage of extended service life, many companies are resorting to leasing rather than selling their equipment. AT&T, for example, used to rent their phones and repair them when they broke. As a result, phones had a lifetime of 30 years. However, after the breakup of the Bell telephone system, the phones were owned by the consumers. Consequently, 20 to 25 million phones are now routinely discarded each year.[12] Computers, copiers, and medical equipment are examples of other products that are frequently leased. This strategy might be better suited for high-value durable products rather than low-value disposable products, but due to high servicing costs it might not be economical to implement this strategy for each individual consumer.

Waste-management Strategies

Waste-management strategies do not reduce pollution, but they do facilitate disposal. Designs are aimed at making products easy to remanufacture, recycle, compost, and incinerate. To facilitate remanufacturing and recycling, products should be easy to disassemble into component parts. A product is discarded after use and ends up in a landfill. More than 15 percent of municipal solid waste constitutes durable goods (see Figure 5.4). About 32 million tons of durable goods were discarded in 1993 alone. Most computers become obsolete after a year, and for every three computers sold, two become obsolete, filling already scarce landfills. Therefore, it is essential to develop ways to recycle them. The concepts of design for recycling and disassembly are becoming formalized. Companies are developing a variety of ways to recycle their manufactured products. For example, three-fourths of the cars in the United States are already refurbished and reused. Used parts dealers are restoring and reselling engines, generators, alternators, and other parts. When a machine is returned, parts are segregated into different plastics, metals, and so on. Parts that are not worn are recycled. However, recycling is not easy. Even adhesives on paper labels can contaminate plastic, making it unfit for recycling. Therefore, companies are developing innovative assembly and manufacturing methods. There are a variety of materials to choose from. By choosing materials that satisfy the correct range of properties and that can be recycled, material selection is speeded up. Recycling is a labor-intensive operation. Therefore, the use of similar materials should be encouraged and materials should separate easily. Paint, label adhesives, and reinforcing foams should be avoided as they adulterate plastic, and because they have a lower melting point than plastic, they present health hazards when incinerated. Another strategy is to mold identifiers on each part.

FIGURE 5.4
Products Generated in Municipal Solid Waste by Weight, 1993
(total weight = 206.9 million tons)

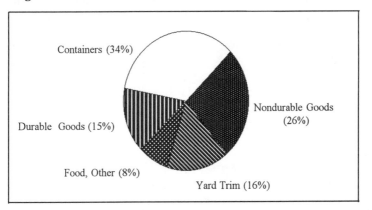

Source: U.S. Environmental Protection Agency, *Characterization of Municipal Solid Waste in the United States: 1994 Update*, Executive Summary, EPA/530-S-94-042 (Washington, D.C.: Government Printing Office, November 1994), p. 8.

Product-differentiation strategy encourages too many varieties of products, which increases recycling and repair costs. In addition, critical assemblies are often sealed and must be returned if a customer wants them to be repaired. Often such assemblies are discarded, significantly increasing solid waste.

Disassembly is a basic requirement for product recycling. Design for disassembly aims at making refurbishment and reuse of materials easier. Companies with products designed for disassembly can achieve significant competitive advantage by taking back their products and recycling them. Durable products such as automobiles, refrigerators, and cooking appliances are currently being designed for disassembly. However, designing for disassembly is not easy. For example, to make disposable diapers easy to disassemble and reclaim pulp and plastics, it should be possible to segregate pulp and plastics from tape tabs, elastic gathers, polyethylene pulp, and so on. The name of the game in designing for disassembly is the development of multifunctional products without the use of multiple components. To improve disassembly, snap fits are preferred over assemblies with screws or glues. However, the expensive tooling required for close tolerances of snap fits increases costs. Minimization of parts promotes faster disassembly. Any product can be designed for disassembly. However, the value of the item determines whether recycling it is economically feasible. Products are often designed to make disassembly harder. While this increases the sturdiness and reliability of the product, the recyclability of the product is compromised. To design for disassembly, consider these suggestions: reduce material variety; use materials that can be recycled as one; reduce the number of parts and assembly steps; standardize parts; highlight separation points and materials; design for easier separation, handling, and cleaning of parts; reduce fasteners; and minimize energy usage.

Remanufacture and reuse can serve the goals of material recycling. The purpose of remanufacturing is to renovate an old product. Remanufacturing extends a product's service life. It promotes the use of subcomponents and parts that would otherwise have been scrapped. Since remanufacturing makes economic sense, kitchen appliances, machine tools, and copiers are currently being remanufactured.

Several design guidelines for product recycling should be heeded. Mark materials for easy identification at the scrap yard. Before replacing materials, evaluate the effects on secondary material industries. Consider disposability of materials and eliminate materials that pollute when incinerated. Develop recycling systems to reclaim strategic materials from low-value scraps. Evaluate coated or composite materials. Finally, consider using recovered materials.

Recycling is difficult to implement in practice as diverse materials need to be separated and purified before they can be used. For example, woolen suits can no longer by recycled into coats and blankets because most new clothes are made out of blends of natural and artificial fibers.[13] Materials need to be upgraded for deterioration from aging and stresses due to recycling. When waste cannot be eliminated or recycled, designs should consider composting or incineration options. Products comprising completely biodegradable materials can safely be disposed of in landfills. Less heavy metals and chlorinated organics can be incinerated.

Wasteful use of materials in products can be significantly reduced by eliminating unnecessary, oversize, and overweight components. Product life can be extended by preventing obsolescence and improving product use. Inflexible product lines and the use of inappropriate materials are a major reason for the waste of scarce materials. After-sales service and encouragement of the reuse of products can significantly reduce mate-rial consumption. Standardization of parts can reduce excessive inventory and production. Green design strategies can be summarized as follows.[14]

Reduce Use of Materials
    Cut down size.
    Stress optimization.
    Improve manufacturing techniques.
    Remove unnecessary parts.
    Standardize parts.
    Use high strength materials.
    Reduce scrap generation.
    Start with raw materials with dimensions close to those of finished products.
    Use powder metallurgy manufacturing techniques.
    Reduce thickness.
    Design for recycling.
    Make functional changes in product.

Replace Critical Materials
    Substitute critical materials with less critical ones.
    Use renewable materials.
    Use recycled materials.

Increase Product Life
    Rework.
    Reuse.
    Remanufacture.
    Reduce obsolescence.
    Reduce failures.
    Improve maintenance.
    Increase corrosion and wear resistance.
    Use a modular design.
    Allow for an after-sale service infrastructure.

Reduce Inventories
    Standardize parts.
    Encourage use of used parts.

Reduce Material Intensity
   Reduce alloy content.
   Reduce coatings.

GREEN DESIGN METHODOLOGIES

Braden Allenby proposes five principles for developing green design methodologies. According to Allenby, methodologies should be system-based.[15] They should involve multiple disciplines. Only technology can reduce environmental degradations and policies and procedures should be developed to encourage green process and product technologies. The free-rider problem should be eliminated by internalizing environmental degradation costs. Policies and regulations must encourage experimentation and research.

Allenby suggests categorizing products into low design–high materials and high design–low materials in order to better develop green design strategies and policies.[16] Low design–high materials products include packaging, cosmetic products, and bulk chemicals. These products involve few materials and therefore are easy to recycle. Their design is generally straightforward. High design–low materials items include automobiles and airplanes. These products involve a variety of materials, making recycling difficult. Evaluating the greenness of these products is also difficult. Policy decisions have different effects on high design–low materials and low design–high materials products. For example, mandatory recycling laws will force high design–low materials products to be constructed for easy disassembly and recycling. However, the same law will make low design–high materials products such as packaging economically impractical because of high transportation costs of used products.

High design–low materials items are typically durable products whereas low design–high materials items tend to be consumable products. There are significant differences in their life cycles. Low design–high materials items are low-technology products that come in all sizes. They generate a high volume of geographically scattered post-consumer solid wastes, most of which are generated during manufacturing. They have a short life-cycle duration, are low in cost, and do not have after-sales service or support. On the other hand, high design–low materials items involve high technology; are large in size; generate less postconsumer solid wastes; produce wastes during all phases of the life cycle; have high potential for recycling, reuse, and remanufacture; are expensive; and have after-sales service and support.

Green design can be implemented either globally for all products or piecemeal for individual products, processes, or inputs. Global analysis includes evaluation to determine whether harmful materials are used in products and their elimination. Substitution of chlorinated solvents by water-based cleaners for all cleaning activities is an example of global analysis. The green design of a product or process involves defining system boundaries, data collection, and data summarization. Defining system boundaries is important as this will determine the depth of analysis that will be done. If system boundaries are drawn widely, a greater number of options will be developed. For example, to analyze a soldering process, the system boundary could be defined as a soldering or joining operation. If the system is defined as a soldering process, then various materials that will be used in soldering will be considered, but if the system is defined as a joining process, then various joining techniques such as welding and riveting will need to be considered.

Gregory Keoleian and Dan Menerey have developed a green design system that utilizes life-cycle assessment as its basis.[17] Their design goals include resource conservation, pollution prevention, equitable distribution of resources and risk, and preservation of the ecosystem. Concurrent design, green quality, design teams, and management commitment are the backbone of effective green design initiatives. Their green design system consists of interrelated steps of needs analysis; formulation of design requirements in terms of environmental, functional, economic, cultural, and regulatory parameters; development of design from concept to detailed versions; and implementation.

The purpose of needs analysis is to determine what customers want from the product. Once the needs are identified, the next step is to outline system boundaries and to establish a project plan. The design team should also consider whether they wish to perform complete life-cycle analysis, partial life-cycle analysis involving narrow system boundaries, or examine only a stage of the product's life cycle. During this step, the team should also decide whether it wants to limit the study only to improving an existing product or simply developing a newer generation model.

The purpose of requirements formulations is to define the expected design outcome. The requirements, in addition to factors such as safety, efficiency, aesthetics, cost, functionality, and reliability should include environmental attributes. The requirements can be categorized into musts and wants. The designs that cannot satisfy musts are rejected outright. Wants are desirable attributes and they form the basis for design selection. Low-priority requirements are grouped into ancillary requirements and are incorporated into the design if they do not adversely affect musts criteria.

For the purpose of life-cycle assessment, Keoleian and Menerey divided product life cycle into raw material acquisition, bulk material processing, engineered materials production, manufacturing and assembly, use and service, retirement, and disposal. They suggested that a requirement matrix be used to compare various design alternatives and that full-cost accounting be used to account for costs of pollution and environmental degradation.

GREEN DESIGN EVALUATION

There are no hard and fast rules for evaluating a design for greenness. One reason for this is that while a multitude of factors point to greenness, there is no definition per se of what constitutes greenness. The greenness of a design is determined by such factors as product performance, safety, reliability, and so on. Increasing varieties of available materials, efficient processes, and the plethora of new regulations have made the selection of optimal designs a long and expensive process. Regulatory requirements — fuel efficiency, building codes, tamper-proof packaging, and safety guidelines, to name a few — are hampering the introduction of products with efficient designs. A design must satisfy marketing needs and production capabilities and must sometimes be compatible with previous designs. In addition, designers must make tradeoffs among various design objectives and environmental objectives.

There are several subjective methods to evaluate designs based on their greenness. Allenby ranks impacts of product, process, and input into various categories such as "not applicable," "positive," "no concern," "minor concern," "moderate concern," and "significant concern." Allenby also suggests ranking uncertainty.[18] Product, process, and input are evaluated from initial production to disposal in four areas — environmental, manufacturing, social/political, and toxicity/exposure. Summary evaluation for each area is then tabulated based on the ranking from initial production, manufacturing, packaging, transportation, consumer use, reuse and recycleability, and disposal.

Green design can significantly influence the manufacture and disposal of a product. Decisions that reduce pollution during these stages are likely to have more impact than decisions to change product composition. However, persuading companies to change manufacture, use, and disposal is not easily accomplished and designers are not given incentives to produce designs that will give the maximum return for their efforts.

The greenness of a design should not be evaluated on the basis of a single criterion. Design decisions involve a variety of factors and therefore rational tradeoffs between various design parameters need to be considered for evaluating greenness of a design. The availability of too many materials makes environmental evaluation difficult and expensive.

The first step in the evaluation of a green design involves identification of wastes generated at different stages of a product's life cycle. For the purpose of analysis, stages of a product's life can be classified into material acquisition, material processing, product distribution, product use, and product disposal. Such a breakdown is required to assess the impact of different pollutants. The wastes generated during the acquisition phase are usually felt by the stores and handling personnel. The pollution generated during manufacturing usually affects manufacturing employees and communities surrounding the facility. The waste generated during use and disposal phases can significantly influence product sales. Materials involved during different phases of a product can be identified from lists of materials, process charts, flow diagrams, and process simulations. Once materials involved during the entire life cycle of a product are identified, the next step is to ensure that these materials and processes do not violate any existing or potential federal, state, and local laws and regulations. Because a company intends to sell products over a long period of time, the evaluation of designs should not be confined to existing laws and regulations. Every effort should be made to ensure that products, processes, use, and disposal are not likely to threaten safety and environmental quality. Product life-cycle analysis is an analytical method for rating environmental costs and benefits of different design choices. The focus of a product life-cycle analysis is on the entire life of a product. The objective is to estimate the sum total of environmental risks arising from input resources and output wastes generated during extraction, material manufacture, distribution, product use, and product disposal. Such an analysis is considered the ultimate yardstick in evaluating greenness of a design. However, life-cycle analysis is hard to perform. Health and environmental effects are difficult to quantify. For example, how do you compare the emission of one pound of nitrogen oxide into the air with the destruction of one tree from a forest? Availability of data presents another problem. The assumptions used in the life-cycle analysis can also affect the results. In addition, limits of analysis should be clearly defined. Even though life-cycle analysis cannot provide precise answers about quantities of waste generated, it can point designers in the right direction. Software packages are also available that can help in the evaluation of product designs.

Because the methodology behind life-cycle analysis is not yet rigorous, other approximate methods to evaluate the greenness of a product can be used. One strategy is to define degrees of greenness at different stages of a life cycle of a product.[19] For example, greenness improves with reduction of solid waste, liquid waste, and air emissions during the manufacturing stage. Incineration is greener than landfilling, recycling is greener than incineration, and source reduction is the greenest of all options. The strategy is to develop a green scoring system that specifies numerical values for various green features. The design is evaluated based on how it achieves various greenness criteria. For example, if a design meets a certain criterion completely, it gets ten points, whereas it might get only five points for partial satisfaction of a criterion. The summary green rating is obtained by summing up all scores and dividing it by the maximum possible scores. Product features that may be used for scoring purposes include material variety, recycled components, compatibility with American Society for Testing and

Materials or International Standard Organization, ease of disassembly and repair, and presence of hazardous chemicals. The scoring system for the manufacturing stage may include such criteria as air emissions, liquid discharges, solid wastes, and energy consumption. The scoring system for the use and disposal stages may include such measures as product life, weight, packaging materials, and biodegradability. Once greenness criteria are identified, they can be used to improve existing product designs.

Another interesting green design evaluation system is the environmental priority strategies (EPS) in product design system developed by the Federation of Swedish Industries, the Swedish Environmental Research Institute, and the Volvo Car Company.[20] This technique translates an "environmental load profile," consisting of energy and raw material consumption and various emissions, into an "environmental impact profile," consisting of the impacts, and then aggregates the impacts and produces a final evaluation. The goal of the EPS system is to highlight environmental impacts through a "transparent eco-calculation" procedure. The crux of the system is the environmental indices for natural resources, pollutant emissions, and materials and processes. The indices for the effects of the natural resources and pollutants are obtained by multiplying environmental indices by the "ecological scores." Environmental load values are obtained by summing up various impacts and making adjustments using an uncertainty factor to account for possible inaccuracies in the data. The environmental indices for natural resources are estimated based on the world per capita known availability of the resources and their uniqueness. The ecological scores that measure the impacts are based on environmental and health effects such as the characteristics and extent of the effect, the severity and frequency, aerial effect, durability, quantity of emission, cost of remediation, and so on.

ORGANIZING FOR GREEN DESIGN

Top management neglect, cost and regulatory constraints, tradition-bound behavior, a slow corporate decision-making process, and cost- rather than engineering-based design evaluations have significantly obstructed green product design. The design of a product must satisfy a variety of goals. Therefore, companies are recognizing that a team approach should replace traditional "chimneys" — so named as organizations look like side-by-side vertical structures that do not interact. A recent Aetna ad, "The pencil costs 14 cents. The eraser, millions," signifies the need for getting the design right the first time. In traditional design function, products are designed and developed in a series of steps. Each step is performed in isolation and changes in design result in dramatic cost overruns. Therefore, companies are employing concurrent engineering in which multifunctional teams work together early in the design process with clear objectives and concurrent decision making. Since product development steps are done in parallel, concurrent engineering reduces design changes and cuts product development time significantly. The product development team consists of personnel from research and development, purchasing, technical services, legal and regulatory department, marketing and sales, and health and safety. The design function is a systematic process that should incorporate considerations of environmental, technical, marketing, legal, and manufacturing groups. Since these factors are in constant flux, product design must be a continuous process. Therefore, the design program must include periodic reviews of products for continuous improvements.

ENCOURAGING GREEN DESIGNS

Senior management commitment is essential for green design. A company should make green design its top priority. Management should set goals, priorities, and strategies to encourage green design. Cross functional teams should be used to ensure systemwide-pollution reduction rather than functional-pollution reduction. Techniques of concurrent engineering and total green management should be utilized to promote crossfunctional teams. Current product lines should be analyzed to identify opportunities for green design. A company should develop green design policies. Green constraints should be treated as opportunities rather than restrictions. Greenness should not be evaluated on the basis of a single criterion but rather on the basis of multiple attributes. Difficulty in obtaining data and a general lack of control generally compel companies to limit their evaluations to within company walls. However, green design efforts should be extended from the raw material extraction stage to the final disposal stage. A design evaluation should be based not solely on constituents of a product but also on impacts on production, use, and disposal. Companies should also allocate adequate resources for green design. Training is essential to promoting green design in an organization. Technology is undergoing tremendous changes and there is less time between innovations. Therefore, designs should incorporate flexibility to respond to technological changes. Designs must satisfy a variety of goals. Therefore, rational tradeoffs between various design alternatives are essential to optimizing a design. An appropriate reward system is necessary to encourage designers to develop green products. In addition, designers should examine whether products outsourced from suppliers can be made green by appropriately changing specifications of components. For example, requiring the use of non-CFC packaging from suppliers can compel suppliers to use green packaging.[21] Design engineers and technical scientists should be encouraged to follow a green code of ethics.[22] Design engineers and technical scientists cannot delegate responsibility for their actions. Responsibility should include care for humanity and society, environmental protection, and economic success. Engineers and technical scientists must have full freedom to do research. Their goal should be promotion of products and technologies that reduce environmental pollution. They should try to increase environmental benefits and reduce environmental risks. The innovations should optimize benefits to risks ratio, raise standards of living, and develop a healthy economy. They should advance technical competence and train others. Engineers and technical scientists should also have an interdisciplinary systems perspective. They should take personal initiative in communicating with the public and they should be truthful with society and themselves.

QUALITY FUNCTION DEPLOYMENT

Quality function deployment, sometimes referred to as the "house of quality," is a tool developed to incorporate customers' needs in the final product and is an excellent way to build environmental goals into the final product.[23] Because several departments with different perspectives are involved in making design decisions, environmental goals are often ignored, resulting in many products that perform poorly in terms of environmental standards. Quality function deployment provides critical linkages between product design and environmental goals.

Information about customer needs is collected for competitors' designs. They are rated according to their importance. The functional attributes represent requirements. The relationships among these attributes are then indicated in the "roof" of the house of quality. The relationship matrix between needs and attributes establishes the optimal ways to satisfy needs. Weights are then used to evaluate various designs (see Figure 5.5).

VALUE ENGINEERING

Value engineering is a systematic procedure to identify unnecessary costs.[24] These costs are typically those that neither improve quality nor additional use, extra life, better appearance, or added attributes. The goal of value engineering is to identify product attributes needed by a customer and achieve them at the least possible cost. Value engineering is much more than cost reduction; it looks at functions and identifies means to achieve them at the least possible cost. Cost-reduction analysis, on the other hand, examines parts, assemblies, and subassemblies with a view toward reducing their costs. Value engineering consists of five steps. The first step is analyzing a product and all its components. The second step is collecting information with a goal of identifying functions and constraints. During this step, the importance of each of the functions will be documented. The third step

FIGURE 5.5
The House of Quality

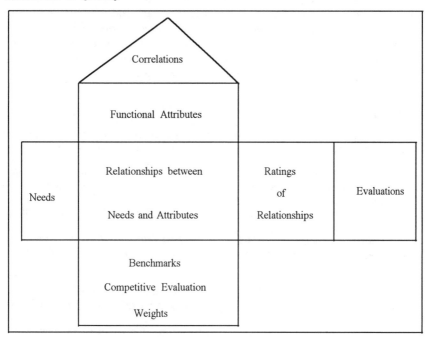

Correlations

Functional Attributes

Needs | Relationships between Needs and Attributes | Ratings of Relationships | Evaluations

Benchmarks

Competitive Evaluation

Weights

is to generate alternatives. Techniques like brainstorming, nominal group technique, Gordon technique, morphological synthesis, and the use of checklists will be used to generate alternatives. The fourth step is evaluation in which the goal is to choose alternatives with maximum value. Once alternatives are chosen, the fifth step is implementing them. Value engineering can be applied in all areas of an organization.

CONCLUSION

A number of companies are forced to retract green claims of their products because these claims could not withstand tough public scrutiny. Since inputs, manufacturing processes, distribution, use, and disposal are decided during the design stage, any green marketing venture should start with green design. Source reduction and waste management are two broad design strategies to reduce wastes. Because source reduction emphasizes prevention rather than cure, it is preferred over waste-management strategies. Green designs reduce waste and are generally efficient. Because they produce less scrap, green designs are consistent with manufacturing designs. Green designs are designed for easy assembly and disassembly. In short, they are efficient, easy to assemble, easy to manufacture, and, above all, superior designs. Even though there are no firm rules for evaluating green alternatives, comparisons of alternatives can provide a product designer with guidance in choosing superior designs. Since a product must meet several criteria, concurrent product development is preferred over a sequential approach. Green marketing ventures will simply not succeed unless such ventures begin with product design.

NOTES

This chapter is a revision of "Green Marketing Begins with Green Design" from the *Journal of Business and Industrial Marketing*, Volume 8, Issue 4, 1993.

1. Robert U. Ayres, "Industrial Metabolism," in *Technology and Environment*, ed. Jesse H. Ausubel and Hedy E. Sladovich (Washington, D.C.: National Academy Press, 1989), p. 26.

2. Gene Bylinsky, "Manufacturing for Reuse," *Fortune*, February 6, 1995, pp. 102–112.

3. John E. Young and Aaron Sachs, *The Next Efficiency Revolution: Creating a Sustainable Materials Economy* (Washington, D.C.: Worldwatch Institute, 1994), p. 15.

4. Ibid.

5. Donella H. Meadows, Dennis L. Meadows, and Jorgen Randers, *Beyond the Limits: Confronting Global Collapse, Envisioning a Sustainable Future* (Post Mills, Vt.: Chelsea Green, 1992), p. 80.

6. David Woodruff, "Detroit's Big Worry for the 1990's: The Greenhouse Effect," *Businessweek*, September 4, 1989, pp. 103–107.

7. U.S. General Accounting Office, *Highway Safety*, GAO/PEMD-92-1 (Washington, D.C.: Government Printing Office, 1992), p. 15.

8. Robert Herman, Siamak A. Ardekani, and Jesse H. Ausubel, "Dematerialization," in *Technology and Environment*, ed. Jesse H. Ausubel and Hedy E. Sladovich (Washington, D.C.: National Academy Press, 1989), p. 59.

9. L. Evans, "Car Size and Safety: Results from Analyzing U.S. Accident Data," in *Proceedings of the Tenth International Conference on Experimental Safety Vehicles* (Washington, D.C.: Government Printing Office, 1985), pp. 548–555.

10. Herman, Ardekani, and Ausubel, "Dematerialization," p. 53.

11. Ibid., p. 52.

12. U.S. Congress, Office of Technology Assessment, *Green Products by Design: Choices for a Cleaner Environment*, OTA-E-541 (Washington, D.C.: Government Printing Office, 1992), p. 58.

13. Ayres, "Industrial Metabolism," p. 35.

14. U.S. Congress, Office of Technology Assessment, *Technical Options for Conservation of Metals: Case Studies of Selected Metal Products*, OTA-M-97 (Washington, D.C.: Government Printing Office, September 1979), p. 55.

15. Braden R. Allenby, "Integrating Environment and Technology: Design for Environment," in *The Greening of Industrial Ecosystems*, ed. Braden R. Allenby and Deanna J. Richards (Washington, D.C.: National Academy Press, 1994), pp. 137–138.

16. Allenby, "Integrating Environment and Technology," pp. 143–145.

17. Gregory A. Keoleian and Dan Menerey, *Life Cycle Design Manual: Environmental Requirements and the Product System*, Project Summary, EPA 600-SR-92-226 (Cincinnati, Ohio: Risk Reduction Engineering Laboratory, April 1993).

18. Allenby, "Integrating Environment and Technology," p. 142.

19.   Patricia S. Dillon, "Implications of Industrial Ecology for Firms," in *The Greening of Industrial Ecosystems*, ed. Braden R. Allenby and Deanna J. Richards (Washington, D.C. National Academy Press, 1994), pp. 143–145.

20.   Sven-Olof Ryding, *Environmental Management Handbook* (Boca Raton, Fla.: Lewis Publishers, 1992), pp. 447–453.

21.   Allenby, "Integrating Environment and Technology," p. 142.

22.   Ralph Saemann, "The Environment and the Need for New Technology, Empowerment and Ethical Values," *Columbia Journal of World Business*, 27 (Fall and Winter 1992): 192.

23.   John R. Hauser and Don Clausing, "The House of Quality," *Harvard Business Review*, 66 (May–June 1988): 63–73.

24.   David J. DeMarle and M. Larry Shillito, "Value Engineering," in *Handbook of Industrial Engineering*, 2d ed., ed. Gavriel Salvendy (New York: John Wiley & Sons, 1992), pp. 354–376.

6

Green Production

According to the *1992 Toxics Release Inventory [TRI]: Public Data Release*, U.S. industries released 3.182 billion pounds of toxic wastes into the environment. This is considerably lower than the 4.85 billion pounds generated in 1988. Two industries, chemicals and primary metals, accounted for more than 60 percent of wastes generated. About six tenths of that total were released into the air. More than one-fifth were disposed of through underground injection (forcing diluted wastes into pockets of rock thousands of feet underground). To reduce pollution, the United States spent $90 billion in 1990, out of which $85 billion was for pollution abatement. Private businesses spent about $50 billion in 1990 for pollution reduction.

A significant amount of waste is generated during the production stage. Therefore, any improvement in production can lead to a considerable reduction of wastes produced. According to a survey of business leaders worldwide, production is the most "critical phase of a product's life."[1] Waste minimization can save substantial amounts of money through better utilization of resources and reduced waste disposal costs. Since minimizing waste lessens environmental risks, waste reduction can also reduce financial liabilities. The goal of production management is to ensure transformation of inputs into outputs using the least amount of resources. Green management achieves production management goals by cutting down on wastes and pollution. A systematic analysis is required in order to reduce pollution generated during production. Waste minimization can be considered for a whole plant or it can be targeted toward particular wastes such as those resulting in material losses, those causing processing problems, those that are hazardous or subject to regulations, and those that require high disposal costs. There are two principal approaches to reducing wastes (see Figure 6.1). Source reduction in the production stage can be categorized under materials management and production-management strategies. Materials management includes inventory control and

FIGURE 6.1
Waste-reduction Approaches

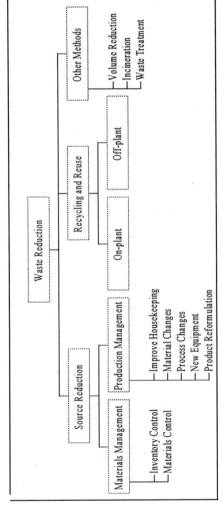

materials control. Production-management strategies include improved housekeeping, material changes, process changes, and installation of new equipment. Recycling involves use, reuse, and reclamation. Incineration, underground injection, and treatment and discharge into the environment are other ways of getting rid of waste. The Pollution Prevention Act of 1990 establishes source reduction as the most preferable approach to managing wastes. The U.S. Environmental Protection Agency (EPA), pursuant to this act, promulgated the following pollution-prevention strategy statement:

Under the Pollution Prevention Act of 1990, Congress established a national policy that:

- Pollution should be prevented or reduced at the source whenever feasible;
- Pollution that cannot be prevented should be recycled in an environmentally safe manner whenever feasible;
- Pollution that cannot be prevented or recycled should be treated in an environmentally safe manner whenever feasible; and
- Disposal or other release into the environment should be employed only as a last resort and should be conducted in an environmentally safe manner.

Pollution prevention means "source reduction," as defined under the Pollution Prevention Act, and other practices that reduce or eliminate the creation of pollutants through:

- increased efficiency in the use of raw materials, energy, water, or other resources, or
- protection of natural resources by conservation.

The Pollution Prevention Act defines "source reduction" to mean any practice which:

- reduces the amount of any hazardous substance, pollutant or contaminant entering any waste stream or other released into the environment (including fugitive emissions) prior to recycling, treatment, or disposal; and
- reduces the hazards to public health and the environment associated with the release of such substances, pollutants or contaminants.

The term includes: equipment or technology modifications, process or procedure modifications, reformulation or redesign of products, substitution of raw materials, and improvements in housekeeping, maintenance, training or inventory control.

Under the Pollution Prevention Act, recycling, energy recovery, treatment and disposal are not included with the definition of pollution prevention. Some practices commonly described as "in-process recycling" may qualify as pollution prevention. Recycling that is conducted in an environmentally sound manner shares many of the advantages of prevention — it can reduce the need for treatment or disposal, and conserve energy and resources.

Pollution prevention approaches can be applied to all pollution-generating activity: energy, agriculture, federal, consumer, as well as industrial sectors. The impairment of wetlands, groundwater sources, and other critical resources constitutes pollution, and prevention practices may be essential for preserving these resources. These practices may include conservation techniques and changes in management practices to prevent harm to sensitive ecosystems. Pollution prevention does not include practices that create new risk for concern.

In the agricultural sector, pollution prevention approaches include:

- reducing the use of water and chemical inputs;
- adoption of less environmentally harmful pesticides or cultivation of crop strains with natural resistance to pest; and
- protection of sensitive areas.

In the energy sector, pollution prevention can reduce environmental damage from extraction, processing, transport and combustion of fuels.

- increasing efficiency in energy use;
- substituting environmentally benign fuel sources; and
- design changes that reduce the demand for energy.

Recycling, energy recovery, and treatment represent less preferred approaches in the waste-management hierarchy. Even though recycling and treatment prevent wastes from going into the air and water, remaining toxic residues are still hazardous and require close attention. Wastes disposed of at landfills or in underground wells turn into disastrous water-pollution problems. Evaporation of solid and liquid wastes can become serious air pollution problems. Only source reduction can eliminate the disastrous effects of hazardous waste. That is why, according to the 1984 Hazardous and Solid Waste amendments to the Resource Conservation and Recovery Act, the policy of the United States is to reduce wastes using source-reduction strategies. The 1984 amendments clearly state that:

The Congress hereby declares it to be the national policy of the United States that, wherever feasible, the generation of hazardous waste is to be reduced or eliminated as expeditiously as possible. Waste that is nevertheless generated should be treated, stored or disposed of so as to minimize the present and future threat to human health and the environment.

The 1984 amendments also require certification by a waste generator that it has a program to reduce the quantity and toxicity of wastes generated. In this chapter, we describe the data requirements and strategies to reduce wastes generated during the production. Because of the overlap among these strategies to reduce wastes, they should be used in combination to maximize the reduction in wastes at the least possible costs.

DATA COLLECTION

Accurate data regarding processes are necessary before waste-minimization strategies can be identified. Quantities of emissions, costs of waste management, and production rates are required to develop comprehensive pollution-reduction programs. Much of this information can be obtained from manifests, emission inventories, and chemical release estimates reported in compliance with right-to-know regulations. Waste-management costs include those of handling, transportation, taxes, fees, insurance, treatment, and disposal. It is advisable that the following data be collected: quantity of wastes generated; list of processes that generate wastes; type of wastes generated; input materials; quantities of input materials going into wastes; efficiencies of various processes; housekeeping procedures; automation and types of process controls used; discharge points for liquid, solid, and gaseous emissions; and maintenance procedures. Design information such as process flow diagrams, piping diagrams, and information about equipment, including operating and maintenance manuals, should also be collected.

The collection of environmental data is also imperative. These data include hazardous waste records; quantities of wastes emitted; prior environmental audit reports; permits and permit applications required under the Clean Air Act, Clean Water Act, Resource Conservation and Recovery Act, and other statutes; and plans to respond to environmental accidents and emergencies. This information is important not only for developing waste-reduction options but also for ensuring compliance with various regulations. Finally, it is important to gather information about production. Input materials, material safety data sheets, inventory records, and production schedules are useful and relevant data.

Once data are collected, the next step is to identify unit operation, which may be defined as a piece of equipment where material inputs are processed into outputs. Unit operation may include storage, rinsing, painting, drying, or waste treatment. Process flow diagrams are prepared by connecting individual unit operations. The flow diagrams are the starting documents for developing waste-minimization options. They are used to identify waste-generation processes and develop material balances. Material balance provides precise information about inputs and outputs of an operation and helps to monitor the progress of waste-minimization efforts as well as provides the basis for estimating the size and cost of new equipment, piping, and instrumentation. Material balance is based on the conservation of mass principle, which states that what goes into a process must come out and can be written as:

$$Input = Output + Accumulation$$

Material balance can be performed for each component of inputs and outputs. It is an extremely useful tool when collecting analytical data proves difficult. Elemental balances for a chemical can be done for a chemical reaction taking place in a system.

Material balance requires a precise definition of inputs to a process or a unit operation. These inputs may include raw materials, water, air, catalysts, electricity or any other form of energy, and any recycled materials. Data about inputs can be obtained from stock rooms and purchasing records. Recycled material, which goes into a process, could be directly from another process, or from another process after some modification. To avoid double-counting of recycled materials, a waste should be regarded as an output from one process and as an input to another. Once the inputs are documented, data about process outputs should be collected. Outputs include primary products; by-products; wastewater; emissions into air, water, and land; and waste transported to other sites. All inputs and outputs need to be converted to standardized units of measurement (pounds, gallons, or tons) on a per day or per batch basis. Inputs and outputs may be displayed as in Figure 6.2. The material balances should be thoroughly reviewed for gaps and inaccuracies and should be refined.

FIGURE 6.2
Process Flow Diagram for Unit Operation

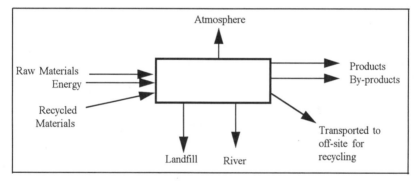

Material balances provide meaningful and precise information about wastes generated and they are a useful way to organize data to identify potential waste-reduction options. However, it is important to precisely define the system across which material balance should be done. Material balances can be performed for individual units, operations, processes, plants, industries, states, or countries. Material balances for a short time span generally require more accurate information about inputs and outputs and more frequent monitoring of streams.

Many facilities discharge significant amounts of wastewater into surface waters directly or indirectly through treatment facilities. Data on water usage should be collected by examining cleaning, cooling, product rinsing, and general maintenance, which are typical areas for inexpensive waste reduction. Reducing water consumption cuts down the volume of wastewater to be treated, resulting in cost savings. A wastewater flow into drains can be reduced by proper analysis of water usage. In addition, wastewater may contain a large quantity of valuable chemicals. Lower water usage can increase the concentration of effluents, making it sometimes possible to reclaim materials, thereby avoiding costly wastewater treatment. Typically, storing and reusing water is cheaper than sending it for treatment and disposal. Therefore, it is important to collect data about wastewater discharges from each unit operation, process, and facility. Wastewater should be analyzed for pH, chemical oxygen demand, biochemical oxygen demand, suspended solids, and other contaminants. Current levels of waste reuse and recycling should be quantified. In addition to wastewater, data about gaseous emissions should also be examined.

While collecting data about inputs, it is a good idea to estimate annual raw material losses as a result of evaporation, spillages, leaks, and so on. In addition to raw materials, energy inputs should also be considered.

MATERIALS-MANAGEMENT STRATEGIES

A significant amount of waste is generated by out-of-date, off-specification, and defective products created with excessive raw materials. Such wastes raise not only a company's disposal costs but also material costs. By improving ordering procedures a company can significantly reduce obsolete inventory. Performing periodic inventories will allow a company to identify out-of-date items. By issuing materials based on expiration dates, deterioration of materials can be avoided. Reducing quantities ordered, purchasing in containers rather than in bulk, and using excess materials are other techniques to reduce material wastage. Just-in-time ordering of materials (just before they are needed for production) can significantly reduce a company's exposure to storage and spillage risks.

Purchasing the right amount of materials at the right time in the right containers is one of the most effective techniques of inventory management. There should be a procedure to dispose of excess inventory. From time to time, a company should review its materials to ensure that obsolete materials do not remain in store. A company should also examine whether surplus materials could be used for some other purposes. If not, suppliers or other users should be contacted to see whether the materials could be sold.

Standard procedures should be developed for material procurement. Every material should be evaluated prior to ordering and checked before acceptance. From time to time, studies should be done to see whether less hazardous materials could be used as a substitute. All items received should be inspected to ensure that off-specification and defective materials or materials with a short life are not accepted.

Every material should be analyzed for its effect on humans and their environment. All materials regulated by various statutes are a good starting point for such an analysis. In addition, analysis should be done to ensure that a company is in compliance with storage, usage, and handling regulations relating to the materials. Material safety data sheets should be acquired from the suppliers. The data should indicate storing procedures, warning labels, and first-aid procedures. Before any new product is produced, an in-depth evaluation of materials and processes should be done.

A company should perform an ABC analysis of materials based on toxicity to identify high risk materials. Most companies find that a small percentage of the materials account for a great percentage of environmental hazards. ABC analysis categorizes the materials into three groups so that each group can be managed differently. Every material should be rated for its risk to humans and the environment. An indicator should then be developed for each material by multiplying the amounts of materials consumed (in the same units) by their risk rating. ABC analysis assumes that roughly 20 percent of items may account for 80 percent of risks. So by concentrating on just 20 percent of these items, a management can effectively control 80 percent of its risk exposure. After performing ABC analysis, the management should develop policies with varying stringency for each category of items.

Storage, handling, and movement of materials during the manufacturing process should be analyzed for spills, leaks, and contamination. Everyone involved in storage, handling, and use should be trained to identify potential accidents and to take corrective actions. Material inventory should be evaluated for its appropriateness. Analysis should be done to determine whether distances between storage and process or between processes can be reduced to cut down on waste during material handling. If the same containers are being used for different raw materials, a study should be done to see whether there is risk of crosscontamination. Security of raw material storage should be examined. Leaking valves and piping, punctured containers, and leaking fill-line connections are some of the potential sources of leakage during loading. Accidents during storage involve overfilling of tanks, leaking containers, and malfunctioning alarms. The materials management strategies to reduce wastes are summarized below:

Buy only exact amounts of raw materials for a production run.

Have a review system to dispose of excess, out-of-date, and no-longer-used materials.

Implement a just-in-time inventory system to reduce the amount of toxic materials stored.

Perform an analysis of inventory to utilize old materials before they become obsolete.

Implement a review system for all materials before they are purchased.

Periodically analyze whether any material can be substituted using less toxic materials.

Rate all materials based on their risk to human health and the environment, and perform an ABC analysis of materials based on the quantity of material consumed times its toxicity rating.

From time to time, analyze material handling procedures for spillage, leaks, and contaminations.

Develop an effective inspection system for materials received.

Evaluate new products before production.

PRODUCTION-MANAGEMENT STRATEGIES

Major production-management strategies to eliminate wastes include improved housekeeping, process changes, material changes, equipment installation, and product reformulation.

Improved Housekeeping

Improved housekeeping can be an economically advantageous way to reduce significant amounts of wastes. However, this approach is usually ignored because of resistance to change. Poor maintenance is often the cause of chemical leaks and emergencies. A strict preventive maintenance program can considerably reduce equipment downtime and prevent accidental releases of hazardous materials. To make a maintenance program cost effective, it should be planned and implemented in a systematic manner. A well-planned schedule and accurate maintenance of records are essential for an effective preventive maintenance program. Periodic reviews of such records should help to identify critical equipment, problem equipment, and other typical problems. Availability of nondestructive testing should considerably help in identifying potential breakdowns before they occur. Nondestructive testing, such as ultrasound and magnetic resonance imaging, can examine critical parts for internal cracks without actually breaking the parts.

In batch processes, the same reaction vessels are used to produce different products. Therefore, residues from one batch must be cleaned out before production of a subsequent batch can be started.[2] Cleanup involving rinsing of reactors, piping, pumps, storage units, and other equipment generates significant amounts of wastes. Reusing rinse water is one way of reducing wastes. Another strategy is to schedule batches so as to reduce equipment cleaning. For example, mixing light paints before dark paints can eliminate the need for cleanup of vats between batches.

Process Changes

Process changes involve the substitution of polluting materials by less polluting materials, redesign of processes, installations of most modern equipment, and product reformulations. The objective of process redesign involves the abatement of pollution at its source. By increasing the efficiency of a process, pollution can be reduced. Simple and inexpensive changes in processes (e.g., eliminating toxic catalysts) and optimizing process variables such as temperature, pressure, and concentrations of liquids can dramatically reduce pollutants.

Another long-term strategy for increasing efficiency is to reduce the number of processing stages either through combining or eliminating processes. Suppose a product is manufactured using a four-stage process with yield efficiencies of 0.8 at each stage. The overall efficiency is 0.41, but if one of the stages can be eliminated, the overall efficiency will rise to 0.51. Hence, elimination of a processing stage will directly reduce costs. Another approach to prevent generation of wastes is to redesign chemical pathways. By altering the series of chemical reactions to produce a product, highly toxic intermediate processes that generate by-product waste and pollution can be avoided. Similarly, inspecting parts before they are processed can also reduce the number of defective parts requiring rework at each manufacturing center.

Material Changes

Substitution of polluting materials with less polluting ones is an effective strategy to reduce wastes. However, such material substitution strategies involve considerable risks. Because of the proprietary nature of material substitution, such strategies need to be tailor-made for each product. Typical examples of material substitution involve the replacement of solvent-based ink with water-based ink and the substitution of chlorinated solvents with nonchlorinated solvents in cleaning products. For existing products, the substitution of materials may lead to changes in the specifications of the finished products and consequently may affect sales.

Product Reformulation

Product reformulations generally require no change in the manufacturing processes. For instance, by manufacturing a product in the form of pellets rather than powder, dust that is generated during handling can be reduced. Switching from dry products to wet products can also reduce dust. However, product reformulations are difficult to implement. Because product reformulations change product specifications, implementing product reformulation is like introducing a new product.

Equipment Installation

Spectacular technological changes have not only boosted the efficiencies of the equipment but have driven down equipment costs as well. As a result, in many instances it is cheaper to install new equipment than to retrofit existing equipment with pollution-abatement outfits. This approach is extremely appropriate in the dry-cleaning industry, for example. Older equipment in the dry-cleaning industry is subject to considerable solvent leakages, and the installation of ventilation and vapor recovery systems in many instances will be costlier than installing new equipment.

OTHER WASTE-MANAGEMENT STRATEGIES

Recovery and Reuse

Recovery and reuse of materials can be either on-plant or off-plant (recycling). On-plant recovery and reuse is one of the simplest methods to curb pollution generation. Through recovery and reuse of polluting materials, a number of companies have transformed an expensive waste-reduction activity into a profitable one. In this strategy, pollutants are recovered and repeatedly reused. This method helps to eliminate waste-disposal costs, to decrease material costs, and to generate revenue from the salable waste. Recovering silver, fixer, and bleach solutions in photographic processing is an example of waste reduction through recovery and reuse. However, not all pollutants can be recycled, particularly if the output contains by-products that are of no use to the processor. In such cases, transporting pollutants to a company that needs them or altering production processes to reduce generation of such pollutants are more attractive alternatives.

When on-plant recovery is not possible because of a lack of equipment, because the amount of waste generated is too little, or because the waste generated cannot be reused in the plant, then firms initiate off-plant reuse and recovery. Feasibility of off-plant recycling depends on the purity of the waste and the market for the waste. Some materials may be salable while others may involve disposal expenses. For those wastes requiring disposal costs, it may be a good idea to try to develop markets using more traditional approaches to product development.

Volume Reduction

Volume reduction essentially involves segregation of hazardous and recoverable wastes from total waste. Volume-reduction methods are used to maximize recoverability and minimize volume, resulting in lower treatment and disposal costs and greater flexibility in disposal.

Waste Treatment and Disposal

This is the ultimate, and generally most expensive, alternative a company can choose when other options have failed. In this strategy, a company tries to treat the waste to make it less toxic so that the waste can be disposed of without the company being subject to legal action. Wastewaters are typically treated and discharged or transported to municipal treatment plants for pretreatment and subsequent discharge, or they are injected into deep wells. On-site treatment may include physical treatment such as allowing solids to settle to the bottom before discharging water, chemical, or biological treatments, which will transform hazardous wastes into less hazardous substances.

WASTE-REDUCTION PRACTICES

Table 6.1 summarizes the pros and cons of various waste-reduction strategies. Even though it is traditionally assumed that releases on land far exceed all other releases, air emissions account for about 60 percent of all releases (see Figure 6.3). Releases on land account for about 10 percent, discharges to surface water about 9 percent, and underground injection about 23 percent. Industrywide analysis presented in Figure 6.4 indicates that chemicals and primary metals generate the greatest amount of wastes. INFORM has performed an in-depth analysis of waste-reduction practices in chemical plants.[3] According to its study, the amounts of hazardous chemicals generated varied significantly between plants, even though some plants used identical chemicals in similar amounts. A variety of processes and chemicals used accounted for much of the differences in the waste generated. Even though it is traditionally assumed that most waste is generated during the production stage and process changes are likely to result in a significant reduction in waste, improved housekeeping can also reduce waste considerably. Even though the INFORM study examined 29 chemical plants for their waste-reduction practices, only two plants utilized the same waste-reduction methods. The differences in input materials and the diversity in production processes make it impossible to use identical waste-reduction practices in different plants. This has significant implications for benchmarking (see Chapter 14). Operational changes are more effective in reducing wastes in batch-processing plants than in continuous-processing plants. On the other

TABLE 6.1
Pros and Cons of Waste-reduction Strategies

Strategy	Pros	Cons
Improved housekeeping	Simple and does not require new capital	Potential reduction in waste is limited
Material changes	Waste prevention is permanent	Likely to affect product specification and implementation is difficult
Process changes	Waste prevention is permanent	May create bottleneck process; employees may require training; work stoppages may be necessary
Install new equipment	Permanent waste elimination	Employee training; capital requirement; work stoppages during implementation
Separate waste	Minimizes waste management costs and easy to dispose	High technology; design changes may be required
Concentrate waste	Easy transportation	No waste reduction
Recover on-plant	Reduces waste-management costs and saves materials' costs	Buyer for waste may not exist; capital investment is required
Recover off-plant	Reduces waste-management costs and generates revenue	Off-plant waste transportation risky; buyer for waste may not exist
Treatment and disposal	Ultimate option	Output needs disposal

FIGURE 6.3
Environmental Distribution of TRI Releases, 1992

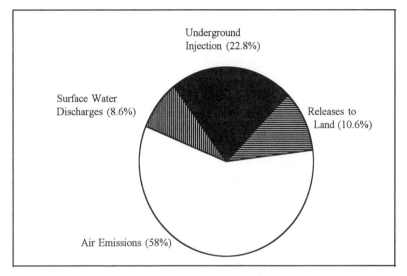

Underground
Injection (22.8%)

Surface Water
Discharges (8.6%)

Releases to
Land (10.6%)

Air Emissions (58%)

Source: U.S. Environmental Protection Agency, *1992 Toxics Release Inventory: Public Data Release*, EPA 745-R-94-001 (Washington, D.C.: Government Printing Office, 1994), p. 4.

hand, equipment changes more often reduce wastes in batch-processing plants than in continuous-processing plants. Reduction in air emissions is easier to achieve than reduction in solid wastes. In addition, process and operational changes reduce more than one type of waste, whereas most other waste-reduction practices reduce only a single stream of waste. It is easier to implement changes in materials to reduce wastes in batch processes than in continuous processes. The study also found that obstacles for waste reduction varied among plants, suggesting that waste-reduction practices should be tailor-made for each plant.

INFORM also analyzed waste-reduction practices of the plants based on their size, age, location, and other factors. Product type can influence the waste-reduction potentials of a plant. For example, plants requiring the use of pure materials are severely restricted from using recycling and reuse options for waste reduction because of the risk of contamination. During manufacturing processes, batch processes typically produced more waste per unit of product produced than continuous processes. Therefore, shifting from batch processes to continuous processes should be an attractive option for reducing wastes. Differences in technical expertise, capital availability, effects of liability, and regulations can influence waste-reduction practices in small and large plants.

FIGURE 6.4
Top Ten Industries for TRI Releases, 1992 (in millions of pounds)

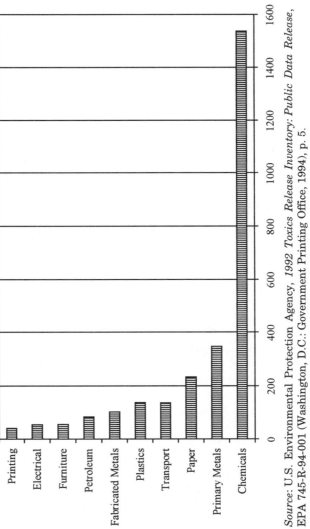

Source: U.S. Environmental Protection Agency, *1992 Toxics Release Inventory: Public Data Release,* EPA 745-R-94-001 (Washington, D.C.: Government Printing Office, 1994), p. 5.

Cost savings due to higher yields and lower waste-management costs encourage companies to support waste reduction, according to the INFORM study. The improved yields reduce costs of materials that otherwise would have been disposed of as wastes. Lower generation of wastes as a result of improved yields minimizes waste management costs. Waste management, which requires equipment, materials, staff, and transportation, dramatically increases costs of production. Often, equipment and personnel involved in waste management are also used for other purposes as well. Therefore, waste reduction does not eliminate fixed costs associated with these resources. This is a significant disincentive for waste reduction. The massive cost disparities between materials used at a facility can be a significant impediment toward implementing waste-reduction activities. For example, raw materials used in the pharmaceutical industry are much more valuable than some of the hazardous wastes they generate. Therefore, more efforts are directed toward recovering valuable materials (irrespective of their harm toward humans or the environment) rather than hazardous wastes.

Corporate liability for problems due to hazardous wastes encourages waste reduction. Several companies have gone bankrupt as a result of environmental liabilities. Because the introduction of new technologies involves risks, however, some companies are inclined to stick to better known traditional technologies to reduce liability risks. In other words, liability risks remain one of the major obstacles to the introduction of new technologies.

The TRI collected under the Emergency Planning and Community Right-to-Know Act (EPCRA) is a valuable source of data on cost-reduction activities. Under section 313 of EPCRA, manufacturing facilities with ten or more employees are required to report to the U.S. EPA amounts of certain toxic chemicals and chemical categories that they release directly into the environment or transfer to off-site facilities. The TRI database, based on reports by more than 23,630 facilities, also includes data on waste-reduction practices.[4] In 1992, 23,630 facilities, reporting in accordance with EPCRA, produced 37.663 billion pounds of wastes, an increase of 0.5 percent over 1991. Figure 6.5 indicates various alternatives by which wastes were disposed. About 52 percent of the toxic chemicals in wastes were recycled, 10 percent were burned to recover energy, 29 percent were treated, and 9 percent were released into the environment. Only 62 percent of the toxic chemicals in waste were used and the remaining 38 percent were either treated or released into the environment. Therefore, significant opportunities continue to exist for waste prevention in U.S. manufacturing facilities.

In spite of stringent regulations and right-to-know laws, only about 36 percent of facilities implemented source reduction for a chemical in 1992. Photographic printing facilities were among the top industries involved in source reduction. Only about one in five facilities in the food and tobacco industries took part in source reduction. The proportion of

FIGURE 6.5
Waste Management, by Activity, 1992

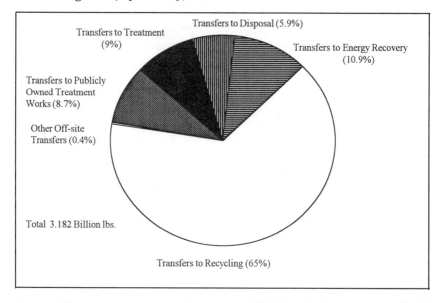

Source: U.S. Enviromental Protection Agency, *1992 Toxics Release Inventory: Public Data Release*, EPA 745-R-94-001 (Washington, D.C.: Government Printing Office, 1994), p. 6.

various source-reduction activities implemented by these facilities are given in Figure 6.6. More than 60 percent of facilities demonstrated good operating practices, process modifications, and preventive spill and leak activities to reduce the generation of wastes. Improved maintenance scheduling, record keeping, procedures, and other changes in operating practices constitute the primary housekeeping practices implemented by facilities to reduce wastes. The major raw material modification strategy is the substitution of raw materials. Modification of equipment, layout, or piping is the most significant waste-reduction strategy under the category of process modifications. Product modifications involve changes in product specifications and therefore involve risk in their implementation. This is the least implemented waste-reduction activity.

Figure 6.7 indicates methods followed by the facilities for identifying source-reduction activities. More than one-half of the ideas for source reduction were a result of participative team management and pollution-prevention opportunity audits. Internal pollution-prevention opportunity audits rather than external audits accounted for most of the ideas for source reduction through audits. State and federal programs were responsible for a mere 0.7 percent of source-reduction

FIGURE 6.6
Frequencies of Source-reduction Activities Reported by Facilities

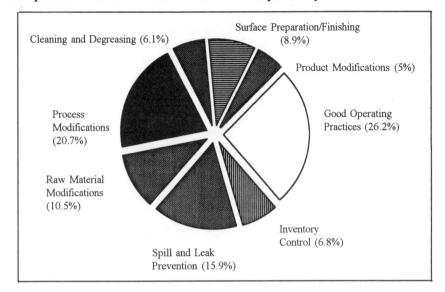

Source: U.S. Enviromental Protection Agency, *1992 Toxics Release Inventory: Public Data Release*, EPA 745-R-94-001 (Washington, D.C.: Government Printing Office, 1994), pp. 138–139.

FIGURE 6.7
Methods Used to Identify Source-reduction Activities

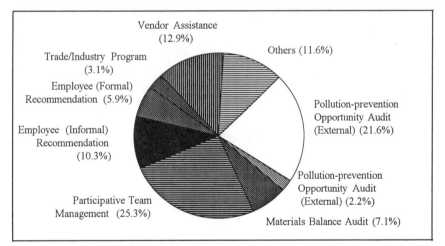

Source: U.S. Enviromental Protection Agency, *1992 Toxics Release Inventory: Public Data Release*, EPA 745-R-94-001 (Washington, D.C.: Government Printing Office, 1994), pp. 134–135.

activities. Vendor assistance generated 11.4 percent, informal employee recommendations 10.1 percent, and the materials balance audit 6.8 percent of source-reduction activities. The EPA also analyzed TRI data provided by the facilities. After accounting for production, facilities that did not report any source-reduction activity had their waste decrease by about 1 percent. However, those facilities that reported having implemented source-reduction activities reduced their wastes by 9.1 percent. These facilities also increased their on-site recycling and energy recovery and at the same time decreased waste discharges and treatments. Industrywide releases and transfers of TRI chemicals in 1988 and 1992 appear in Figure 6.8

FIGURE 6.8
Industrywide TRI Releases in 1988 and 1992

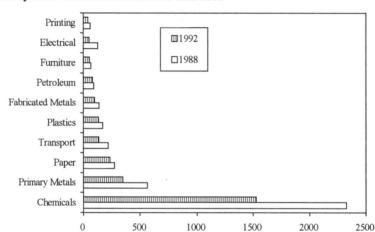

Source: U.S. Enviromental Protection Agency, *1992 Toxics Release Inventory: Public Data Release*, EPA 745-R-94-001 (Washington, D.C.: Government Printing Office, 1994), p. 191.

OBSTACLES TO WASTE PREVENTION

There are several obstacles to waste prevention. Fixed costs and small savings are two major factors that prevent waste reduction. Research and development costs are another barrier. Pollution-reduction activities can increase costs that consumers may be unwilling to pay. Sometimes the products produced using lesser polluting processes may be of an inferior quality, also dissuading consumers. Liability costs of waste handling and disposal are difficult to estimate. A company's short-term vision may prevent investments in equipment that take a long period of time to pay off. Some companies can save money by not investing in pollution-reduction technologies. This creates an uneven playing field in the short run. Low profitability can also discourage companies from investing in pollution prevention. The option of process changes is inefficient for many older plants. In addition, outdated management accounting systems can conceal high environmental costs among overhead costs.

Pollution-reduction technologies should be tailored for each organization. It is not generally possible to copy a pollution-prevention technology from another plant and expect a spectacular reduction in pollution. Unavailability of technology for specific applications inhibits the implementation of pollution-reduction technologies, especially in small plants. Even though it is easy to say that pollution can be reduced by substituting a toxic material with a less toxic one, it is often difficult to find such alternative materials.

Initiation and implementation of waste-reduction alternatives require good managers and employees. In a time of technical personnel shortages, companies are not inclined to use engineers for pollution-reduction activities rather than production activities. Waste-prevention activities typically involve changes. However, waste treatments using "end-of-pipe" solutions do not involve changes because they typically focus on treating what comes out of the pipe or smokestack. This inhibits companies from supporting pollution-reduction projects.

Regulatory hurdles prevent companies from opting for recycling rather than outright incineration or landfilling. Permits and waivers emphasize pollution control rather than pollution prevention. Uncertainty about future environmental regulations encourages companies to wait until regulations are passed before taking action. This attitude favors end-of-pipeline treatment technologies rather than pollution prevention.

The risks involved in introducing new methods often inhibit companies from venturing into waste prevention. Management attitude poses another problem. Resistance to change prevents management from trying new approaches. Lack of reliable information about waste reduction is another obstacle to waste prevention. Emphasis on compliance has forced management to think only in terms of regulated wastes rather than all wastes.

Operational problems can also obstruct pollution-reduction activities. Pollution-reduction activities can slow down production, creating a bottleneck operation. With subsequent process changes, equipment may need more intensive maintenance requiring, in turn, a higher skilled labor force. Rework of defective products and lower quality can increase workload. Work stoppage during implementation is a major disincentive for carrying out pollution-prevention projects. Inadequate utilities, such as electricity, could also be an obstacle to pollution reduction.

INFORMATION SOURCES FOR POLLUTION PREVENTION

Information is essential for identifying appropriate technologies for pollution prevention. Newsletters, case studies, technical journals, and electronic databases are valuable sources for information on pollution prevention.[5] In addition, there are several programs dealing with pollution prevention and waste reduction. The U.S. EPA, the Department of Energy, and national laboratories such as Los Alamos National Laboratory and Pacific Northwest Laboratory are important federal government sources of information on pollution reduction. State environmental protection departments and universities are invaluable as information sources. Most states have information clearinghouses, waste exchanges, and technical assistance programs for waste reduction, and can also supply information on grants and tax incentives. Trade associations, corporations, and nonprofit research organizations are other information sources.

There are several databases, on-line services, and Internet bulletin boards that provide information on environmental matters. The EPA's Electronic Information Exchange System maintains an electronic directory of federal and state environmental experts, pollution-prevention legislation databases, an international cleaner production information clearinghouse, and information on waste exchanges. EcoNet provides access to many conferences on environmental topics and huge environmental databases for a fee. Envirolink, a free service that can be accessed through the Internet, provides a database on Supreme Court rulings, information about the Environmental Law Alliance Worldwide, full texts of multilateral trade treaties, and so on. SAFETY is an Internet discussion group that deals with environmental and occupational health and safety issues. Other discussion groups include CMTS-L (chemical management and tracking system) on the Internet, SAFETYNET (dealing with chemical and environmental hazards), and OSHA on CompuServe. *FedWorld*, managed by the National Technical Information Service, and *Labor News*, maintained by the Department of Labor, are other sources for information on environmental and safety issues.[6]

CONCLUSION

Green initiatives can reduce costs by increasing efficiency, saving materials, and reducing waste-management costs. They can provide greater flexibility to companies by helping them define problems, set priorities, and develop effective solutions. Proactive waste-prevention activities, in addition to helping companies comply with regulations, improve competitive advantage. A company with well-developed green expertise can take advantage of growing opportunities in green products, services, and technologies. Increasing investor confidence and employee morale and improving public image can raise company performance immensely. In spite of the many advantages of waste reduction, about 40 percent of the waste in 1992 was discharged into the environment either before or after treatment. According to the Office of Technology Assessment, "over 99 percent of Federal and State Environmental spending is devoted to controlling pollution after waste is generated. Less than one percent is spent to reduce the generation of waste."[7]

Source-reduction strategies include materials and production-management strategies. Better management of materials, improved housekeeping, equipment changes, material changes, process changes, and so on are some of the approaches to waste reduction. Recycling and recovery can reduce wastes discharged into the environment. Treatment, which makes possible benign waste disposal, is one of the least preferred pollution-reducing alternatives.

There are still several obstacles to implementing waste-reduction strategies that must be overcome. Operational difficulties, resistance to change, lack of information, and too much emphasis on compliance are some of the reasons for low participation of facilities in waste reduction.

NOTES

1. McKinsey & Company, "The Corporate Response to the Environmental Challenge," in *Transnational Environmental Law and Its Impact on Corporate Behavior*, ed. Eric J. Urbani, Conrad P. Rubin, and Monica Katzman (Irvington-on-Hudson, N.Y.: Transnational Juris Publications, 1993), pp. 217–262.

2. Harry M. Freeman, *Hazardous Waste Minimization* (New York: McGraw-Hill, 1990), p. 33.

3. INFORM, *Cutting Chemical Wastes* (New York: INFORM, 1985).

4. U.S. Environmental Protection Agency, *1992 Toxics Release Inventory: Public Data Release*, EPA 745-R-94-001 (Washington, D.C.: Government Printing Office, 1994).

5. See, for example, *Pollution Prevention Review*, a quarterly publication of Executive Enterprise Publications Co., Inc., 22 West 21st Street, New York, N.Y. 10010-6990; *Waste Minimization and Recycling Report*, a monthly publication of Government Institutes, Inc., 4 Research Place, #200, Rockville, Md. 20850; and *Reference Guide to Pollution Prevention Resources: Prevention, Pesticides, and Toxic Substances* (TS 792), EPA 742-B-93-001, an annual publication of the U.S. Environmental Protection Agency.

6. "Clean and Green on the Information Superhighway," *Environmental Forum*, 11 (July–August 1994): 34–37.

7. U.S. Congress, Office of Technology Assessment, *Serious Reduction of Hazardous Waste: For Pollution Prevention and Industrial Efficiency* (Washington, D.C.: Government Printing Office, 1989).

7

Green Packaging

The packaged-goods industry is a multibillion dollar business in the United States. According to the *Packaging* magazine, the top 100 U.S. packaged brands purchased $12 billion in materials and containers in 1993.[1] For consumers, packaging is one of the most visible forms of waste. Packaging is the single largest contributor to municipal solid waste. Therefore, the environment is a critical issue for the packaging industry. Packaging companies must consider the environmental impact of their products in every aspect of their strategic and business plans. Shrinking landfills and growing packaging waste make green packaging one of the pressing issues for many corporations. Between 1960 and 1993, the per capita generation of municipal solid waste rose from 2.66 to 4.4 pounds per day in the United States. The number of landfills decreased from 20,000 in 1978 to a mere 6,000 in 1986 and many of these remaining landfills will be closed by the year 2000. Consequently, more and more towns are adopting policies to encourage source reduction and recycling. The amount of municipal solid waste recycled or composted rose from 6 percent in 1960 to 17 percent in 1990. Still, the tipping fees to unload at disposal sites continue to rise. In 1990, almost one-third of the municipal solid waste consisted of packaging materials. The United States generates one of the largest amounts of municipal solid wastes per capita among the developed countries.[2] Therefore, even a small decrease in the generation of packaging waste could have significant impact on the garbage crisis.

Packaging has cultivated a negative image. It uses scarce resources and generates pollution. Products are overpackaged. Packaging is generally not biodegradable and it cannot be properly disposed of. However, packaging has several benefits as well. It maintains products in good condition until they are bought and it provides the general public with products fit for use. Without packaging, products cannot be transported away from a factory or a supermarket. Packaging is an excellent communication and marketing tool. It makes products look more attractive and appealing. Packaging helps manufacturers display the identity of a product, its ingredients, its use and misuse, expiration dates, and instructions for disposal.

Two-thirds of all packaging is currently used for food preservation. The primary function of packaging is to protect a product from spoilage. Packaging reduces deterioration of foods by acting as a barrier between food products and the external environment. Packaging also preserves food products. Frozen food would not be available to consumers without developments in packaging. Without packaging, self-service grocery stores would not exist. Packaging has dramatically improved the efficiency and effectiveness of distribution systems. According to a study by H. Alter, the amount of food waste is inversely related to the quantity of packaging materials in municipal solid waste.[3] However, reduction in food waste varies with packaging types. For every 0.1 percent increase in plastics packaging, the food waste is reduced by 0.165 percent. In addition, packaging also cuts down on waste by reducing the breakage of products in transit. For instance, the World Health Organization reports that in several developing countries, there is 30 to 50 percent food wastage because of a lack of modern distribution and packaging systems, as compared with only 2 to 3 percent in Europe and the United States.[4] Yet, packaging represents one of the most obvious targets of environmentalists. Market pressures typically determine packaging. However, one of the difficulties in responding to the packaging waste problem is that the dimension of the problem involves local, regional, and global effects. However, landfill toxicity, litter, pollution, ozone depletion, and wildlife endangerment are among the many concerns providing the impetus for green packaging.

Packaging can be categorized into three types. Primary packaging has direct contact with the product, protecting it from external hazards. Primary packaging is made from metals, glass, plastics, and paper. Secondary packaging typically found in products delivered, is used to pack individual products. Tertiary packaging facilitates the safe and efficient handling of products that are transported from the factory to the warehouse and ultimately to the retailers.

The number of products stocked in the supermarkets has risen from about 2,500 in 1960 to more than 15,000 in 1993.[5] Relatively low-cost transportation and distribution of such a large number of products would not have been possible without packaging developments. Primary packaging has reduced labor costs by making it unnecessary to weigh or measure a product. It has also helped to make self-service possible. Transportation of a product to the home is made easier by packaged goods. Secondary packaging has facilitated grouping, display, and in-store handling of products. Tertiary packaging has dramatically cut down labor and transportation costs.

PACKAGING DESIGN

In the 1960s, packaging was essentially designed to improve convenience. Lightweighting was the packaging strategy during the energy-shortage decade of the 1970s. Safe packaging became the predominant concern of the 1980s, due in part to criminal product tampering. The 1990s began an era of green packaging. Packaging consumes energy and high-grade materials. It is an R&D-intensive industry. In 1986 the cost of food packaging was more than that of the crops in the United States.[6] Packaging must satisfy a variety of objectives. It must preserve and protect a product and help to prolong product life by creating a modified atmosphere. Packaging should be microwave- or oven-ready. It must be tamper-proof. It should be difficult for a child but easy for an elderly person to open it. Packaging should be so designed as to help pour out a measured quantity of a product. It should attract consumers. The goal of environmental packaging is to satisfy customer needs with the least amount of harm to the environment. Green packaging should use fewer materials, consume less energy, reduce air pollution, avoid the use of ozone-depleting materials, be non–water polluting, encourage recycling, and reduce solid waste. Environmental degradation may be caused directly as a result of manufacture and distribution. Because this is usually within the control of an organization, manufacturers of packaging materials should make every effort to reduce this type of environmental degradation. Indirect harm includes that which happens outside the organization, such as raw material acquisition and final product use and disposal.

Green packaging design begins with needs analysis. Packaging specifications must meet those needs. The next step is to design packaging and select appropriate materials. Manufacturing operations and their impact on the environment must be a consideration when selecting materials. The final step is packaging evaluation.

Needs Analysis

The first step in packaging design is identifying customers and their needs. Separating actual needs from temporary desires is a challenging task of packaging design. Defining customer needs is very difficult. Convenient and environmentally responsible packaging such as plastic bottles and pump sprays for deodorants, instead of aerosol sprays, are examples of customer needs.

Green Packaging Design

The first strategy for green packaging is to determine whether packaging is required at all. Many nonfood items do not need any packaging at all. Lightweighting is another strategy. Milk bottles currently weigh about 245 grams as compared with 570 grams in 1920 and 400 grams in 1950. The weight of a typical food can was reduced to 56.6 grams in 1990 from 69.9 grams in 1970. A beer can currently weighs only 17 grams as compared with 91 grams in 1950. Concentrating a product can reduce its packaging requirements significantly. Increasing the size of packaging can reduce packaging material consumption. For example, a large container consumes less material than two smaller containers. A 16-ounce can comprises 40 percent less metals than two 8-ounce cans.

Each product has a different lifetime. For example, polystyrene cups may last for minutes. High-density polyethlyene gas tanks, however, can last for years. Prolonging the life of a package is a simple strategy to reduce waste. Therefore, packaging that consumes more material is not environmentally harmful if it can be used several times. Reducing materials consumption per usage is an effective strategy.

To encourage recycling, plastic bottles and cups need to have coding to identify their polymers. The coding system of the Society of the Plastic Industry (SPI) assigns a number of each polymer category: 1 for PET (polyethylene trephthalate), 2 for HDPE (high-density poly-ethylene), 3 for PVC (polyvinyl chloride), 4 for LDPE (low-density polyethylene), 5 for PP (polypropylene), 6 for PS (polystyrene), and 7 for Other. The code, a number surrounded by a triangle and an abbre-viation for the resin type must be indicated on each plastic product. It is mandatory in 39 states to have a plastic coding system consistent with the SPI resin code. Elimination of cadmium, lead, and chromium pigments in packaging is another strategy for avoiding contamination during recycling and emission during incineration. Using more recycled materials in packaging can save energy and costs of disposal. A breakdown of the composition of 70.6 million tons of containers and packaging materials constituting municipal solid waste in the United States in 1994 is as follows:

Paper and paperboard	50.1%
Glass	17.3%
Wood	13.5%
Plastics	11.9%
Metals	7.0%[7]

Packaging Material Selection

Selecting materials for packaging is an important environmental decision. Designers generally choose packaging materials based on such attributes as attractiveness to consumers, convenience, cost, and so on. However, consumer pressure is forcing designers to consider the envi-ronmental effects of their packaging materials during acquisition, manufacture, use, and disposal stages.

It is traditionally considered that returnable packaging is greener than expendable packaging. However, this may not be the case. Returnable containers are sent back to the supplier empty. Metal racks, returnable bins, rigid plastic racks and dunnage, and totes are some examples of returnable containers. Expendable packaging is used only once and discarded, but it may be recycled. Types of expendable packaging include corrugated boxes, shrink-wraps, and wood skids. Expendable packaging costs little but is generated in large quantities.

Aluminum is typically used for cans, semirigid containers for food, and foils used in flexible packaging. Its low density and resistance to oxidation, as well as the availability of plenty of raw materials, makes it an ideal packaging material. Ease of decoration and low cost make aluminum an excellent material for beverage and food cans. Low recycling costs, the substantial reduction in energy requirements to produce aluminum from used cans, and the high residual value of aluminum packaging have substantially increased the recycling of aluminum. More than half of all aluminum packaging in the United States is currently recycled. Lightweighting strategy has reduced the weight of aluminum cans by more than 60 percent over the last 30 years. Currently, one ton of tinplate can produce as much as 30,000 cans as compared with 24,000 cans in 1985. However, production of aluminum from virgin material is extremely energy intensive and purification of aluminum involves considerable pollution.

Steel is typically used in open-top food and beverage cans. It is tough and unaffected by water and air. As a result, steel is used as packaging material for bandages and foods. About half of steel packaging materials are recycled. Steel is easy to recycle because of its magnetic properties. However, its low cost and high transportation cost discourage steel recycling. Raw material availability, tamper resistance, ease of recycling, and high reusability make steel an ideal packaging material. However, high-energy consumption, pollution, low scrap value, and high transportation costs are some of the weaknesses of steel as a packaging material.

Paper and paperboards make up more than half of all U.S. packaging materials. They have a long history of recycling. About 44 percent of all paper and paperboard packaging was recycled in 1993. Even though paper is biodegradable if exposed to air and water, most paper in airtight and watertight landfills takes a long time to degrade. Wax and plastic coatings decelerate degradation. Paper packaging can be grouped into corrugated boxes, folding and setup boxes, paper bags, and so on. About half of all corrugated boxes are currently recycled. Household paper packaging is not extensively recycled because of the lack of a collection infrastructure; it is difficult to segregate because of its many varieties. Producing paper is extremely energy intensive. Producing paper takes more than twice the energy than producing the same weight of glass. In addition, paper production generates significant quantities of waste due to bleaching and other chemical treatments. Recycling can reduce air pollution, water consumption, and energy usage.

Glass makes up about one-fourth of all packaging materials in the United States. Sand, soda ash, and limestone, which are used to manufacture glass, are readily available. Glass is an ideal packaging material for foods and beverages. It is easy to recycle and does not lose any of its properties after recycling. About 25 percent of the glass disposed of by consumers was recycled in the United States in 1993. Recycled glass must be segregated by color and also by shape (e.g., flat glass must be separated from glass containers). The labor intensity of the segregation process reduces the proportion of glass recycled. Since glass bottles made of thick materials require more energy to manufacture and ship, they are recycled rather than refilled. Advanced technology has made it possible to produce less thick glass without reducing its strength. Since the 1950s, there has been a 30 to 50 percent reduction in weight as a result of lightweighting strategy. Unlike metals and other materials, glass is inert, making it an ideal packaging material for many products. Most developed countries have a well-developed infrastructure to recycle glass. However, glass does have several drawbacks as a packaging material. It is energy intensive. Furnaces used to manufacture glass are pollution intensive. Glass is heavy and can break in transit. In addition, glass bottles require more filling time than cans. Consequently, glass is steadily losing its market share as a packaging material for beverages.

Plastics account for about 12 percent of all packaging materials. The term *plastics* is used to include various polymeric compounds. Plastics include a variety of chemical compounds with several applications, making them one of the most versatile of all packaging materials, but their diversity makes their environmental consequences hard to understand. Plastics commonly used for packaging include LDPE used to produce trash bags, HDPE used in milk bottles, PS used in foam cups, polypropylene used in drugs and mouthwash bottles, PET used in soft drink bottles, and PVC used in cosmetics and vinegar bottles. Plastics are excellent packaging materials because of their diversity, durability, and flexibility. They are extremely well suited for individual packs. Except for HDPE, which is hazy, PET and PVC are transparent. They are excellent packaging materials for foods and beverages. Unlike glass, plastic containers do not break in transit. Significant amounts of heat can be recovered from plastics through incineration. In addition, plastic containers can be reused. Since only about 6 percent of plastics are recycled in the United States, most consumers believe that plastics cannot be recycled. Thermoplastics used in consumer packaging and disposables can be recycled and reused. To facilitate easy segregation of plastics, SPI has developed labels to be placed on the bottom of plastic containers. LDPE (31.9 percent), HDPE (28.9 percent), and PS (12.1

percent) now constitute more than 70 percent of plastics in plastics packaging.[8]

Plastics have several disadvantages, however. They are derived from nonrenewable fossil fuels. They are difficult to recycle and do not degrade easily. Their manufacturing process may emit chlorofluorocarbons, which have been known to damage the earth's ozone layer. Incineration of PVCs has the likelihood of dioxin emission. Since plastics are porous to water vapor, oxygen, and other gases, penetration of these gases can spoil some food items. In addition, high-pressure contents cannot be stored in plastic containers. Since lack of contamination cannot be guaranteed for recycled plastic, recycled plastics are typically used in construction, automobiles, and so on rather than for food packaging. Some of the strengths and weaknesses of various packaging materials are as follows:

Strengths	*Weaknesses*
Aluminum	
Abundant supply	Energy intensive
Easy to reuse	Purification involves pollution
High residual value	
Easily recycled	
Does not rust	
Nonmagnetic	
Light, strong, and durable	
Glass	
Abundant raw materials	Energy intensive
Hygienic	Relatively heavy
Refillable	Production involves pollution
Well-developed infrastructure	Can break in transit
Paper and Board	
Renewable raw materials	Energy intensive
Well-developed infrastructure	Production involves pollution
Degradable	Difficult to recover all
Energy recoverable through	recyclable paper and board
paper incineration	Low residual value
	High cost of recovery
Plastics	
Versatile packaging material	Made from nonrenewable raw
Excellent for individual packs	materials
Hygienic packaging for food	Does not degrade
and beverages	Difficult to recycle
Safe in transit	Multilayer materials are hard
Energy recoverable through	to recycle
incineration	
Steel	
Abundant raw materials	Production involves pollution
Excellent for individual packs	Energy intensive
Safe in transit	Low residual value
Easy to segregate because of	
magnetic property	
Can be reused indefinitely	

PACKAGING EVALUATION

Environmental degradation by packaging occurs because of resource depletion, pollution, and the generation of solid wastes. The environmental degradation by packaging begins with the extraction of raw materials and ends with the disposal of packaging. Packaging needs to be evaluated using multiple criteria. According to a 1994 *Packaging* magazine survey, 19 out of 20 respondents believe that keeping a product in good condition until it is bought is the most important packaging benefit.[9] Keeping a product in good condition after the package is opened and providing "just enough" packaging were other highly touted packaging benefits. Total environmental impact, cost, liability, technical feasibility, customer appeal, and ease of handling are some of the factors that need to be considered in evaluating packaging. Life-cycle assessment is supposed to provide a cradle-to-grave estimate of the environmental impact of packaging materials. Environmentalists, law makers, and others have yet to reach agreement on a methodology with which to conduct life-cycle analysis to identify optimal strategies for packaging improvements. Typically, life-cycle assessment estimates the extent of environmental degradation for the given raw materials and their relative costs, manufacturing processes, distribution, and disposal methods. However, life-cycle assessment can also be used to answer questions relating to various packaging decisions.[10] Figure 7.1 analyzes four strategies for improving the packaging for 1,000 liters of a single-strength liquid fabric conditioner.

The most appropriate packaging improvement strategy is chosen based on the reduction in energy usage in process, transport, and feedstock and the reduction in emissions into air, water, and land. Figure 7.1 indicates concentration strategy is more effective than the use of recycled inputs and recycling. Combining concentrations and using refills can significantly reduce energy consumption and emissions.

A number of organizations have developed guidelines for evaluating packaging based on current industry know-how. Guidelines developed by the Institute of Packaging Professionals are concerned with five main areas: source reduction, recycling, degradability, disposal methods, and legislative considerations. These guidelines, which appear in the appendix at the end of this chapter, use a question format and are approached from theoretical, practical, and technological levels. The guidelines are flexible enough to accommodate future changes.

The Source Reduction Council of the Coalition of Northeastern Governors suggests that industry follow a packaging hierarchy, which, in order of priority, includes no packaging, minimal packaging, consumable or returnable packaging, recyclable packaging or packaging made of recycled materials.[11] To ensure that packaging meets public health criteria, the Institute of Food Technologists suggests a consideration of safety, quality, and nutrition aspects of packaging; an analysis of the effects of taxes and bans on packaging materials on safety, quality, and nutrition; the implementation of integrated waste management; and encouragement of source reduction to reduce municipal solid waste.

FIGURE 7.1
Percentage of Decrease in Energy Usage and Emissions for
Four Packaging Improvement Strategies

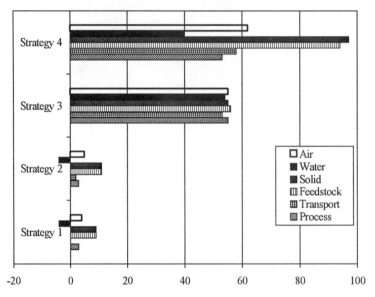

Strategy 1: Add 25 percent recycled HDPE into the virgin HDPE bottle
Strategy 2: 25 percent recycling of the virgin HDPE bottle
Strategy 3: Threefold concentration of the product
Strategy 4: Threefold concentration and virgin paper carton to refill HDPE bottle

Source: Council on Plastics and Packaging in the Environment, "Issues in Life Cycle Assessment," *COPPE Info Backgrounder* (Washington, D.C.: Council on Plastics and Packaging in the Environment, September 1991).

ENVIRONMENTAL LAWS

Even before environmental laws were passed, the packaging industry was subject to various regulations. The packaging and labeling of meat and poultry products were regulated by the Department of Agriculture since 1906 in accordance with the Meat Inspection Act of 1906. The Food and Drug Administration regulated packaging and labeling of pharmaceutical, food, and cosmetic products. The Federal Trade Commission enforced regulations relating to deceptive packaging and labeling. The transportation of containers carrying dangerous products is regulated by the Interstate Commerce Commission. Until the passage of the Solid Waste Disposal Act of 1965, there were no significant federal regulations regarding solid wastes. States and localities were responsible for regulating solid wastes, and, as a result, regulations were disorganized and uncoordinated. The emphasis of the 1965 act was on research, demonstration, and training. The Resource Conservation and Recovery Act of 1970 focused on the recovery of materials and energy from solid waste. However, when the EPA realized that waste-disposal guidelines were not consistently applied by the states, it added enforcement to the Resource Conservation and Recovery Act by setting minimum criteria for solid waste disposal facilities and prohibiting open dumps.

Rising reclamation and waste-disposal costs and difficulty in dealing with packaging waste forced the government to introduce regulations to control a variety of packaging wastes. There are basically two types of legislation. One consists of market-based measures; the other stresses command-and-control measures. Market-based measures essentially use economic carrots and sticks, including deposit requirements and packaging charges, to encourage the reduction of packaging waste. For example, several states in the United States levy deposits for beverage containers to encourage reuse and recycling. Some countries have or are planning to impose taxes on certain types of packaging to encourage the use of green packaging. Command-and-control measures include control of packaging wastes. Legislation bans certain packaging materials; requires products to contain a certain proportion of recycled materials; and mandates the return of packaging to manufacturers, or minimum level of reuse, recycling, or recovery. For example, California and Oregon require a certain proportion of recycled content in plastic and glass containers. Germany's Ordinance on the Avoidance of Packaging Waste is an example of reuse and recycling requirements. Banning the use of multilayered aseptic packaging in Maine is an example of a command-and-control measure of legislation.

CONCLUSION

Packaging plays a vital role in the distributions and uses of products. Even though packaging has a significant impact on municipal solid waste, packaging designers should consider several factors in addition to environmental impact. The most important factor for green packaging design managers to keep in mind is not to compromise packaging effectiveness for the sake of greenness. It is essential to encourage R&D to develop new forms of packaging. An integrated rather than piecemeal approach to reducing municipal solid waste is recommended for achieving maximum waste reduction. The use of recycled materials in packaging can significantly reduce municipal solid waste. A team approach on plant, company, and industry levels is required to reduce solid waste. Consumer education and public relations programs ensure that decisions are made based on accurate information. The lack of a recycling infrastructure has significantly thwarted recycling. Therefore, industry and government should cooperate together to develop an effective recycling infrastructure. To ensure that policy making does not force industry to choose suboptimal options, it is essential for companies to become actively involved in government policy making.

APPENDIX: IoPP PACKAGING REDUCTION, RECYCLING, AND DISPOSAL GUIDELINES
(July, 1990)

SOURCE REDUCTION

Source reduction is an on-going materials and energy conservation process to reduce post-consumer solid waste by developing and adopting a wide variety of functional systems and techniques that minimize the use of materials and energy resources. Of all the environmental considerations packaging professionals must evaluate, none more directly affects municipal solid waste than source reduction. This is the EPA's highest priority solid waste management option and should be the first and most important consideration. Depending on consumer acceptance of recycling programs, a package which achieves significant source reduction goals may actually have a better environmental impact than a highly recyclable package which, nonetheless, never gets into recycling system.

Among questions packaging professionals should ask are:

1. Can the package or any of its components be eliminated entirely (i.e. does the product really need an individual package or can it be sold as is or in bulk)?
    ☐ Yes, the package can be eliminated.
    ☐ Yes, a component of the package can be eliminated.
    ☐ No, neither the package nor any of its components can be eliminated.
2. Are measurable source reduction benefits made possible by the reuse of the package without remanufacturing?
    ☐ Yes   ☐ No
3a. Can source reduction goals be achieved by packaging geometry or structural design changes (e.g. lower packaging surface area to product volume ratios)?
    ☐ Yes   ☐ No
b. Can overall packaging volume be reduced by using different packaging or container forms?
    ☐ Yes   ☐ No

c. Can overall packaging weight be reduced by using different packaging or container forms?
☐ Yes   ☐ No

4a. Does a reduction in materials in one part of the package system require as much or more materials to be used in another part of the system?
☐ Yes   ☐ No

b. Is it possible to increase secondary or tertiary packaging to reduce primary packaging and achieve a net overall reduction?
☐ Yes   ☐ No

5. Through product design changes (e.g. liquid concentrates, improved product ruggedness), can the package be redesigned to use less material without compromising the product?
☐ Yes   ☐ No

6. Can the package or one of its components be designed to be safely refilled or reused by the consumer?
☐ Yes   ☐ No

7. Can source reduction goals be met by replacing a number of smaller packages with a single larger, more efficient package size (e.g. family-size or bulk containers rather than individual portion packages)?
☐ Yes   ☐ No

8. Is it possible to reduce or eliminate secondary or tertiary packaging or wrapping?
☐ Yes   ☐ No

9. Are customer suggestions on source reduction possibilities for secondary and tertiary packaging through the distribution system solicited and encouraged?
☐ Yes   ☐ No

10. Does a product or package change which results in source reduction cause an increase in solid waste in other areas (e.g. an increase in the amount of food spoiled and thrown away as result of changing from smaller to larger packaged servings)?
☐ Yes   ☐ No

11. Can source reduction be achieved by changing the distribution process or transportation modes?
☐ Yes   ☐ No

RECYCLING

Recycling of packages or using recycled material in packages is generally considered the second most desirable alternative for reducing the environmental impact of the package.

However, using a material that can be technically recycled may not be preferable to other means of reducing environmental impact if there is not a commercially viable recycling system in place. Too often, the term "collectable" is confused with "recyclable," and there is a very big difference between the two.

Because some municipalities have established recycling systems while others have not, the package's distribution area must be considered.

Recycling is an issue that necessarily involves individuals outside the packaging community as well as those within it. Suppliers, users, environmental groups, government personnel, consumers, and legislators must work together to establish and coordinate recycling programs and help create real markets for recycled materials.

As a practical matter, to be recyclable a material must have an existing economically practical and functional commercial recycling system through which it can be processed. If there is not such a system in place, but the technology and market exist to have one, then all parties involved should work together to develop such a system if it is economically feasible.

Note: In the committee's opinion, new package forms and packages made of materials not currently being recycled will probably be subjected to higher levels of scrutiny than traditional package forms and materials that are already being recycled.

12a. Does the technology exist to collect packaging from consumers and recycle it commercially?
☐ Yes   ☐ No

b. If not, is the necessary research being conducted to develop this technology — either alone or in conjunction with industry, government officials or academia?
☐ Yes   ☐ No

13a. Is the package or one of its components reusable as the same item without remanufacturing?
☐ Yes   ☐ No

b. Is there a system in place to collect and reuse these used packages?
☐ Yes   ☐ No

c. If not, is there active development of such a system?
☐ Yes   ☐ No

14a. Is the package recyclable (i.e. is there a system in place to recycle the package)?
☐ Yes   ☐ No

b. If so, are a symbol and instructions used on the package to encourage recycling?
☐ Yes   ☐ No

15. Can the material be identified on the package (e.g. the plastic resin recycling code) to aid collection and recycling?
☐ Yes ☐ No

16a. Has an in-house or in-plant resource recovery or recycling system to use waste products generated from the manufacture of your product or package been established?
☐ Yes, into the same product.
☐ Yes, recycled into a secondary product or single material.
☐ Yes, recycled into secondary product or commingled material.
☐ Yes, materials must be reclaimed by a chemical or other process.
☐ Yes, and the material is sold or given to an outside vendor to be recycled.
☐ No

b. If not, is there active development of such a system?
☐ Yes ☐ No

17a. Is the outer and inner packaging used for shipment and distribution of goods recyclable?
☐ Yes ☐ No

b. Has a resource recovery and recycling system been established in co-operation with customers to collect and reuse distribution packaging waste that does not reach the ultimate consumer?
☐ Yes ☐ No

c. If not, is there active development of such a system?
☐ Yes ☐ No

18a. Are programs in place to require reusable or recyclable secondary packaging from suppliers?
☐ Yes ☐ No

b. If not, is there active development of such programs?
☐ Yes ☐ No

19a. If the technology does exist to collect and recycle post-consumer packaging, are systems in place to collect and recycle the packaging?
☐ Yes ☐ No

b. If not, is the development of such systems being actively pursued — either alone or in conjunction with industry, government officials or academia?
☐ Yes ☐ No

20a. Are recycling systems established for the packaging material in all the regions in which the package will be sold or distributed?
☐ Yes ☐ No

b. If not, is participation in the creation of such regional recycling systems being pursued?
☐ Yes ☐ No

21a. Is there a viable commercial market for these post-consumer recycled packaging materials?
☐ Yes ☐ No

b. If not, are any projects or programs to increase demand for this recycled material being initiated — either alone or in conjunction with industry, government officials or academia?
☐ Yes ☐ No

22a. Is the package mono-material or multi-material (e.g. laminated or coextrusion)?
☐ Mono-material ☐ Multi-material

b. If the package is multi-material:
1) Are current recycling systems set up to handle these multi-material packages?
☐ Yes ☐ No

2) If there is not a recycling system in place to process the multi-material package, is your company pursuing the development of such a system — either alone or in conjunction with industry, government officials or academia?
☐ Yes ☐ No

3) Is this combination of materials the most environmentally sound structural design possible without compromising product integrity?
☐ Yes ☐ No

4) Do the materials need to be further separated to increase their recycling value or to avoid impeding the recycling process?
☐ Yes ☐ No

23a. Does the primary, secondary and/or tertiary package currently use recycled material?
☐ Yes ☐ No

b. If so, is there a symbol and statement on the package to indicate that recycled material has been used?
☐ Yes ☐ No

24a. Have the effects that the use of recycled materials on the physical properties of the package (stacking strength, printing quality, etc.) been thoroughly considered?
☐ Yes ☐ No

b. Will the use of recycled materials require more materials or an increase in the overall volume/weight of the package to maintain an acceptable level of package performance?
☐ Yes ☐ No

c. Has the impact of recycled material use on your manufacturing/production processes been researched (e.g. will recycled materials run on our existing machinery; will the use of recycled materials require significantly more energy/labor consumption)?
☐ Yes ☐ No

DEGRADABILITY

Degradability is perhaps the most misunderstood concept in the solid waste field. A package may have the characteristics that make it biodegradable, photodegradable, or chemically degradable, but if it is not disposed of properly (under the right environmental conditions), it will not degrade and will remain a waste product in the municipal solid waste system. For instance, essentially no degradation takes place in a landfill. Biological degradation occurs in composting and sewage treatment plants.

Because successful applications of degradable packages are limited, the desirability of degradability follows source reduction and recycling. In most cases, degradability follows source reduction and recycling. In most cases, degradability may actually be undesirable. It would not be appropriate to switch a package to material that is degradable from one that is recyclable and for which a recycling system exists.

Before a degradable system is considered as a viable option, all the impacts of that system on the environment must be fully understood and considered. Moreover, the issues of proper exposure conditions, time frames required, and levels of break-down should be established.

25a. Is the package technically biodegradable?
     ☐ Yes   ☐ No
  b. If yes, does the packaging material need to be separated before it can be considered biodegradable?
     ☐ Yes   ☐ No
  c. Will the package be intended to be disposed of in a composting or some other specified treatment facility to ensure that biodegradation occurs?
     ☐ Yes   ☐ No
  d. Will it produce any by-products through degradation which are harmful to the environment?
     ☐ Yes   ☐ No
  e. Has research been conducted to evaluate the positive and negative aspects of using biodegradable material?
     ☐ Yes   ☐ No
26a. Is the package photodegradable?
     ☐ Yes   ☐ No
  b. If yes, does the package material have to be separated before photodegradation?
     ☐ Yes   ☐ No
  c. Will it produce any by-products through degradation which are harmful to the environment?
     ☐ Yes   ☐ No

d.   Has research been conducted to evaluate the positive and negative aspects of using photodegradable materials?
☐ Yes   ☐ No

27a. Is the package chemically degradable?
☐ Yes   ☐ No

b.   If yes, does the package material have to be separated before chemical degradation?
☐ Yes   ☐ No

c.   Will it be disposed of in a sewage treatment plant to ensure that chemical degradation occurs?
☐ Yes   ☐ No

d.   Will it produce any by-products through degradation which are harmful to the environment?
☐ Yes   ☐ No

e.   Has research been conducted to evaluate the positive and negative aspects of using chemically degradable materials?
☐ Yes   ☐ No

DISPOSAL

When a package finally reaches the end of its life cycle, it must be disposed of properly. This is a problem that each geographic region must handle according to its own needs and resources. However, the package should be designed to facilitate its safe, and if possible, easy disposal. This may require instructions on the proper disposal method. Co-operation between industry and governments must be pursued to ensure that proper disposal is achieved.

28a. Has the package and its components (i.e. inks, dyes, pigments, stabilizers, solders and adhesives) been made without the inclusion of toxic materials, such as heavy metals including cadmium, lead, mercury and hexavalent chromium?
☐ Yes   ☐ No

b.   If the package material currently uses toxic materials, can they be removed without compromising the package's functions?
☐ Yes   ☐ No

29a. Can the package be landfilled safely without leaching hazardous by-products or otherwise causing harm to the environment?
☐ Yes   ☐ No

b.   If no, can the package be designed to avoid problems in landfill disposal?
☐ Yes   ☐ No

30.   Can the package be made smaller and/or designed to be compacted by consumers or waste management companies so that it takes up less collection/landfill space?
☐ Yes   ☐ No

31. Can the package be incinerated safely to recover the energy value of the packaging materials without harmful ash residue or emissions?
    ☐ Yes   ☐ No
32. Does the package contain sufficient combustible materials to be reprocessed for safe burning and energy recovery?
    ☐ Yes   ☐ No

LEGISLATIVE CONSIDERATIONS

Legislation which will directly impact packaging is being written and proposed in every part of the country. This legislation varies from area to area and, therefore, must be carefully considered in conjunction with the proposed distribution of the product/package.

33. Will existing or proposed legislation (i.e. package taxes, bans, deposits, solid waste bills, etc.) affect the package?
    ☐ Yes, on the federal level.
    ☐ Yes, on the state level.
    ☐ Yes, on the local level.
    ☐ No.
34a. Does your company act in an advisory capacity to federal, state and/or local governments to ensure that they have access to accurate packaging data?
    ☐ Yes   ☐ No
b. If yes, are the packaging structural design requirements fully considered by corporate lobbyists?
    ☐ Yes   ☐ No
c. Have you catalogued and considered all current and pending legislation in markets where your package will be sold or distributed?
    ☐ Yes   ☐ No

NOTES

1. "Top 100 Packaged Brands Buy $12 Billion," *Packaging*, 39(1) (January 1994): 37.

2. Organization for Economic Cooperation and Development, *Reduction and Recycling of Packaging Waste*, Environment Monograph, No. 62, (Paris: Organization for Economic Cooperation and Development, 1992).

3. H. Alter, *The Greatly Growing Garbage Problem* (Washington, D.C.: Government Printing Office, 1988).

4. World Health Organization, *Nutrition: Facts and Hopes* (Washington, D.C.: World Health Organization, October 1984).

5. Jane Bickerstaffe and Elaine Barrett, "Packaging's Role in Society," in *Packaging in the Environment*, ed. Geoffrey M. Levy (London: Blackie Academic and Professional, 1993), p. 38.

6.   Lester R. Brown, *State of the World 1990 — A Worldwatch Institute Report on Progress Toward a Sustainable Society* (London: Unwin Hyman, 1990).

7.   U.S. Environmental Protection Agency, *Characterization of Municipal Solid Waste in the United States: 1994 Update*, Executive Summary, EPA 530-S-94-042 (Washington, D.C.: Government Printing Office, November 1994), p. 8.

8.   "Filling New Needs in Packaging," *ChemicalWeek*, 147(3) (July 25, 1990): 32.

9.   Chris Baum, "10th Annual Packaging Consumer Survey, 1994," *Packaging*, 39(8) (August 1994): 43.

10.   Council on Plastics and Packaging in the Environment, "Issues in Life Cycle Assessment," *COPPE Info Backgrounder* (Washington, D.C.: Council on Plastics and Packaging in the Environment, September 1991).

11.   Lewis Erwin and L. Hall Healy, Jr., *Packaging and Solid Waste Management Strategies* (New York: American Management Association, 1990), pp. 69–76.

8

Green Marketing

Manufacturers are realizing that price, quality, and convenience are not the only means of competing in a cutthroat market. Greenness is becoming a potent marketing weapon. Purchasing decisions are affected by the environmental attributes of a product. As a result, more manufacturers are incorporating green claims in their labeling and advertising. In 1991 two out of five new household products included green claims in either labeling or advertising. Rising sales for green products are forcing marketers to respond to the environmental concerns of their consumers. Companies belonging to traditionally polluting industries, such as those that produce chemicals, petroleum, and household products, are aggressively carrying out marketing strategies to win customers. They are developing greener products with superior performance, added convenience, and lower prices. According to the Marketing Intelligence Service, the number of green products introduced skyrocketed from 24 in 1985 to 810 in 1991. The number of green products as a share of all new products introduced rose from a mere 0.5 percent in 1985 to 13.4 percent in 1991.[1] The Gallup Poll reports that 68 percent of marketers made packaging changes in 1991 to make products green as compared with 59 percent in 1989. Environmentalism has no boundaries. Any company wishing to remain competitive in a global market must develop environmentally sound products. Growing green consumerism in Europe and Japan will force companies in the United States to introduce more green products in the future in order to remain competitive.

GREEN CONSUMERS

The 77 million baby boomers born between 1946 and 1964 form a core segment of green consumers. They are one of the most educated age groups. As they become older, their priorities shift from quantity to quality. They prefer durable rather than disposable products. As the population above age 35 grows, the demand for green products will rise. Green customers, based on their commitment to the environment, can be categorized into various segments. The Roper Organization classifies people as true-blue greens, greenback greens, sprouts, grousers, and basic browns based on their commitment to the environment.[2] The Simmons Market Research Bureau groups people into premium greens, reds, whites, and greens, no-cost ecologists, convenient greens, and unconcerned.[3] About 25 to 40 percent of the U.S. population are active environmentalists. They tend to be older (median age of about 44), richer (median income of $33,000 in 1990), consist primarily of women (about 60 percent), and are married with children under age 13. The active environmentalists as a group recycle regularly, favor product boycotts, and are willing to pay premiums for green products. About 30 to 40 percent of the U.S. population are unconcerned about the environment. They tend to belong to lower income groups, live in the South and rural areas, and have a median age of about 39. The rest of the population belongs to the swing group. They are not antienvironmentalists per se. They believe in recycling but do not regularly practice it. They are not willing to pay premiums for green products and are uncertain when they must choose between convenience and the environment.

GREEN MARKETING STRATEGIES

Unlike traditional marketing, green marketing involves the development of high-performance, low-cost, high-convenience, and environmentally less harmful products. In addition, products should project an image of greenness. However, green marketing is affected by various factors, which are discussed below.

Public Distrust

Only 13 percent of Americans believe companies to be trustworthy sources of environmental information.[4] Recent industrial accidents and oil spills have made the public skeptical about a company's ability to prevent future environmental disasters. Most people perceive that companies have no incentive to reduce pollution. Shortly after the *Valdez* oil spill, 41 percent of Americans were angry enough to consider boycotting Exxon.[5] A product manager must therefore match words with deeds to overcome public skepticism about her company's products.

Varied Perceptions

Understanding the differences in risk perception by the consumers, government agencies, and industry affects marketing success. The public can correctly estimate the rank order of various causes of deaths.

However, they make significant errors when estimating the actual number of deaths. They overestimate the number of deaths from rare risks and underestimate the number from common risks. They typically underestimate the number of deaths from hunting, firearm accidents, suicide, and diseases, and they overestimate the number of deaths from fire fighting, floods, vitamin poisoning, vaccinations, and bites and stings.[6] Perceptions about alar and nuclear energy highlight these differences in risk perception and the importance of perception in marketing. Alar is a chemical substance used on apples to keep them longer on trees and to help them develop firm, red fruits. When alar residues were found in the fruit, the public panicked. The U.S. Environmental Protection Agency (EPA) and the company manufacturing the chemical unsuccessfully claimed that the chemical was of no risk to the public and that it would continue to be used until reviewed. However, mounting public pressures and bad publicity forced the company to stop its sale even before the EPA could complete its review.

Overregulation

The growing volume of environmental laws are bringing more products under a regulatory sweep. In 1971, the *Environmental Law Reporter* summarized the federal environmental laws in 33 pages. In 1989, it took 3,500 pages to do the same.[7] In addition, states and local agencies are passing their own laws. To reduce the generation of solid waste, legislators are imposing higher packaging taxes and heavier disposal fees. Some states are trying to redefine such terms as "recyclable," "biodegradable," and "photodegradable." Several states intend to pass legislation regarding packaging and labeling requirements. These regulations make the product design task extremely complex.

Confusion about Green Claims

There are no perfectly green products. Every product consumes scarce resources and energy and generates waste during distribution and use that must be disposed of. However, Madison Avenue has developed a wide array of confusing terms to describe the greenness of its products: degradable, biodegradable, environmentally friendly, ozone safe, pH-balanced, and so on. Unfortunately, these terms mean different things to different people. For example, Mobil has claimed that its Hefty trash bag was biodegradable. However, these bags break down extremely slowly when packed tightly in landfills, and consequently, Mobil was forced to withdraw its biodegradability claim. Amoco Corporation's consumer products division touted the recyclability of its polystyrene cups. However, the plant that could recycle them was located only in New York as of early 1990. Consequently, these cups were not recyclable for consumers in the other parts of the United

States. Scores of such environmental claims have made the consumers extremely skeptical of green products. According to a preliminary study of environmental advertising claims, most claims were judged to be vague.[8] Therefore, a product manager should take special care not to antagonize consumers or annoy regulators by merely pasting on a green label. Another problem concerns the subjective nature of the life-cycle costing. Several companies have switched from polystyrene packaging materials to paper as polystyrene is not recyclable, uses nonrenewable energy resources, and requires the use of ozone-depleting chlorofluoro-carbons (CFCs). Life-cycle analysis presented by Martin B. Hocking and environmental consultant Franklin Associates, Ltd., point out that polystyrene containers are "greener" than paper alternatives.[9] The assumptions made in life-cycle analyses can easily influence the "greenness" measurement of a product. Therefore, a product manager should label products very carefully. Claims must be precise, factual, and supported by solid research. Claims must conform to specific legislation requirements and should not be misleading.

The U.S. Federal Trade Commission (FTC) and a task force of attorneys general from 11 states — California, Florida, Massachusetts, Minnesota, Missouri, New York, Tennessee, Texas, Utah, Washington, and Wisconsin — have issued guidelines for environmental market-ing.[10] The FTC guidelines comprise administrative interpretations of laws administered by the FTC and as such are not legally enforceable. However, they provide an excellent starting point for marketers trying to comply with legal requirements. The FTC guidelines require marketers to disclose whether environmental claims refer to a product, package, or a component of either. It advises marketers not to overstate environmental claims. When comparative claims are made, FTC guidelines mandate that the marketer should substantiate the claim. Broad environmental claims should be avoided. The environmental claims about degradability, biodegradability, photodegradability, com-postability, recyclability, recycled content, source reduction, refillability, and ozone-free and ozone-friendly products should be substantiated. The FTC guidelines do not preempt state laws and several states have passed their own regulations relating to green marketing. *The Green Report II* issued by the attorneys general of 11 states provides guidance for environmental marketing so that companies do not violate state deceptive advertising laws. Like the FTC guidelines, the recommenda-tions of the attorneys general are not laws and have neither the force nor effect of law.

Consumer Education

Based on environmental attitudes and behavior, Americans can be divided into three categories — visionary greens, hard-core browns, and maybe greens.[11] Visionary greens, which make up 5 to 15 percent of the population, are consistent buyers of green products. Hard-core browns, forming 15 to 30 percent of the population, are antienvironmentalists and cannot be influenced to buy green products. Therefore, green marketing efforts should be focused on the maybe-greens, constituting 55 to 80 percent of consumers.

Consumer education should not be restricted solely to advertisements and labels. Product managers should also prepare brochures to reinforce claims made in the advertisements. Involving environmental and other nonprofit groups in promoting a product should also be considered. Product-stewardship programs used by chemical companies to inform distributors and consumers about the proper handling and use of their products is an excellent example of a consumer-education program.

Dwindling Sales

According to an often quoted CBS/*New York Times* poll conducted in March–April 1990, 74 percent of respondents said that the environment must be protected regardless of cost, up significantly from 45 percent in 1981. However, one dilemma facing several product managers is that green product sales seem to be withering.[12] According to a *Wall Street Journal*/NBC poll conducted in July 1991, only 46 percent of those surveyed purchased any product during the six months preceding the poll specifically because the product or manufacturer had a good reputation for protecting the environment. In other words, consumers may be depicting themselves in a greener light than their actions indicate.

Green marketing has not been successful for all products. Consumers typically seem to appreciate environmental considerations in those products where the effect on the environment is easy to see. According to a survey by the Roper Organization conducted in 1993, consumers value greenness in declining amounts in lawn and garden products, household-cleaning products, paper products, gasoline, personal-care products, cars, and fast-food restaurants. The greenness value is less than the average for all personal-care products, cars, and fast-food restaurants. However, this does not mean that companies should give up on green marketing. According to the Roper Green Gauge Study, experience, price, quality, advertisements, environmental record, and sponsorship are some factors that influence buying decisions.[13] Between 1989 and 1993, environmental record increased by 6 points from 12 to 18 as a factor that influenced buying behavior of a consumer. Quality and experience with brand fell during the same period. Figure 8.1 indicates the proportion of consumers whose buying is influenced by various factors.

FIGURE 8.1
Factors Influencing Purchase of a Brand

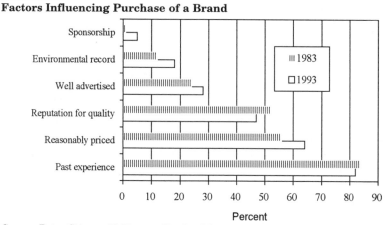

Percent

Source: Peter Stisser, "A Deeper Shade of Green," *American Demographics*, 16 (March 1994): 14–29.

Consumer Support for Life-style Changes

When people opt for a green product, sometimes they must give up some benefits. For example, if people choose energy-saving small cars, they sacrifice some of the protection a larger car would offer them in the event of an accident. Recyclable packaging consumes time for sorting and recycling. Disposable diapers, which account for 85 percent of the diaper market, are convenient, but they fill scarce landfills. Cloth diapers are cheaper and recyclable but are considerably less convenient. The American Academy of Pediatrics and the American Public Health Association recommend disposable diapers in out-of-home child-care programs to prevent public health problems. Consumers, therefore, must make tradeoffs between environmental consequences and convenience, health, and economic factors. However, because harmful environmental effects had no significant impact on the sales of disposable diapers, this probably indicates that consumers are not willing to change their life-styles. Consumers consider several factors while deciding and the environment is just one of these factors.

Market Share versus Niche Marketing

Green marketing is an excellent way to increase market share. Economies of scale, because of an increased market share, can reduce costs. In addition, green products should lead to reduced costs because of improved yields, lower liability costs, and so on. Therefore, a company offers its green products at a lower price. However, any market-share strategy should take into account the financial strength of a company and should only be pursued if a company has enough financing to withstand competitors' actions. Niche marketing is another strategy. It allows a company to avoid confronting a competitor. In addition, a company can identify marketing channels overlooked by competitors.

LAUNCHING GREEN MARKETING

All else being equal, green products have an edge over traditional products in today's market. According to the 1993 Roper Organization survey, consumers were willing to pay zero to 0.8 percent higher real prices, or 4.2 to 5 percent higher prices before inflation, in 1991 for green products over traditional products.[14] Green marketing begins with a green audit, green design, green product development, green operations, and green distribution. The first step in green marketing is strategic planning. The goal is to develop plans that go beyond compliance. The next step is to identify products and services that can satisfy environmental requirements. The EPA's Design for Environment program cycle can be used to identify such products or services. The first step is identifying "use clusters" in the industry or product line. A use cluster consists of a group of products, processes, and technologies all of which perform a specific function. For example, paint stripping for maintenance, paint stripping for commercial purposes, and paint stripping for original equipment manufacturing are three use clusters in the paint-stripping industry. Alternatives for paint stripping may not be similar at all. In maintenance function, paint stripping can be done using chemical solvents, sandblasting, and plastic pellet blasting. The next step is to rate each of these alternatives using human and ecological factors. The third step is to perform a substitutes assessment of alternatives based on factors such as risk, releases, costs, and performance. At this point, alternatives can be categorized for their potential based on markets and greenness. The strategy is to choose alternatives with high market value and green potential (see Figure 8.2). Some green attributes include little or no packaging, energy efficient operations, toll-free numbers to answer consumer questions, lack of CFCs, less waste generation from extraction to disposal, easy recyclability, less postconsumer waste, and so on. However, companies should be careful not to select trivial attributes. Attributes should be specific and carefully defined. Advertisements should emphasize values rather than product benefits. To promote the product, it might be a good idea to team up with environmental groups that will complement a company's strengths.

FIGURE 8.2
Green Product Selection Method

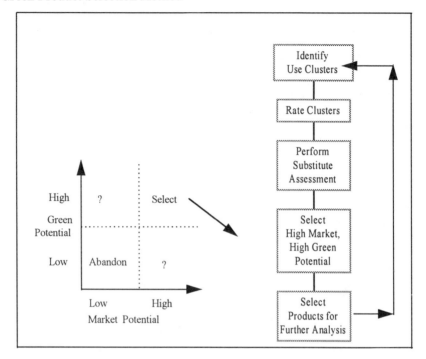

GREEN LABELING

To satisfy rising demand for green products, companies are
introducing green products and making green claims for their existing
products. According to a recent poll, more than 3,000 of the 12,000 new
household products introduced in 1990 boasted that they were
environmentally friendly in some way.[15] This has resulted in deceptive
and false claims. One car company was awarded a Green Con Award by
Friends of the Earth for asserting that one of its cars was environmentally friendly because its air-conditioning system did not use
CFCs.[16] In most states, "recycling," "biodegradable," and other environmental labels have not been defined. A large segment of the U.S. population believes that environmental claims are "mere gimmickry." As a
result of the increase in green marketing, governments have passed
laws regulating environmental marketing.

Green labels consist of seals or symbols placed on a product or
package to convey to the consumer that the product is environmentally
less harmful than other functionally similar products. They make it
easy for consumers to recognize environmentally friendly products.
Green labels were first introduced in West Germany in 1978. Green
labels are now awarded in most of the European countries including

Austria, Denmark, France, Germany, Norway, Spain, Sweden, and the United Kingdom. Japan and South Korea also award green labels and Singapore, Brazil, Colombia, India, Poland, and China plan to establish green labeling soon. The purpose of green labels is to steer consumers toward green products and to provide incentives to manufacturers to develop environmentally friendly products. Green labels make markets more efficient by providing information to consumers and generally improve sales by projecting an image of a safe product.

There are three categories of green labels. Single-issue voluntary labels convey information about one aspect of a product such as "energy efficient," "CFC free," "ozone friendly," and so on. In most countries, if claims are true, there are only a few restrictions on using a single-issue label. Single-issue mandatory labels provide either positive or negative information on one aspect of a product such as "flammable," "eco-toxic," "biodegradable," and so on. The third category of green label is supposed to indicate the overall environmental quality of a product. Other than in the United States, government agencies generally award green labels.

The purpose of green labeling programs is to convey to consumers that labeled products are relatively environmentally less harmful than others in the same category. However, because most products harm the environment during some stage of their production, distribution, use, and disposal, only a few products can be considered green. Therefore, making such relative evaluations requires estimates that take into account a product's overall environmental impact.

Most green labeling programs follow similar procedures. They identify the product group to be labeled such as printing paper or lightbulbs. The critical areas of environmental impact are then identified using life-cycle analysis, and green labeling criteria are established. For example, 90 percent of the environmental consequences stemming from a washing machine occur during a use stage. Therefore, criteria for awarding green labels for washing machines are generally based on use-related environmental impacts. Public comments are considered before final decisions about the awarding criteria are made. Then criteria for awarding green labels are publicized and manufacturers are encouraged to apply for the label. Only about 10 to 20 percent of the market share qualify for green labels. There is a fee for a green label and a green labeling contract is valid for a fixed duration.

A comprehensive survey about environmental labeling can be found in *Environmental Labelling in OECD Countries*.[17] Figure 8.3 presents the green labels of some of these countries. West Germany awarded Blue Angels to products on the basis of seven criteria: recyclability, low hazardous substances, low emissions, low noise, water efficiency, energy efficiency, and biodegradability. These criteria are stringent. To get a Blue Angel label, for example, recycled paper must be made from 100 percent scrap paper with a tolerance of 5 percent and should

FIGURE 8.3
Green Labels in Different Countries

Canada (Environmental Choice)

Nordic Countries (White Swan)

Germany (Blue Angel)

Japan (EcoMark)

United States (Scientific
Certification Systems)

United States (Green Seal)

Source: U.S. Congress, Office of Technology Assessment, *Green Products by Design: Choices for a Cleaner Environment*, OTA-E-541 (Washington, D.C.: U.S. Government Printing Office, October 1992), p. 12.

contain at least 51 percent low- or medium-grade scrap paper and wastes containing sulfate pulp papers.

As of 1991 Canada has awarded Environmental Choice labels to 14 product categories based on safety, performance, and environmental standards. Besides publicizing awarding criteria, the Canadian program outlines the environmental burden of the product and environmental benefit of the labeled product. For example, according to ECP-14-89 (a document that describes criteria for labeling), disposable diapers constitute the third largest item in municipal solid waste and consume "65,000 tonnes of pulp, 8,800 tonnes of plastic and 9,800 tonnes of packing materials in a year." On the other hand, reusable cloth diapers require less than 20 kilograms of cotton to satisfy the diaper needs of a baby who spends two and one-half years in diapers. Criteria for issuing the Environmental Choice label for reusable diapers include that they should be washable at home and reused at least 75 times.

Japan awards EcoMark for products designed to reduce kitchen waste and for recyclable and energy-efficient products. The award of EcoMark requires that the environmental impact during production, use, and disposal be minimal; the product comply with quality and safety regulations; and the price not be higher than a comparable product.

There are no government-sponsored green labeling programs in the United States. However, computer manufacturers satisfying requirements of the EPA's Energy Star Computer program can use the Energy Star[SM] logo to label their equipment. In addition, the U.S. Department of Energy governs an energy-efficiency labeling program for household appliances — such as refrigerators, heat pumps, air conditioners, washing machines, and dishwashers — that consume about one-fifth of the electricity consumed in the United States. In addition, any marketer making claims about recycled content; source reduction; and degradable, biodegradable, photodegradable, compostable, recyclable, refillable, ozone-safe, and ozone-friendly products should satisfy the FTC guidelines for environmental marketing and *Green Report II* to avoid litigation. Several states, including Rhode Island, New York, Connecticut, Wisconsin, and New Hampshire, have passed laws regulating the use of such terms as "recycling" and "ecologically sound."

There are two major private green labeling programs in the United States. The Scientific Certification System allows manufacturers to use Green Cross symbols on their products after verifying manufacturers' claims. To reduce the environmental impacts of consumer products, Green Seal, an independent, nonprofit organization, issues its seals to products that meet its criteria. The criteria emphasize reduced toxic chemicals, reduced harmful effects on fish and wildlife and their habitat, reduced destruction of natural areas, increased energy efficiency, and so on. Green Seal has issued standards on lighting, printing and writing papers, tissue papers, and water-efficient fixtures.

PRODUCT STEWARDSHIP

The goal of product stewardship is to reduce product risks from cradle to grave. Traditionally, companies implemented product stewardship through green design and packaging. Companies are now extending the concept of product stewardship beyond factory walls by promoting safe use and disposal or recycling of their products and by improving communication with distributors and consumers. This concept is spreading. Community right-to-know laws and Occupational Safety and Health Agency regulations are forcing companies to divulge the health and environmental risks of their products. Manufacturers are required to provide material safety data sheets and labeling for their customers. They are routinely training and providing customers with information on safe handling, use, and disposal of their products. Companies are also providing after-sale service on customer request. Companies are providing technical assistance and expertise on pollution reduction and green auditing to their suppliers and customers. Purchasing contracts and product specifications incorporate environmental performance standards. In addition, suppliers are chosen not only based on their prices but also on improved operating practices and environmental records. Customers are forming partnerships with suppliers to develop solutions to environmental problems.

The idea of product stewardship is spreading and companies are being forced to reduce the environmental impacts of their products during use and disposal stages. The principles set forth by the Coalition for Environmentally Responsible Economies state that companies "will inform their customers of the environmental impacts of their products or services and try to correct unsafe use." The Business Charter for Sustainable Development requires companies "to advise, and where relevant educate, customers, distributors and the public in the safe use, transportation, storage and disposal of products provided; and to apply similar considerations to the provision of services." Chemical Manufacturers Association has a comprehensive code of management practices. This code requires companies "to make health, safety and environmental protection an integral part" of all aspects of a company's operations. Product-stewardship programs require strong management leadership and commitment. Written policy, participation, and communication are essential for strong leadership. Performance measurement is another crucial element of the program. Allocation of adequate resources for the program demonstrates the management's strong commitment. Product stewardship requires companies to develop data on health, safety, and environmental effects of their existing and new products.

To make a product-stewardship program successful, a cradle-to-grave analysis of products must be done (see Figure 8.4). An effective product and process design and improvement system should be

FIGURE 8.4
Product-stewardship Program

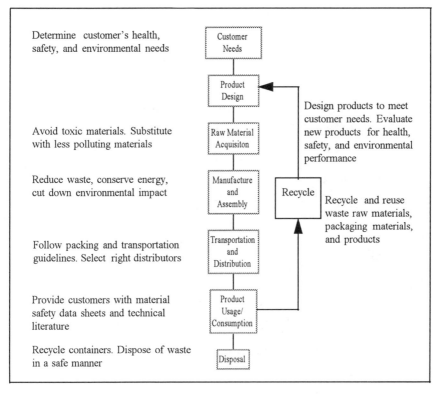

established to improve the greenness of products. A risk-management system will help document health and environmental risks and develop procedures to mitigate those risks. Employee education is critical for the successful implementation of product-stewardship programs. All employees should understand the need for it, its purpose, and its potential benefits. A product-stewardship training program should introduce the program with concrete examples, hazard communication, regulations, and life-cycle analysis. Unlike other green programs, a product-stewardship program is not facility oriented. It extends far beyond the four walls of a facility. The focus should include contractors, suppliers, distributors, and customers. A company should demand contract manufacturers to follow practices that are healthy, safe, and green. They should be provided with information about products to make handling safe. Environmental factors should be significant considerations when choosing suppliers. A company should periodically review distribution practices and suggest methods to enhance greenness and improve safety. Customers should be provided with technical literature and materials safety data sheets. Companies should encourage customers to call a toll-free number if they have questions about the product. When companies are extending their stewardship of products from cradle to grave, they are sometimes concerned about taking on more liability. However, product liability risks will be lower, as there will be fewer accidents, fewer risks, and more satisfied customers.[18]

FEDERAL TRADE COMMISSION GUIDELINES FOR ENVIRONMENTAL MARKETING

Consumers can help prevent pollution by considering the environmental impacts of the products they purchase. In July 1992 the FTC, with input from the EPA, issued the following national guidelines to address application of section 5 of the Federal Trade Commission Act to environmental advertising and marketing practices.[19]

Environmental claims must be substantiated by reliable scientific evidence.

Qualifications and disclosures should be sufficiently clear and prominent on a product to prevent deception.

Environmental claims should make clear whether they apply to the product, the package, or a component of either.

Environmental claims should not overstate the environmental attribute or benefit.

A claim comparing the environmental attributes of one product with those of another should make the bases for the comparison clear and should be substantiated.

The guidelines cover the following environmental claims being made by advertisers for products in the U.S. marketplace.

General Environmental Benefit

Unless substantiated, claims of general benefit such as "environmentally friendly" or "environmentally safe" should be avoided.

Degradable, Biodegradable, and Photodegradable

Claims should be substantiated by evidence that the product will completely decompose into elements found in nature within a reasonable time after consumers dispose of it in the customary way.

Compostable

Claims should be substantiated by evidence that all materials in the product or package will break down into usable compost such as soil-conditioning material and mulch in an appropriate composting program or facility or in a home compost pile or device.

Recyclable

A product or package should not be marketed as recyclable unless it can be collected, separated, or recovered from the solid waste stream for use in the form of raw materials in the manufacture of a new product or package.

Recycled Content

Materials should have been recovered or diverted from the solid waste stream, either during manufacture or after consumer use.

Source Reduction

Claims that a product or package has been reduced or is lower in weight, volume, or toxicity should be qualified to avoid deception about the amount of reduction and the basis for any comparison asserted.

Refillable

Claims should provide for collection and return of the package for refill or for later refill of the package by the consumer with a product subsequently sold in another package.

Ozone Safe and Ozone Friendly

Claims should not be advertised as ozone safe, ozone friendly, or as not containing CFCs, if the product contains any ozone-depleting chemical.

While the guidelines themselves do not have the force of law, failure on the part of companies to follow them can result in the FTC bringing suit against offending companies. Between July 1991 and July 1992, the FTC announced consent agreements in eight such enforcement actions. In three cases, products containing CFCs or ozone-depleting chemicals claimed to be ozone friendly. Four cases involved unsubstantiated claims of the biodegradability of plastic trash bags and disposable diapers. The eighth case dealt with a manufacturer's improper claim that a product was pesticide-free. The settlements of these cases have prevented the companies from using misleading claims in the future.

GREEN REPORT II GUIDELINES

Environmental claims should be specific and not general, vague or broad.

Environmental claims should be precise about the environmental benefit that the product provides.

The promotion of an existing or unadvertised green attribute should not create the perception that the product has been recently modified or improved.

The promotion of a product from which few environmentally harmful ingredients are removed should not give the impression that the product is good for the environment in all respects.

Environmental attributes should be specific whether they refer to a product or its package.

Recycled content claim should specify whether it is post-consumer or recaptured factory material.

When comparative claims are made, they should be complete and should include basis for comparison.

Product life cycle assessment results should be used to advertise until uniform method for conducting them are developed.

Promotion of green certifications must be done with great care.

Source reduction claims should be specific, clear and complete.

Claims about disposability should include availability of such option where the product is sold.

Products currently disposed in landfills or through incinerations should not claim to be degradable, biodegradable and so on.

Compostable claim should not be made unless a significant portion of the product is currently composted.

Recyclability claim should not be made unless a significant portion of the product is currently recycled.

Product should specify what environmentally dangerous material has been eliminated instead of vague claims about disposal.

Claims should be substantive.

Insignificant and irrelevant claims should be avoided.

Single-use product promotion on the basis of environmental attributes should be done carefully.

All environmental claims should be based on reliable scientific evidence.[20]

CONCLUSION

Because green consumers tend to be better educated and more affluent than other consumers, an aggressive and targeted action to win green consumers is necessary to increase market shares and profits. Their proportion among consumers is rising. Green products have an edge over traditional products in today's market. Therefore, companies should put in place a system for identifying and promoting green products. Companies should also initiate product-stewardship programs to reduce environmental risks and degradations.

NOTES

1. Jacquelyn A. Ottman, *Green Marketing* (Lincolnwood, Ill.: NTC Business Books, 1994), p. 13.

2. Peter Stisser, "A Deeper Shade of Green," *American Demographics* (March 1994): 14–29.

3. Ottman, *Green Marketing*, Chap. 2.

4. Carl Frankel, "Blueprint for Green Marketing," *American Demographics* 14 (April 1992): 28.

5. David Kirkpatrick, "Environmentalism: The New Crusade," *Fortune*, February 12, 1990, pp. 44–50.

6. Conservation Foundation, *Risk Assessment and Risk Control* (Washington, D.C.: Conservation Foundation, 1985).

7. Alan J. Miller, *Socially Responsible Investing* (New York: Institute of Finance, 1991), p. 117.

8. N. Kangun, L. Carlson, and S. J. Grove, "Environmental Advertising Claims: A Preliminary Investigation," *Journal of Public Policy and Marketing* 10 (Fall 1991): 47–58.

9. Martin B. Hocking, "Paper versus Polystyrene: A Complex Choice" *Science*, February 1, 1991, pp. 504–505; David Stipp, "Life-cycle Analysis Measures Greenness, But Result May Not be Black and White," *The Wall Street Journal*, February 28, 1991, pp. B1, B5.

10. Council on Environmental Quality, *Environmental Quality, Twenty-third Annual Report* (Washington, D.C.: Government Printing Office, 1993), pp. 176–177; Attorneys General of California, Florida, Massachusetts, Minnesota, Missouri, New York, Tennessee, Texas, Utah, Washington, and Wisconsin, *The Green Report II: Recommendations for Responsible Environmental Advertising,* 1991 (available from the Office of the Attorney General for the respective state).

11. Ottman, *Green Marketing*, Chap. 2.

12. V. Reitman, "Green Product Sales Seem to be Wilting," *The Wall Street Journal*, May 18, 1992, p. B1.

13. Stisser, "A Deeper Shade of Green," pp. 14–29.

14. Ottman, *Green Marketing*, p. 43.

15. Jaclyn Fierman, "The Big Muddle in Green Marketing," *Fortune*, June 3, 1991, pp. 90–101.

16. Jim Salzman, "The Trade Implications of Eco-labelling in OECD," *Life-cycle Management and Trade* (Paris: Organization for Economic Cooperation and Development, 1994), pp. 41–49.

17. Organization for Economic Cooperation and Development, *Environmental Labelling in OECD Countries* (Paris: Organization for Economic Cooperation and Development, 1991).

18. Susan J. Ainsworth and Ann M. Thayer, "Chemical Manufacturers Welcome Challenges of Product Stewardship," *Chemical and Engineering News*, 72 (October 17, 1994): 10–31.

19. Council on Environmental Quality, *Environmental Quality, Twenty-third Annual Report* (Washington, D.C.: Government Printing Office, 1993), pp. 176–177.

20. Attorneys General of California, Florida, Massachusetts, Minnesota, Missouri, New York, Tennessee, Texas, Utah, Washington, and Wisconsin, *The Green Report II: Recommendations for Responsible Environmental Advertising,* 1991.

9

Recycling

According to a study by the U.S. Bureau of Mines, material flows in the United States accounted for a staggering ten metric tons per person in 1990.[1] If the rest of the world follows the same level of consumption, material flows and wastes generated from extraction, manufacturing, distribution, use, and disposal will have dangerous consequences given the world population and its anticipated increases. According to Donella H. Meadows, Dennis L. Meadows, and Jorgen Randers, population, food production, industrial production, resource consumption, and pollution have been rising exponentially since the early 1960s.[2] The average North American uses 40 times as much commercial energy as the average person in a developing country, and the average European uses 10 to 30 times as much. Only 8 percent of the world's population own an automobile. Natural gas per capita consumption in the United States is 184 times that of India, aluminum per capita consumption is 34 times, and copper is 45 times.[3] Rising population, standards of living, and investments in highways and schools will increase demand for products dramatically. Every one ton of garbage at the disposal stage can cause five tons of waste at the manufacturing stage and 20 tons during resource extraction.[4] If wastes cannot be reduced through source reduction, recycling is the second-best benign solution for managing wastes. The goal of recycling is to use materials again. Recycling waste is reduced by its conversion into useful products. Recycling involves collecting and using wastes as raw material in manufacturing processes that will create new products or raw materials. Therefore, a successful recycling program will consist of waste collection, the manufacture of wastes into useful products, and the consumption of products made up of recycled materials. Recycling programs depend on all three activities.

ADVANTAGES OF RECYCLING

Recycling has several advantages. By reducing the processing of virgin materials, it saves energy. As much as 95 percent reduction in energy use can be achieved by recycling aluminum. Figure 9.1 presents the ratio of energy saved by recycling to energy saved by incineration. Since no virgin ore has to be mined, recycling conserves natural resources. Recycling also reduces pollution. Without recycling, the waste will be either incinerated or disposed of in the landfill. By eliminating the need for treatment or disposal, recycling reduces costs. New environmental regulations are reducing available landfills and recycling can significantly reduce requirements of landfill space. Because recycling involves waste materials that must be collected, sorted, and processed in small quantities, this creates jobs. According to a study commissioned by the State Office of Waste Reduction, recycling supports about 9,000 jobs or 0.027 percent of the state's total employment in North Carolina.[5] Recycling also produces revenue for wastes that otherwise would have been discarded. It is an effective way to mitigate the solid waste crisis.

FIGURE 9.1
Energy Savings Ratio of Recycling to Incineration

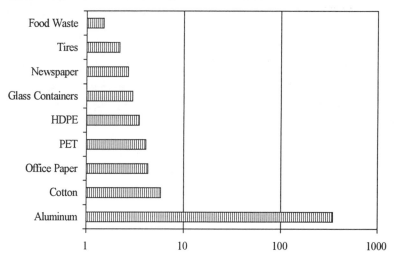

Source: John E. Young and Aaron Sachs, *The Next Efficiency Revolution: Creating a Sustainable Materials Economy* (Washington, D.C.: Worldwatch Institute, 1994), p. 21.

RECYCLING MANAGEMENT

From management's point of view, the purpose of recycling is to recover as much value as possible from used and scrapped products, parts, and materials. By doing so, a company can increase revenue and reduce wastes to a minimum. Recycling may be used to recover pre- or postconsumer waste. Preconsumer waste consists of overruns, rejects, and scraps generated during production outside the manufacturing process. Postconsumer waste is a product discarded after use. Recycling can be either closed loop or open loop. In the former, a material is used repeatedly to produce the same part or product. Repeated reuse of aluminum cans to produce new cans is an example of closed-loop recycling. Closed-loop recycling can significantly reduce the need for virgin materials. Contamination and degradation during use make it very hard to recycle postconsumer waste in a closed loop. However, waste generated during production can be recycled in a closed loop. In open-loop recycling, recycled material is used to produce a different product. For example, food packages made out of polystyrene are used to manufacture benches and combs. As a result, open-loop recycling does not reduce the need for virgin materials. The United States generated 13 billion tons of nonhazardous solid waste in 1992.[6] However, the annual output of the top 50 commodity chemicals is only 0.3 billion tons per year.[7] Therefore, solid waste is a potential source of materials for industry.

Planning for the Recycling of Production Wastes

Though recovery of production waste is not waste prevention, it does reduce the environmental impact of the waste. Waste recovery eliminates waste-management costs, reduces costs of materials, increases revenue, and saves energy by using wastes as fuel. According to the *1992 Toxics Release Inventory*, U.S. companies recycled 51.8 percent of their production-related wastes in 1992 and are likely to increase to 54.3 percent by 1994.[8] Stringent regulations, rising waste-management costs, and new technologies are likely to encourage increased recovery of production wastes in coming years. Production waste may be recovered either on- or off-site. Recovery of silver in photographic processing and copper in printed circuit board manufacturing are some examples of waste reclamation efforts. Lack of data, low waste value, secrecy about the composition of wastes, and regulations are some barriers toward waste recycling and recovery.

The *1992 Toxics Release Inventory* also revealed that 42.5 percent of production related waste is recycled on-site.[9] On-site recovery reduces the chance of contamination with other waste materials and eliminates handling and transportation risks. Centrifuge, batch-distillation, electrolytic recovery, and reverse osmosis are some methods of recovering production wastes.

Low volume, high equipment costs, difficulty in using recovered materials in-house, one-time generation of wastes, uneven generation of wastes, and lack of expertise encourage companies to opt for off-site recovery. However, increased handling and transportation of residue, along with the risk, make it essential that this alternative is carefully evaluated. For many small businesses, this may be their only recycling option.

An old saying, one man's meat is another man's poison, may be true for waste generated during production in any given plant, as it may be used by another plant in its manufacturing operations. For example, oil sludges can be used in asphalt manufacturing, tires can be used as fuel, and waste oil can be rerefined as lube oil. Waste exchanges and recyclers can help identify potential partners and match waste generators with waste users. Waste exchanges are typically nonprofit organizations funded by state governments. Many waste exchanges provide on-line computer database listings. Recyclers, unlike waste exchanges, buy wastes, reprocess them, and sell them to others.

Planning for off-site waste recovery includes determining the quantities of wastes generated, the on-site uses of recovered materials, identification of potential customers for wastes generated, reprocessing requirements of wastes, selection of potential partners, and negotiation of recycling agreements. Since waste generators are responsible for the wastes they generate, every recycler or potential partner should be carefully screened to ensure that he has the permits required under the law, does not have any recent violations, meets industry standards, and has the expertise and equipment to recover the materials.

Typically, costs of recovery from wastes are inversely related to the concentration. Therefore, low-value items require concentrated wastes to make recycling economically feasible. Source segregation and concentration methods can be used to increase concentration. Though these volume-reduction approaches do not reduce wastes, they do make it economical to recover raw materials by reducing disposal costs and increasing waste-management alternatives. Segregation of hazardous wastes from nonhazardous wastes can significantly simplify management of wastes. Evaporation, ultrafiltration, and reverse osmosis are some methods of concentrating wastes. Using data on metal prices, economically recoverable concentration level, national hazardous waste data, and the 1986 rate of recycling, David T. Allen and Nasrin Behmanesh concluded that there is significant potential to increase metal recycling.[10]

Planning for Recycling of Solid Wastes

The United States generated 13 billion tons of nonhazardous solid waste in 1992, out of which 200 million tons were municipal waste. The EPA estimates that the costs of managing nonhazardous solid waste will be about $75 billion in the year 2000 as compared with $8.4 billion in 1972.[11] Falling disposal capacity, rising waste-management costs, and increasing pressures from local residents against placing disposal facilities in their towns are forcing state and local governments to demand large waste generators to come up with plans to reduce wastes. Many states have set aggressive recycling goals. Rhode Island mandates businesses to recover materials that are on the recycling list. Other states have imposed sales bans, disposal bans, advanced disposal fees, deposit laws for containers, recycling content requirements, mandatory recycling, taxes on trash, high tipping fees, and so on. The proportion of all municipal solid waste recovered by recycling increased from a mere 7 percent in 1960 to 22 percent in 1993. In addition, for several materials, the energy savings from use of recycled rather than virgin materials are significant.[12]

Planning for solid waste recycling includes collecting data, determining the potential for reducing wastes, studying market conditions, assessing recycling options, performing feasibility analysis, and implementing the plan. Information should be collected about the quantities and types of wastes generated, the sources and locations of waste generated, the methods of waste collection and disposal, and the estimate of waste-reduction and recycling potential. Once data are collected, the next step is to develop alternatives to reduce wastes and set up a system for internal flow of materials. Changes in purchasing practices, changes in consumption and use, and education are some methods of reducing wastes.

Identifying markets for wastes is the next step. Local recycling companies and waste exchanges may be contacted to evaluate whether they would accept the wastes produced. The yellow pages, trade publications, and state recycling agencies are excellent sources of information on markets. They are also good sources of information on recycling equipment, collection and processing of wastes, and prices. The various percentages of municipal solid wastes recycled in 1993 are as follows:

Paper and paperboard	34.0%
Glass	22.0%
Ferrous metals	26.1%
Aluminum	35.4%
Plastics	3.5%
Total materials in products	24.5%
Total municipal solid waste	21.7%[13]

Paper and paperboards have the maximum potential in reducing landfill space as they generate about 38 percent of all municipal solid waste. Their recycling can save considerable amounts of energy and reduce air and water pollution. Among paper and paperboard, corrugated boxes are extensively recycled because of their ease of identification and collection. Because of the high capital investment required to de-ink newsprints, newsprint recycling suffers from inadequate processing capacities. An adequate infrastructure does not exist to recycle paper other than corrugated board and newsprint. Paper recycling suffers from several obstacles including weak markets for mixed papers, inability to recycle paper indefinitely without deterioration, and difficulty in de-inking photocopy and laser-printed papers. Though plastics form 9.3 percent of the solid waste, only 3.5 percent of the plastics is recycled. Collection difficulties; sorting problems, including the high cost of sorting equipment; and readily available cheap virgin plastics are some causes of their low recycling rates. Polyethylene trephthalate (PET) has the strongest recycling infrastructure among plastics. The high market value for used PET and a mandatory recycl-ing requirement of beverage containers in several states are the reasons for its high recycling rate. However, even minor contamination of PET by polyvinyl chlorides, for example, can spoil an entire batch of recycled PET. Drainage pipes, toys, carpets, and sleeping bags are some products made out of recycled plastics. Contaminants do not pose major hurdles for glass recycling, as they burn off in furnaces. However, glass recycling faces different challenges, among them breakage during sorting and the need for hand sorting by color. Metals are extensively recycled because they are easy to collect and separate. Since the market for scrap aluminum is strong, recycling of aluminum is a major source of income for many municipal recycling programs. Demand for steel scrap is strong as steel foundries and steel makers use the scrap to produce new steel products.

Recycling cannot succeed unless there is demand for products made out of recycled materials. Recycled products are expensive, their quality is inferior, and they are not readily available are all myths that reduce the demand for recycled products. As a result, market prices for recycled materials are much lower than their collection and processing costs. Aluminum is the only material that can be recycled profitably.[14] Once market conditions for recyclables are determined, the next step is to choose among different alternatives of recovering wastes. Wastes can be separated either at or close to the point where they were generated or at a centralized processing facility. Typically, less contaminated recyclables can be obtained by separating wastes close to their source, resulting in more revenue generated. Separating wastes at a centralized location, however, means that greater quantities of recyclables can be recovered. In addition, centralized processing requires very little modification of existing material-handling procedures. Once the recycling options are chosen, a feasibility analysis, which should address financial, technical, marketing, administrative, and logistical dimensions of the options, must be developed. Once the feasibility analysis has been performed, recycling programs may be implemented.

Planning for Recycling of Postconsumer Waste

According to a 1994 McKinsey survey, more than 80 percent of the senior executives indicated their agreements with the premise that a company has responsibility for its product even after it has left the plant.[15] However, only a very few companies have taken responsibility to control the environmental consequences of their products. The German initiative, *Rucknahmeverpflichtung* (take back your obligation), requires retailers to take back packaging from customers, manufacturers to recover it from the retailers, and packaging companies to reclaim it from the manufacturers. However, most products are not designed for reclamation. Since customers often base their buying decisions on initial costs rather than costs over the life cycle of the product, companies have very little incentive to design products to reduce costs over the course of the life cycle. Currently, governments and customers are demanding that companies develop products to reduce resource consumption and costs. Corporate average fuel economy standards as well as energy act sheets on refrigerators, washers, and dryers in the United States are some examples of pressures put on companies to develop products that reduce life-cycle costs. Some buyers of large quantities of durable products such as computers and tires require sellers to take back discarded products. Managers recognize that product waste generated during use and disposal stages are threats to their companies and they are developing strategies to recycle their finished products.

Recycling is a labor-intensive process. The first step in organizing a recycling program is to collect information about related environmental laws and regulations. The Resource Conservation and Recovery Act describes the prerequisites for obtaining recycling permits. The next step is to develop objectives. For any recycling program to be successful, public support is essential. Therefore, education is the cornerstone of any recycling program. For any company to develop a recycling strategy for their finished products, they must collect information about wastes generated by their products; quantities of finished products that will be returned after usage; markets for reused products, parts, and materials; and recycling operations. Data collection begins with the analysis of the composition of finished products. The objective is to identify materials, calculate their quantities, determine their values, evaluate their hazards, and assess the feasibility of their recovery. The next step in data collection is to estimate the quantities of finished products that can be recovered after use. Products exported to another country are typically hard to get back even if economically feasible. Leased products, cars and copy machines, for example, can easily be recovered at the end of their lease term. Since products sold will be used over different periods by different buyers, estimating the quantities of these products that will be returned is difficult. It is also difficult to estimate the number of products that will be returned because of their failure to function. Companies can encourage users to return their products by offering buybacks and giving discounts on new products to those who return their used products. Manufacturers of cars and vacuum cleaners frequently use this strategy. For any recycling program to succeed, there must be a demand for products manufactured using recycled prod-ucts and materials. Usually there is no difference between products made out of virgin materials and those made from recycled materials. One notable exception is paper; the recycled product is inferior to virgin paper for certain uses. Companies can use or sell recovered products to others, who then can sell recycled products through other distribution channels.

Because recycling involves the collection of products from frag-mented sources, companies should analyze recycling operations in terms of organizations, obstacles, revenues, and costs. Recovered prod-ucts can be repaired, refurbished, remanufactured, cannibalized, or recycled, besides being incinerated and landfilled.[16]

The returned product is repaired to bring it back to working order. Repair, which generally involves fixing and replacing broken and worn out parts, is not always possible. Repairs can be done either at the customers' site or at repair centers. The decision to either repair or retire a product is based on the useful life remaining and costs of repair. Refurbishing can improve the quality of a used product. Refurbishing involves inspection of all critical parts and their replacement. Older models may be refurbished with newer technologies. Remanufacturing involves much more than repair and refurbishing. Disassembly, inspection, and replacement of worn out parts can make a used product as good as new. In other words, remanufacturing restores an old product by renovating old parts and adding new components if necessary. Expensive equipment and products undergoing slow technological changes are ideal candidates for remanufacture. Common remanufac-tured products include buses, copying machines, telephones, jet engines, machine tools, construction equipment, and railcars. Remanufacturing is generally feasible for products with large sales volumes, excellent after-sale servicing or trade-in networks, low collection costs, and so on. The inspection in remanufacturing is more intensive than in refurbishing and repair. The remanufacturing process is extensive, involving the examination of every part, material, and structure. Core housing or casting is usually retained, but critical components are replaced with technologically superior products. Unlike repair, refurbishing, and remanufacturing, in which most of a used product is reused, only a small portion from a used product is reused in cannibalization. Cannibalization is selective recycling. In cannibalization, expensive parts are disassembled and used for repair, refurbishing, or remanufacturing. In recycling, instead of using assemblies and parts, the goal is to reuse materials from components and parts.

Generally, the original equipment manufacturers do recycling. An entrepreneur will find it difficult to recycle postconsumer waste because of difficulty in getting replacement parts. In addition, the need for a constant supply of recycled products can also hamper remanufacturing. For instance, to remanufacture a single tractor, six salvage tractors may be needed. Therefore, anyone who plans to recycle postconsumer waste should be sure to have a steady source of supplies.

One of the most effective recycling programs in the United States is that of automobiles. About 7 million automobiles are recycled every year saving 80 million barrels of oil, 15 million tons of cast iron and steel, 500,000 pounds of aluminum, and about 200,000 Troy ounces (12 Troy ounces = 1 pound) of platinum.[17] The recycling of automobiles begins with a dismantler that removes battery cables, distributors, fuel pumps, starters, and so on. Dismantled parts are then cleaned, tested, and inventoried. Since automobiles are not designed for easy disassembly, these recovery operations are extremely labor intensive. The dismantler sells what remains of the automobile to a shredder. The automobile is stripped and shredded by machine and the metals are segregated by magnetic and other methods. The remaining mixture of about 600 pounds, called fluff, consists of plastics, glass, rubber, and dirt; these are landfilled. The United States generates about 3 million pounds of fluff a year. Shredding is generally capital intensive. Other methods of automobile recycling include incineration, hand dismantling, and cryogenics. Even though automobiles are not designed for recycling, nearly 100 percent of all automobiles are recycled. Regulations such as corporate fuel economy standards have increased substitution of metals by plastics. Too many varieties of plastics in automobiles have effectively increased the weight of fluff. This exemplifies how command-and-control regulation to reduce fuel consumption can increase wastes to be landfilled. Material suppliers, parts manufacturers, car manufacturers, retailers, dismantlers, repair shops, shredding companies, and consumers are involved in automobile recycling. If automobile designs were changed to facilitate recycling, then the volume of fluff generated would decrease. This would significantly reduce incentives for shredders and dismantlers to engage in recycling. The strategies of design for manufacture include easy assembly, fewer integrated parts, small production runs, use of low-weight materials, and custom designs for different applications. However, green design strategies include easy disassembly, easy repair, standardized parts, and fewer variety of parts. Because some of these green strategies are inconsistent with automobile design strategies, it is essential to come up with designs reconciling both objectives.

RECYCLING OBSTACLES

In spite of the several advantages that it offers, recycling faces many obstacles. Consumer participation is necessary for recycling to work. Therefore, educating consumers about the advantages of recycling is essential. Consumers believe that recycled products are inferior compared with those made from virgin materials, but finding differences between aluminum cans made out of new metal and recycled material, for example, is impossible. Often, a product's quality is judged on its appearance rather than its performance. As a result, people are sometimes not willing to buy recycled products.

Legal barriers to recycling also exist. The Food and Drug Administration prohibits recycled plastic from coming into direct contact with food. The Food and Drug Administration has recently permitted the Coca-Cola Company to bottle products in recycled containers if regenerated rather than recycled plastic is used to manufacture these bottles. Government procurement guidelines demand the use of virgin materials even though they are not always necessary for product performance. Some of these guidelines are being modified, however, to accommodate recycled products. The Resource Conservation and Recovery Act regulations make the recycling of hazardous wastes more expensive than their disposal. In addition, the Resource Conservation and Recovery Act does not differentiate between high-risk and low-risk chemicals and waste streams.

National commitment is essential for successful recycling. Although there are several pieces of federal legislation that promote recycling, enforcement and funding are left to the states. Since federal tax laws allow deduction for the depletion of resources, they indirectly subsidize the use of virgin materials. For successful recycling, products must be designed for easy disassembly and separation. However, a significant number of durable goods such as computer equipment, televisions, and so on are not designed for easy recycling. For glass to be used as a raw material, it must be nearly pure in order to produce a flawless finished product. Plastics must be sorted before they can be used to create useful products. Disposal is almost always cheaper than labor-intensive recycling. However, technological developments coupled with the rising costs of landfills are reducing economic barriers to recycling.

COMPOSTING

Composting is another form of recycling. It is a controlled process of allowing microorganisms to convert organic matter into humus. Composting begins with visual inspection of the wastes to ensure that they do not contain toxic materials. Home composting can be done by piling wastes at least three feet wide and three feet tall. The pile must be turned periodically and watered. After several months, depending upon pile size, aeration, and moisture content, waste is turned into soil additives. The biggest hurdle for composting is odor, which can be controlled by periodically turning the pile and controlling the type of waste entering the pile.

INCINERATION

Incineration involves the burning of wastes under controlled conditions. At high temperatures, most organic materials break down into simple substances such as carbon dioxide and moisture. Since incineration reduces waste volume significantly, it has been used by many towns. However, the ash remaining after incineration must be landfilled. Incinerators are expensive to build and can emit a variety of dangerous substances including fly ash, sulfur dioxides, dioxins, hydrogen chloride, and nitrogen oxides. Since not all municipal solid waste can be recycled, incineration is one alternative to landfilling.

CONCLUSION

This chapter has explored various resource-capturing strategies. Though recycling does not prevent wastes, it does prevent the depletion of resources, reduce impacts on the environment, save money, and preserve waste-disposal capacity. For recycling to be successful there must be a demand for recycled products, a stable supply of recyclable materials, and a willingness to manufacture products using recyclable materials; recycling is not simply the collecting of recyclable materials. Recycling in the United States is currently in trouble because the processing costs of recyclable materials are high compared with their market value, and the demand for recycled products is not sufficient to make full use of collected recyclable materials. This lack of demand for recycled products, however, gives smart companies a splendid opportunity to build competitive advantages by *creating* a demand.

NOTES

1. D. Rogich (and staff), Division of Mineral Commodities, U.S. Bureau of Mines, *Material Use, Economic Growth and the Environment*, paper presented at the American Council for Capital Formation Symposium, September 30, 1992.

2. Donella H. Meadows, Dennis L. Meadows, and Jorgen Randers, *Beyond the Limits: Confronting Global Collapse, Envisioning a Sustainable Future* (Post Mills, Vt.: Chelsea Green, 1992), Chap. 1.

3. *World Resources* (New York: Basic Books, 1994–95), p. 17.

4. Meadows, Meadows, and Randers, *Beyond the Limits*, p. 83.

5. Michael Shore, "Recycling Impact on Jobs," *Biocycle Journal of Composting & Recycling* 36(4) (1995): 36–37.

6. U.S. General Accounting Office, *Solid Waste: State and Federal Efforts to Manage Nonhazardous Waste*, GAO/RCED-95-3 (Washington, D.C.: Government Printing Office, February 1995), p. 8.

7. "Chemical Production Resumed Growth in 1992," *Chemical and Engineering News*, 71(26) (June 28, 1993): 40–41.

8. U.S. Environmental Protection Agency, *1992 Toxics Release Inventory: Public Data Release*, EPA 745-R-94-001 (Washington, D.C.: Government Printing Office, April 1994), p. 7.

9. Ibid., p. 25.

10. David T. Allen and Nasrin Behmanesh, "Wastes as Raw Materials," in *The Greening of Industrial Ecosystems*, ed. Braden R. Allenby and Deanna J. Richards (Washington, D.C.: National Academy Press, 1994), p. 68.

11. U.S. General Accounting Office, *Solid Waste*, p. 8.

12. John Schall, "Does the Solid Waste Management Hierarchy Make Sense? A Technical, Economic and Environmental Justification for the Priority of Source Reduction and Recycling," PSWP working paper #1 (New Haven, Conn.: Yale University, School of Forestry and Environmental Studies, 1992), p. 63.

13. U.S. Environmental Protection Agency, *Characterization of Municipal Solid Waste in the United States: 1994 Update*, Executive Summary EPA 530-S-94-042 (Washington, D.C.: Government Printing Office, November 1994), p. 5.

14. David Biddle, "Recycling for Profit: The New Green Business Frontier," *Harvard Business Review* 71 (November–December 1993): 145–156.

15. McKinsey & Company, "The Corporate Response to the Environmental Challenge," in *Transnational Environmental Law and Its Impact on Corporate Behavior*, ed. Eric J. Urbani, Conrad P. Rubin, and Monica Katzman (Irvington-on-Hudson, N.Y.: Transnational Juris Publications, 1994), pp. 217–262.

16. M. C. Thierry, *Strategic Production and Operations Management Issues in Product Recovery Management* (Rotterdam, Netherlands: Erasmus University, Rotterdam School of Management, 1993).

17. David R. Powelson and Melinda A. Powelson, *Recycler's Manual for Business, Government, and the Environmental Community* (New York: Van Nostrand Reinhold, 1992), p. 61.

10

Green Communication

Rising demands for green products, tougher regulations, public pressures, skyrocketing liability costs, accident and environmental press reports, and competitive pressures are forcing companies to develop coherent communication programs with stakeholders. The exponential growth of environmental laws has made green concerns a priority in corporate boardrooms. The Toxics Release Inventory requires facilities to report emissions of more than 300 chemicals. The Emergency Planning and Community Right-to-Know Act (EPCRA) requires companies to disclose to local planning committees information about substances they store and emit. The 1992 Earth Summit brought international attention to environmental problems. Though several companies have improved their environmental performance, few companies have received credit for it. Therefore, more companies feel a need to express their environmental performance to the public. However, any mistake in communication strategy can easily backfire on the company. Therefore, a company should treat green communication with the same care and rigor as it handles other business functions. According to an international survey, about two-thirds of companies published material and safety data sheets indicating risks associated with their products.[1] A majority of companies include on their product labels safety information and product contents. Emergency planning was revealed to be one of the significant public relations activities for more than one-half of the companies surveyed. One in two companies financed environmental organizations, held annual meetings with environmental officials, issued separate environmental annual reports, made donations to local green societies, and established formal environmental policy. However, fewer than one-third of these companies disclosed product- and process-risk information or provided the public access to environmental R&D results. Even though public relations activities practiced by different companies varied significantly, all demonstrated efforts to satisfy stakeholders' needs. Therefore, any company planning for green public relations should begin by identifying those stakeholders — consumers, community and neighbors, employees, investors, media, environmental groups, legislators, and so on — with whom it wants to communicate.

STAKEHOLDERS

Customers

Without consumers, no organization can exist. Because consumers play a significant role in the existence of an organization, they should be involved in any green public relations strategy. While consumers support environmentalism by segregating and recycling wastes, initiating environmental activities, and encouraging the development of green products, they are often misinformed about the details of environmentalism. Most consumers prefer paper to plastic because they believe paper is degradable and plastic is not. However, nothing degrades in airtight, watertight landfills. Consumers also believe that plastics constitute 69 percent of the solid waste stream, even though plastics make up only 13 percent of the waste stream.[2] Education therefore is the key to the consumers' communication program. Consumers need information to choose, use, and dispose of products in an environmentally compatible manner. By providing environmental information on labels, a company can help consumers to use and dispose of products safely. To ensure safe handling of products from cradle to grave, many companies are starting product-stewardship programs. For example, Chemical Manufacturers Association recently unveiled its product-stewardship code of management practices to encourage chemical companies to support product stewardship.[3] Product-stewardship programs require companies to incorporate health, safety, and environmental protection in their products.

Community

Community relations can make or break a company. Community right-to-know regulations have made mandatory public disclosures of environmental issues and risks. As a result, anyone can access information about waste discharges, chemical spills, emissions, and hazardous chemical inventories. In addition, private parties can sue for enforcement of regulatory requirements. Community approval is frequently required to get permits under different statutes. Unfortunately, often emotion plays a major role in the permit process. Therefore, a company must be careful in developing appropriate communication programs. Focus groups can help in developing communication programs. Polling is another method to elicit the community's reaction toward the permit process. Regulators also play a major role in the outcome. Therefore, data collected on public health and safety and submitted to the regulators should be carefully evaluated. A company should keep records of all issues brought to its attention by community groups. Credibility is crucial in any community relations programs. The purpose of laws and regulations is to ensure health, safety, and environmental protection so the goal of the company should be to project an image of competence in meeting safety and health standards. A company will be judged by what it communicates and that is why it is important for a company to have effective community relations programs. A company can lose its credibility if its communication program is poor and if its past performance is shoddy. If a company wants to overcome a negative image, it should first start with actions to correct past errors and improve greenness. Second, to avoid credibility problems, it should not project a greener image of itself than it really is. It should from time to time put out press releases about its environmental performance. It should open up its facilities for public viewing, and it should conduct regular discussions with community leaders.

EPCRA mandates community reporting. Any facility that uses and stores above-threshold-level chemicals for which material safety data sheets (MSDSs) need to be maintained under the Hazard Communication Standards must report annually to the State Emergency Response Commission, the local emergency planning committee, and local fire departments. Section 311 of the EPCRA deals with the submission of MSDSs. A facility should send copies of the MSDSs on chemicals or a list of all chemicals grouped by hazard category to the State Emergency Response Commission, the local emergency planning committee, and local fire departments. Section 312 mandates the annual reporting of chemicals grouped by hazard category. Section 313 requires the reporting of toxic chemical emissions from certain facilities. The purpose of these reports is to determine the chemical dangers confronting communities and to prepare emergency plans to respond in case of an accident. The 1990 Clean Air Act amendments require chemical plants to develop risk-management plans to respond to hazards posed by the plant. The Toxic Substances Control Act requires 90 days' notice before importing and manufacturing new chemical substances.

A community advisory panel is one way of fostering continuous dialog with the community and helping a facility understand the needs of the community. Its members should come from a broad cross section of the community and be independent of the facility it advises. A steering committee should be formed to select panel members, set panel objectives, and establish ground rules for the panel's operation. Finally, panels should be committed to improving the quality of life of the community.

Employees

Employees are critical for successful implementation of green public relations programs. Employees can be staunch allies or enemies of a company depending on how they are treated. Therefore, every public relations program should involve employees beginning with recruitment. Recruiting employees with green attitude is an important element of green communication strategy. Several companies project an environmental image in their employment advertisements. It is a good idea to include green questions in recruitment interviews. Every employee who joins an organization should be told about green responsibilities and expectations. A green image is an excellent tool to retain employees. Environmental training is a valuable asset for any employee. Senior-level managers should be trained in global environmental issues and company policies. They should be mindful of future changes in the regulations and their likely impact on the company. Training for line managers should include environmental issues relating to products, packaging, recycling, community relations, and so on. Technical specialists need to update their knowledge in clean technologies, recycling, energy-saving techniques, and regulatory requirements. Communication professionals must be kept up-to-date on issues relating to environmental performance and achievements. Training is critical for any company wishing to improve its green image and is useful for increasing employee participation in pollution reduction. Informing employees about chemical-handling procedures can reduce workplace accidents. Green performance as one factor in deciding raises and promotions should help companies improve overall environmental performance. In addition, a company should encourage employees to get involved in community activities.

To boost employee morale, a company should strive to keep its workplace safe and healthy. The company must inform its employees about environmental hazards and risks. Protecting workers from diseases and injuries in the workplace should be management's primary responsibility. A variety of chemicals used in the workplace today are toxic and dangerous. Exposure to these substances can cause cancer and other diseases. Noise and vibrations can lead to hearing loss. Ultraviolet radiation is detrimental to eyesight, lasers can cause blindness, and nuclear radiation can cause cancer. It is important for a company to identify such hazards and take action to prevent them. In addition, companies should identify actions that need to be taken to satisfy federal occupational safety and health standards. Stringent internal safety and health standards and periodic evaluations of working conditions can prevent hazards. Workers should be regularly screened for specific environmental hazards; a physical examination should be a part of such screening.

Green laws require companies to communicate with their employees. The Occupational Safety and Health Administration (OSHA) has a hazard communication policy for workers handling chemicals. It requires employers to inform workers about hazardous chemicals in the workplace and how to handle them.

OSHA's hazard communication standard starts with manufacturers and importers. All chemicals produced, imported, and used must be evaluated for their hazards. Manufacturers and importers must inform their employees and employers who purchase the chemicals about physical and health hazards. Manufacturers and importers should produce MSDSs and supply them to all users. These MSDSs should identify chemicals and describe their characteristics and hazards, health effects, exposure limits, handling and control measures, first-aid procedures, and so on. It is the responsibility of manufacturers and importers to maintain up-to-date data sheets. Users must maintain similar data sheets for all chemicals used.

According to an international survey of companies, about 82 percent of companies incorporate health and safety responsibilities in an employee's job description. Two out of three companies train employees about the environmental impact of their operations and consider safety records in performance evaluation. Most companies provide worker safety training programs.[4]

The Media

Environmental stories can boost ratings of the evening news. A story about a beached whale can run several days, but a chemical company's decision to drop a billion-dollar product may not make the news at all. Media influence people. South American rain forests, endangered species, and spotted owls are well known because environmental groups have been successful in getting their stories out to the public. However, industry groups have not been so successful in conveying their achievements. The result is that the public holds a negative view of industries. The corporate message to media should be simple and short, emphasizing what the company is doing to reduce risks. The company should take responsibility for its share of the problems; it is wise not to blame others. The message should project trust and credibility by conveying empathy, competence, honesty, and commitment. Messages should address health, safety, economic, fairness, legal, and environmental concerns. Companies should not treat the environment as simply another public relations issue but rather as a technical issue requiring technical input. A company should only discuss serious environmental issues; focusing on trivial issues may result in a loss of credibility. It should be specific about its claims.

Responding to media distortions is one of the most difficult communication problems. For example, the media frequently overstate cancer risks from synthetic chemicals, food additives, pollution, radiation, pesticides, and hormone treatments. The media also dramatically overstate risks from nuclear plants, radon, and chemicals in homes.[5] Corporate response should be to set the record straight, ensuring that all counter-claims can be factually substantiated.

Investors

Annual reports are the primary documents through which companies communicate with their investors. Typically, companies spend a paragraph or a page showing their commitment to the environment. Some companies also distribute publications highlighting what they are doing to reduce pollution. Many companies publicly affirm their commitment to the environment by adopting the Business Charter of Sustainable Development (see Chapter 2), Responsible Care® guiding principles, and Coalition for Environmentally Responsible Economies (CERES) principles. The CERES principles set forth the following commitments:

Protection of the Biosphere
We will reduce and make continual progress toward eliminating the release of any substance that causes environmental damage to the air, water, or the earth or its inhabitants. We will safeguard all habitats affected by our operations and will protect open spaces and wilderness, while preserving biodiversity.

Sustainable Use of Natural Resources
We will make suitable use of renewable natural resources, such as water, soils, and forests. We will conserve nonrenewable natural resources through efficient use and careful planning.

Reduction and Disposal of Wastes
We will reduce and where possible eliminate waste through source reduction and recycling. All waste will be handled and disposed of through safe and responsible methods.

Energy Conservation
We will conserve energy and improve the energy efficiency of our internal operations and of the goods and services we sell. We will make every effort to use environmentally safe and sustainable energy sources.

Risk Reduction
We will strive to minimize the environmental, health, and safety risks to our employees and the communities in which we operate through safe technologies, facilities, and operating procedures and by being prepared for emergencies.

Safe Products and Services
We will reduce and where possible eliminate the use, manufacture, or sale of products and services that cause environmental damage or health or

safety hazards. We will inform our customers of the environmental impacts of our products or services and try to correct unsafe use.

Environmental Restoration

We will promptly and responsibly correct conditions we have caused that endanger health, safety, or the environment. To the extent feasible, we will redress injuries we have caused to persons or damage we have caused to the environment and will restore the environment.

Informing the Public

We will inform in a timely manner everyone who may be affected by conditions caused by our company that might endanger health, safety, or the environment. We will regularly seek advice and counsel through dialogue with persons in communities near facilities. We will not take any action against employees for reporting dangerous incidents or conditions to management or to appropriate authorities.

Management Commitment

We will implement these Principles and sustain a process that ensures that the Board of Directors and Chief Executive Officer are fully informed about pertinent environmental issues and are fully responsible for environmental policy. In selecting our Board of Directors, we will consider demonstrated environmental commitment as a factor.

Audits and Reports

We will conduct an annual self-evaluation of our progress in implementing these Principles. We will support the timely creation of generally accepted environmental audit procedures. We will annually complete the CERES Report, which will be made available to the public.

Accounting disclosures form a significant part of communication with shareholders. Some developments in this area were evident from a Price Waterhouse survey of corporations about their accounting of environmental costs.[6] In 1992 about one in four companies had environmental oversight in place at the board of directors level. The environmental management group reported to high-level management in about six out of ten companies. One in three companies had written accounting policies regarding environmental costs. Disclosures of future cleanup costs were guided by the Financial Accounting Standard Board's FAS 5 "accounting for contingencies." More than one-half of the companies analyzed environmental exposures on a quarterly basis for accounting purposes. Contractors' costs, reimbursed cost of regulatory agencies' claims for site cleanup, remedial investigation, and feasibility study costs were some costs that were often included as environmental costs. Only about one in ten companies used discounted present values of the future environmental liabilities to estimate environmental liabilities. Among those who used discounted present values, most used their costs of funds and market rates for discounting purposes and 70 percent incorporated inflation in their computation. About three in four included cleanup costs in operating expenses. Environmental liabilities were disclosed in financial statement footnotes, management discussion and analysis, and legal proceedings. General environmental matters were often disclosed under business description. The disclosure requirements of environmental liabilities in various regulatory filings are described in the "Staff Accounting Bulletin No. 92."[7]

Based on a 1992 survey of investors conducted by the Global Environmental Management Initiative and the Investor Responsibility Research Center,[8] environmental disclosure by companies should include liability information, compliance information, policy and programs, and public relations activities. Information required by investors, in order of priority, includes liabilities, litigation, policy, compliance programs, auditing, goals, expenditures, chemical emissions, accidental spills, environmental codes of conduct, and so on. The environmental report should be concise and should include both worldwide and U.S. activities. The investors preferred aggregate information about the whole company rather than individual plants and divisions. The report should include environmental information regarding penalties, capital expenditures, discretionary spending, projected environmental costs, compliance, emissions, and spills. Information relating to the corporate policy, corporate structure, environmental programs, and community relations should also be included in the report.

The Public Environmental Reporting Initiative guidelines suggest the inclusion of organizational structure, environmental policy, environmental management, emissions, resource-conservation activities, risk-management activities (including audit programs, compliance information, and product stewardship activities), employee reward programs, and involvement of stakeholders in environmental reports.[9]

Many investor organizations rate companies on environmental performance. The Investor Responsibility Research Center evaluates companies based on Superfund sites, spills, total emissions, enforcement actions, and penalties under various environmental statutes. Kinder, Lydenberg, Domini & Company Inc. includes donations to charity; employee stock ownership; environmental performance such as chlorine use, recycling, adoption of the CERES principles, and total quality management programs; the presence of women and minority employees; and other factors to decide companies to be included in its Domini 400 Social Index. The United States Trust Company of Boston uses performance in such areas as policy, compliance, energy conservation, emergency preparedness, and so on to select companies in its portfolios in the Calvert Social Investment Fund. Table 10.1 presents a summary of the disclosure guidelines of various organizations.

Environmental Groups

While environmental groups were perceived as radical in the 1960s, they have since won popular support in several countries. In the United

TABLE 10.1
Environmental Disclosure Guidelines of Various Organizations

	GEMI/IRRC FOCUS GROUP	PERI	UNEP	CERES
Air Emissions:				
Toxics Release Inventory	•	•	•	•
Greenhouse Gases		•		•
Ozone-Depleting Substances		•		•
Audit Information	•	•	•	•
Charitable Contributions		•	•	
Company Profile		•	•	•
Compliance Programs	•	•	•	•
Corporate Goals	•	•	•	
Corporate Policy	•	•	•	•
Customers/Consumers Programs		•	•	
EH&S Management Systems		•	•	
Emergency Response Plans		•	•	•
Employee Education/Involvement		•	•	•
Energy Consumption		•	•	•
Enforcement Actions	•	•	•	•
Environmental Awards			•	•
Environmental Staff Information	•	•	•	
Env. Impact Assessment/Risk Management		•	•	•
Expenditures	•	•	•	
Habitat Protection/Management		•	•	•
Hazardous Waste		•	•	•
Industry Associations	•	•	•	
Liabilities:				
Superfund	•			•
Remediation	•		•	
Litigation	•	•		
Lobbying Activity	•			
Management Systems	•	•	•	•
Materials Conservation/Recycling		•	•	•
Packaging			•	•
Permit Restrictions	•			•
Product Impacts		•	•	•
Product Stewardship		•	•	•
Research & Development	•	•	•	•
Solid Waste		•	•	
Spills/Incidents	•	•	•	•
Stakeholder Involvement	•	•	•	
Statement by Chief Executive			•	
Supplier Education/Cooperative Programs		•	•	•
Third-Party Verifiers Statement	•		•	
Water Conservation		•	•	
Water Effluents		•	•	
Workplace Hazards		•	•	•

Source: Global Environmental Management Initiative, *Environmental Reporting in a Total Quality Management Framework: A Primer* (Washington, D.C.: Global Environmental Management Initiative, 1994).

States, support for them among consumers has risen from 15 percent in 1987 to 42 percent in 1992.[10] Their influence has risen along with their membership. A recent story in the *Wall Street Journal* describes how Greenpeace outsmarted one of the world's largest oil companies, Royal Dutch/Shell, by forcing it to dispose of its Brent Spar oil-storage rig on land rather than at sea.[11] The manufacturer of Alar was forced to withdraw the pesticide as a result of a campaign by the Natural Resources Defense Council. More than 10 million dolphins have died in the tuna nets since 1960. The environmental group Earth Island Institute has forced tuna manufacturers to use only dolphin-safe tuna since 1990. Though the objectives of the environmental groups and companies can sometimes be in conflict, companies can form strategic alliances with environmental groups for purposes of green marketing, public relations, and image improvement. The first step in forming such a partnership with an environmental group involves establishment of objectives for partnership. Educational programs, donations to the environmental group based on the quantities of product sold, employee-matching gifts, plant-a-tree promotions, and vehicle-owner education are some examples of alliances between environmental groups and companies. Such alliances help companies extend the reach of their products' marketers. In addition, such alliances also help companies to access expertise and marketing information and to increase influence. Based on the objectives, the next step is to choose an environmental group. There are several worldwide environmental groups with local chapters. It is advisable to choose an environmental group that is compatible and noncontroversial. The environmental group should strengthen the company's ability to achieve its objective. When selecting a partner, the company should aim to develop a long-term relationship. The company should evaluate the partnership from a financial perspective. Alliances between environmental groups and companies are often subject to in-depth scrutiny. Therefore, both parties should be expected to fully disclose organization and financial information.

Legislators

Like any public policy matter, environmental issues go through a series of developmental, legislative, executive, and judicial stages.[12] Environmental issues typically arise from a gap between corporate environmental performance and the public's expectation about the performance. Dramatic events like accidents or widening expectation gaps can cause people to form opinions about issues. When an issue is beginning to develop, typical communication strategies include annual reports, television and radio talk shows, advertising, and direct meetings. During the developmental stage, the issue is widely debated in the media and a politician may introduce legislation to establish new agencies that will oversee the performance. Once the law is passed, the issue moves into the executive stage. Once the issue moves into a legislative stage, strategies to thwart legislation include building alliances with like-minded groups, lobbying, contributing to political action committees, and so on. Cooperating with agencies, litigation, and compliance are strategies that are employed after regulations have been passed. If the corporation is not happy, it may challenge the legislation in the courts.

PLANNING GREEN COMMUNICATIONS

Like any other function, green public relations requires effective and systematic planning. This iterative planning process begins with identification of goals and objectives.[13] A company should determine what it wants to get out of the communication and how it is going to measure success. Communication always requires an audience. The second step is to identify target audiences. Audiences could be customers, investors, employees, environmental groups, or legislators. To develop an effective communication program, it is essential to collect information about potential audiences. The third step is selection of communication media. Public meetings, seminars, public displays, press releases, pamphlets, and videotapes are some channels of communication. The fourth step is to develop themes for communications, which should be tailored to objectives, potential audiences, and channels of communication. During this step, messages will be developed, tested, and delivered. Programs will then be implemented by introducing them to target audiences and monitoring their reactions. The next step is to initiate dialogue with the target audience. The final step is reviewing the communication program for the purpose of determining whether the program is achieving its intended objectives. If a program is not achieving its goals, it must be modified.

FRAMEWORKS FOR GREEN COMMUNICATIONS

Several models can help to develop green communications. The total quality management model of the Global Environmental Management Institute,[14] E. Bruce Harrison's quality model, [15] the R.A.C.E. (Research, Analysis, Communication, and Evaluation) process,[16] and the Responsible Care® program of the Chemical Manufacturers Association are some frameworks with which to develop green communications programs.

The total quality management framework of the Global Environmental Management Institute begins with an internal management system consisting of planning, doing, checking, and acting. Planning identifies consumers and their aspirations, doing implements measurement and reporting plans, checking identifies gaps between achievements and performance goals, and acting chooses options to make up shortfalls. Consumers could be employees, shareholders, customers, and the general public. Each of these consumers has different aspirations. Employees, for example, may prefer a safe workplace free from accidents and health risks and would welcome strong management commitment toward the environment. Shareholders, bondholders, and insurers will like efficient operations and fewer future liabilities. Customers will favor green products with very little packaging. The public, especially those living close to company plants, will demand compliance with the laws and regulations and insist on safe operations. These objectives are not always consistent with each other. Therefore, one goal of management should be to make tradeoffs among objectives. Self-evaluation is crucial and can be accomplished by measuring performance against the Business Charter for Sustainable Development, or various codes of management practices developed by the Chemical Manufacturers Association as a part of their Responsible Care® program, or the CERES principles.

It will also be necessary to generate two types of reports, one that focuses on results and one that focuses on activities. For example, a number-of-spills report focuses on results whereas reports containing data on the number of employees trained in inspecting leakages, preventive maintenance activities, and the number of inspections conducted deal with activities. These reports can form the basis for modifying actions in order to achieve the original objectives.

Corporations must divulge enormous amounts of information to their stakeholders. External reports should be generated using the same procedures as internal reports: identify stakeholders' needs, develop management systems, assess shortfalls between goals and achievements, and take actions to close the shortfalls.

Harrison's seven-step quality model refers to *q*uantification of audiences, *u*nderstanding of audiences' needs, *a*sking the right questions and getting responses from audiences, *l*istening to their aspirations, *i*nterpreting their responses and taking appropriate actions, *t*aking charge of the public relations process, and *y*ou playing the key role in the communication process. According to Harrison,[17] a company can achieve sustainable communication by following a five-step process that begins with the development of a green mentality. The second step is to observe what winning companies are doing. They typically ensure compliance and establish written policies that clearly state environmental protection as the paramount goal, source reduction as the primary means of pollution reduction, open dialogue as the means by which to achieve understanding with employees and the public and cooperation with regulatory agencies. The third step is to empower employees. Because community members play a vital part in a company's success, it is essential to bring them to a company's side for sustainable communication. The fifth step is to actively participate in the public policy making.

The R.A.C.E. process for community relations consists of four steps. Research collects data about community needs. Analysis identifies audiences, determines key message points, and develops long- and short-term strategies. Communication involves initiating dialogue with the public through community meetings, plant tours, and so on. Evaluation involves measuring the effectiveness of the program through questionnaires, media monitoring, and so on. The Chemical Manufacturers Association's Responsible Care® guiding principles, reproduced here, is an excellent basis on which to develop community relations programs.

Chemical Manufacturers Association member companies pledge to manage their business according to these principles:

to recognize and respond to community concerns about chemicals and operations;

to develop and produce chemicals that can be manufactured, transported, used, and disposed of safely;

to make health, safety, and environment considerations a priority in our planning for existing and new products and processes;

to report promptly to officials, employees, customers, and the public information on chemical-related health or environmental hazards and to recommend protective measures;

to counsel customers on the safe use, transportation, and disposal of chemical products;

to operate our plants and facilities in a manner that protects the environment and the health and safety of our employees and the public;

to extend knowledge by conducting or supporting research on the health, safety, and environmental effects of our products, processes, and waste materials;

to work with others to resolve problems created by past handling and disposal of hazardous substances;

to participate with government and others in creating responsible laws, regulations, and standards to safeguard the community, workplace, and environment; [and]

to promote the principles and practices of Responsible Care® by sharing experiences and offering assistance to others who produce, handle, use, transport, or dispose of chemicals.

Recognizing and responding to community concerns about chemicals and our operations is one of the guiding principles of the Responsible Care® program. Community awareness and the emergency response code of management practices of the Responsible Care® program require companies to maintain a dialogue about safety, health, and the environment and to have emergency response programs in place to protect employees and communities effectively. Management practices should include communication training for key employees, education about emergency response plans, continuous dialogue with employees, and evaluation of communications efforts with employees. A similar program is also required for communication with the community. An emergency response and preparedness program requires a written emergency response plan, training programs for employees, facility tours, emergency exercises, and so on.

CONCLUSION

Businesses have made significant improvements in environmental performance. Still, the public perceives businesses as environmental villains. One reason for this perception is the lack of effective communication. Green communication essentially involves identifying stakeholders, analyzing their needs, evaluating a company's performance, determining the gap between needs and performance, taking actions to close this gap, and reporting the performance to the stakeholders. Companies that take communication seriously will be rewarded with an improved image in the eye of the public.

NOTES

1. United Nations Center on Transnational Corporations, *Environmental Management in Transnational Corporations* (New York: United Nations Center on Transnational Corporations, 1993), pp. 75–77.

2. Jacquelyn A. Ottman, *Green Marketing* (Lincolnwood, Ill.: NTC Business Books, 1994), p. 76.

3. Susan J. Ainsworth and Ann M. Thayer, "Chemical Manufacturers Welcome Challenges of Product Stewardship," *Chemical and Engineering News*, October 17, 1994, pp. 10–14.

4. United Nations Center on Transnational Corporations, *Environmental Management in Transnational Corporations*, p. 85.

5. U.S. House of Representatives, Committee on Science, Space, and Technology, "How Safe Is Safe Enough? Risk Assessment and the Regulatory Process," 103d Cong., 1st sess., July 27, 1993, pp. 252–259.

6. Price Waterhouse, *Accounting for Environmental Compliance: Crossroad GAAP, Engineering, and Government, A Survey of Corporate America's Accounting for Environmental Costs* (Pittsburgh, Pa.: Price Waterhouse, 1992).

7. "Staff Accounting Bulletin No. 92," *Federal Register*, 58 (112) (June 14, 1993): 32842–32847.

8. Investor Responsibility Research Center, "Institution Investor Needs for Corporate Environmental Information," report prepared for the Global Environmental Management Initiative Stockholder Communication Workgroup, Washington, D.C., September 1992.

9. Public Environmental Reporting Initiative, *Guidelines*, Washington, D.C., May 1994.

10. Ottman, *Green Marketing*, p. 87.

11. "How Greenpeace Sank Shell's Plan to Dump Big Oil Rig in Atlantic," *Wall Street Journal*, July 7, 1995, pp. A1, A4.

12. Mike H. Ryan, Carl L. Swanson, and Rogene A. Buchholz, *Corporate Strategy, Public Policy and the Fortune 500: How America's Major Corporations*

Influence Government (New York: Basil Blackwell, 1987), pp. 40–45.

13. Vincent T. Covello, "Communicating Risk Information: A Guide to Environmental Communication in Crisis and Noncrisis Situations," in *Environmental Strategies Handbook: A Guide to Effective Policies and Practices*, ed. Rao V. Kolluru (New York: McGraw-Hill, 1994), pp. 535–538.

14. Global Environmental Management Initiative, *Environmental Reporting in a Total Quality Management Framework: A Primer* (Washington, D.C.: Global Environmental Management Initiative, 1994).

15. E. Bruce Harrison, *Going Green: How to Communicate Your Company's Environmental Commitment* (Homewood, Ill.: Business One Irwin, 1993).

16. Cynthia Leslie-Bole and Stephen J. Nelson, "Environmental Community Relations: A Vital Component in TQEM," in *Environmental TQM*, ed. John T. Willig (New York: Executive Enterprises Publications, 1994), pp. 111–118.

17. E. Bruce Harrison, "Achieving Sustainable Communication," *Columbia Journal of World Business* 27 (Fall and Winter 1992): 242–247.

11

Green Strategies for Research and Development

Pollution is an uncertainty facing many research and development (R&D) managers today. Materials, products, and processes are constantly changing; small quantities of waste are generated sporadically; and semiautonomous research groups operate with little or no supervision. Growing public pressures, stricter enforcement of environmental laws, skyrocketing cleanup costs, and shrinking disposal options are forcing R&D facilities to rethink waste minimization. The support for waste-minimization strategies among R&D personnel can encourage environmentally sound designs of products and processes, thus diminishing potential for future waste generation. In spite of the vast amount of literature in waste minimization, only a small fraction of it is applicable to R&D facilities. The unique nature of R&D activities makes planning for waste reduction extremely difficult. Diverse projects on which R&D personnel work generate a variety of wastes, all of which must be treated environmentally. Constantly changing aqueous waste streams, solvents, by-products, and wastes present a complex disposal dilemma and environmental properties of new materials, processes, contaminated materials, and test-sample wastes may not be known. This chapter describes a systematic procedure for preparing green plans and strategies to combat pollution. The four-step procedure to systematically reduce pollution involves collecting information, generating alternatives, evaluating alternatives, and implementing options.

PLANNING FOR POLLUTION REDUCTION

Collecting Information

The first step is to gather facts. Data about waste streams, current waste-minimization practices, and current and proposed federal, state, and local regulations are required to prepare waste-reduction plans. A long-range R&D plan is necessary for identifying potential future wastes and their quantities. This plan should describe objectives, priorities, existing projects to be continued and terminated, new projects to be initiated, and so forth.

In order to generate waste-minimization alternatives, a detailed description of products, processes, and operations is required. Information about wastes generated, processes and operations from which these wastes are emitted, whether these waste are hazardous, existing treatment and disposal procedures, operating and management practices, and health statistics of the employees and communities surrounding the facilities need to be collected. This information will be useful for setting goals and priorities and for comparing available waste-reduction options.

Collecting data about products and processes is difficult because many raw materials, processes, and projects must be analyzed in detail. Data collection should include information about all areas of environmental concern including air pollutant emissions, waste water discharges, and so on. It is essential to review each material used in the facility for potential hazards. Acids, organic solvents, unused chemicals, reaction products, contaminated materials, and photographic wastes are some of the pollutants generated by an R&D facility. It may be a good idea to computerize all data about materials at this stage. To analyze and develop a database for processes, flow diagrams can be used. Such diagrams should include information about inputs, outputs, and wastes generated at each process. The flow diagrams should indicate raw materials that are in the final products; those transformed in the process; those released in the form of solid, liquid, and vapor wastes; any by-products produced; and so on. Material balance for complex processes involving recycle streams is hard to develop, but process simulation software is well-suited for this purpose.

Rising liability and increasing complexity of environmental laws make collecting external information an important step in the planning for pollution reduction. This step ensures compliance with permits, guidelines, licenses, environmental laws, and reporting and labeling requirements. Chapter 3 provided an overview of federal environmental statutes in the United States. Most of these laws are written for manufacturing facilities where pollutants are generated continuously. Therefore, interpreting and complying with these laws in an R&D facility is difficult and expensive as R&D facilities generate a particular pollutant only temporarily. In addition, because more items are being brought into the regulatory sweep, more facilities are required to comply with regulations. Permits are much more restrictive and the patchwork of state and local regulations makes environmental laws complex to understand and costly to implement. Environmental standards are set based on health and safety risks or standards achievable using existing technologies. Therefore, when technology improves or when more information about the health or safety risk of a product becomes available, the standards change. Keeping up-to-date on relevant environmental standards is one of the biggest challenges for R&D facilities. Regulations that apply beyond specific volumes of pollutants typically favor R&D organizations and those that apply beyond certain concentrations irrespective of the volumes represent a barrier for R&D organizations. Most laboratories may not emit large quantities of pollutants into the air to be subjected to regulations. However, many laboratories discharge chemicals such as chloroform, methylene chloride, and benzene, which are all regulated.

Generating Alternatives

Once sources and causes of pollution have been identified, the regulations that affect the facility have been ascertained, and waste problems have been defined, the next step is to generate a comprehensive set of options for minimizing waste. Pollution-reduction options may be broadly organized into categories of improving operating procedures, substituting materials, separating wastes, concentrating waste, recycling, and treatment and disposal.

Improving Operating Procedures

Several R&D professionals recognize that improving operating procedures can significantly reduce waste generation and its economic consequences. The severity of the Bhopal accident could have been prevented or dramatically lessened had operating personnel followed simple procedures. The intensity of the accident could have been lessened had smaller quantities of materials been stored. An effective emergency plan would have reduced the number of victims. Many victims could have been saved had they simply been instructed to breathe through wet towels.[1] Operating procedures can be broadly categorized into material management practices, R&D facility practices, and the establishment of preoperational project reviews.

Excess, expired, contaminated, and off-specification materials are the major sources of waste in an R&D facility. For example, 40 percent of waste disposed of by the Los Alamos National Laboratory in 1988 comprised a surplus of laboratory chemicals.[2] The cost involved in two kinds of waste includes not only disposal costs but also the cost of the lost materials. An effective materials-management practice can reduce waste significantly. Centralized purchasing, review of each material requisition before purchasing, sharing of materials among common users, ordering smaller quantities in exact amounts, and issuing materials based on expiration dates are some of the strategies to reduce waste. Creating an internal exchange to swap materials among departments and returning excess materials back to the supplier can also reduce waste. Risk of spillage can be lessened by cutting down on the amount of stored materials. An R&D facility should also institute a system for identifying hazardous wastes in the facility.

According to an Occupational Safety and Health Administration directive contained in the hazard communication regulations, R&D organizations are required to communicate the health and safety hazards of materials by means of labels on containers, material safety data sheets, and training programs. This is a difficult program for an R&D facility, which uses thousands of materials, to implement. For example, the Los Alamos National Laboratory purchased more than 19,000 laboratory chemicals in 1988.[3] Labeling programs, in addition to providing information about potential hazards to employees, can reduce worker injury and illness. All materials used in a facility must be labeled. All wastes after separation should also be labeled. In addition to labeling, every hazardous material must be accompanied by a material safety data sheet that describes significant hazardous properties and information in order to protect personnel. These data sheets should be kept at the facility for quick and easy reference by all R&D personnel. C. J. Kmetz described an on-plant container-labeling program at the Chevron Research Company.[4]

Every R&D project must be reviewed for its environmental, safety, and hygienic aspects. By reviewing each project before it is initiated, the most cost-effective alternatives can be developed to cut down waste. Each project should be reviewed for products and by-products that will be produced, emission of pollutants, wastewater discharge, ground contamination, and so on. The review must be done by impartial personnel not involved with the project. A detailed review procedure followed by Dow Chemical Western Division is described by M. DesJardin and colleagues.[5] Similar reviews must be performed whenever any changes to a project are made or any changes in the regulations take place. Reducing scale will also reduce chemical and energy costs as well as cut down on storage and equipment requirements. Another method to reduce chemical generation is to use computer simulations to replicate chemical reactions. The elimination of wastes and the speed at which R&D results can be obtained will encourage more computer simulations of chemical reactions, resulting in a substantial drop in pollution generation.

Substituting Materials

Substituting hazardous material with less hazardous material is an effective approach to waste reduction. The Emergency Planning and Community Right-to-Know Act requires R&D facilities to report the routine and accidental release of toxic chemicals into the environment. Since material substitution strategy eliminates the need for such disclosures, this is an excellent public relations technique. J. S. Bridges and colleagues suggest substituting sodium hypochlorite for sodium dichromate, alcohol for benzene, and detergents for a chromic acid solution with which to clean glassware.[6] While substitution strategy may not always eliminate or reduce the amount of waste generated, it may make waste handling and disposal easier and more economical.

Separating Wastes

Separating wastes is a simple and economic waste-reduction technique. Separating hazardous from nonhazardous waste reduces the volume of hazardous waste, thereby increasing recoverability, expanding disposal options, and reducing disposal costs. For example, by combining all flammable wastes, they can be disposed of through incineration, eliminating the need for the less preferred option of burying them.

Concentrating Waste

Concentrating wastes reduces volume, reducing disposal costs and increasing management options. There are several methods for concentrating waste, including filtration, vaporization, and heat drying. Aqueous solutions of heavy metals such as chromium, lead, copper, and selenium can be concentrated through evaporation. Simply cutting down the volume of waste does not constitute waste reduction, however, unless the waste material can be reused.

Recycling

Recycling waste is an effective waste-management alternative. Recycling saves waste disposal costs, reduces material procurement costs, and generates income from salable waste. For example, the Los Alamos National Laboratory saves $50 for every pound of material recycled in addition to the cost of replacing that material.[7] Unlike a large manufacturing plant, an R&D facility finds it difficult to find commercial firms to recycle its waste as these firms prefer large volumes. By recovering materials such as metallic mercury, silver, platinum, and other valuable metals, significant cost savings can be achieved. Organic solvents are recovered from contaminated solvents by distillation. Electrolysis is another method for recovering waste. At photographic and X-ray facilities, silver can be recovered using electrolysis. Heat can be recovered from a flammable material by burning it as fuel. An R&D facility must make storage space available and publicize its program to make recycling successful.

Treatment and Disposal

If waste generation cannot be prevented, then waste must be treated and disposed of. Treatment of waste is not a waste-reduction alternative but rather a way to dispose of waste legally, safely, and in an environmentally sound manner. Therefore, this option should be chosen only after all other options are found unsuitable. Since R&D facilities produce small quantities of waste, it is a good idea to centralize treatment of wastes. This way an R&D facility can take advantage of economies of scale and also relieve scientists and engineers from treatment responsibility. There are several treatment alternatives. Waste acids and bases can be neutralized and disposed of through the sewer. Toxic waste can be made nontoxic using oxidizing agents. For example, cyanide salt can be detoxified by treating it with an oxidizing agent. Several procedures for converting hazardous wastes to less hazardous wastes are outlined by the National Research Council.[8] Hazardous wastes are segregated by compatibility of contents and are buried in lab packs. Lab packs typically hold less waste than their capacity allows. The remaining content of the drum consists of an absorbent cushion to protect the contents against breakage and to absorb liquids in the event of breakage. These absorbent materials can be vermiculite, diatomaceous earth, or fuller's earth. Lab packs are also used to transport waste materials to a disposal site. Before any waste can be buried, the chemical composition of hazardous waste must be identified. The drum to be buried must be made of metal. Waste-management professionals do not approve of burying wastes in lab packs as this method does not really dispose of wastes but rather simply hides them. Another way to dispose of wastes in an environmentally acceptable manner is to incinerate them. By combining all flammable wastes in a single drum for incineration, the amount of chemicals disposed of in landfills can be reduced. Wastes to be incinerated must be packed in a flammable material. Getting a license for an incinerator is very difficult. Not all chemicals can be burned. Mercury, gallium, and arsenic, for example, can produce toxic fumes when incinerated. An R&D facility that generates small quantities of waste can use a contractor to burn its wastes.

Evaluating Alternatives

Once the alternatives have been generated, the next step is to evaluate them in order to select the best remedy. The evaluation process involves technical, economic, regulatory, and public relations considerations. Technical evaluation ascertains whether the proposed alternative will perform in a specific application. The technical evaluation process examines issues relating to worker safety, special expertise that may be required, new environmental problems that may be created, and so on. Financial criteria such as net present value, internal rates of return, and so on are used for economic evaluation. Regulatory screening explores whether the proposed alternative violates any current or proposed regulations. Waste-reduction alternatives must also be evaluated for acceptability by employees, communities surrounding the facility, and so on.

Implementing Options

Management commitment is essential for any waste-reduction program to be successful. Management commitment should include a letter signed by the head of the R&D facility describing the waste-minimization program. Using a consultant who has done similar work can significantly improve planning and options generation. Since employees are the persons most familiar with materials and processes, their involvement should be encouraged. Employee training must be a part of any implementation program. In addition, R&D facilities should establish an incentive system to encourage employees to come up with ideas for waste minimization. R&D facilities should also institute a hazard communication system to inform employees about the waste-minimization program. Internal seminars, presentations, brochures, and videos are some effective ways of reaching employees. The amount of waste generated should be compared with the planned generation of wastes. Since waste generation is sporadic, R&D facilities need to develop a waste tracking and reporting system. Facilities should review procedures whenever there are changes in materials, an increase in waste-management costs, enactment of new regulations, introduction of new technology, or the occurrence of an environmental tragedy.

CONCLUSION

Rising disposal costs, restrictions on the use of landfills, future liability concerns, and the availability of options are forcing R&D facilities to consider waste-minimization strategies. The four-step planning procedure for waste minimization presented in this chapter can help those R&D facilities to develop programs that not only comply with regulations but also help reduce accidents and improve employee safety. Because of the sporadic nature of waste generation, a continuous, rather than periodic, environmental review procedure should be instituted.

NOTES

1. Daniel D. Chiras, *Environmental Science: A Framework for Decision Making* 2d ed. (Menlo Park, Calif.: Benjamin/Cummings, 1988), p. 302.

2. P. Josey, *Segregation for Recycle and Rescue of Hazardous Chemical Material at Los Alamos National Laboratory*, LA-UR-90-1116. (Los Alamos, N. M.: The Laboratory, 1990).

3. Ibid.

4. C. J. Kmetz, "An In-plant Container-labeling Program," *Chemical Engineering Progress*, 6 (March 1990): 33–36.

5. M. DesJardin, M. D. Gustafson, R. Helling, M. J. Ladd, K. Steele, and D. Vanderhoof, "Dow Chemical Western Division Research Pre-Operational Review of New Projects," *Plant/Operations Progress*, April 1991, pp. 69–80.

6. J. S. Bridges, C. A. McComas, T. Foecke, and L. Swain, "Results from a Cooperative Federal, State and Trade Association Waste Minimization Research Program," *Hazardous Waste and Hazardous Materials* 6(1) (1989).

7. DesJardin et al., *Plant/Operations Progress*, pp. 69–80.

8. National Research Council, *Prudent Practices for Disposal of Chemicals from Laboratories* (Washington, D.C.: National Academy Press, 1983).

III

GREEN TOOLS

12

Total Green Management

Over the last two decades, the concept of green management has changed dramatically. Instead of retrofitting existing plants with cleaning equipment, the emphasis now is on eliminating waste generation itself. The rising demand for green products has made greenness a source of revenue. The global impact of pollution has made the environment a global competitive weapon. Productivity growth and innovation associated with green management have forced companies to consider a total quality management approach. The responsibility for pollution reduction lies not with one department but rather with the entire organization. Green management is becoming a philosophy. This chapter describes a variety of total quality management tools and shows how they can be used to achieve total green management. The goals of total green management include reduction of environmental waste; conservation of resources and energy; and satisfaction of customers, employees, and other stakeholders. Using techniques from total quality management, the strategy of total green management is continuous improvement. The framework for total green management is based on ideas developed by Philip B. Crosby and W. Edwards Deming.[1]

TOTAL GREEN MANAGEMENT COSTS

The costs of total green management are determined by an aggregate sum of all costs incurred to maintain greenness. Typically, the costs of total green management do not stem from the environmental department alone but rather all departments. These costs include finance, personnel, and any other expense incurred for environmental purpose.

Since management decisions are guided by costs and benefits, accounting for total costs is an important element of successful total green management. Accounting involves identifying all direct expenditures related to environmental activities and estimating other indirect costs such as goodwill, liability, and so on. This information can be used by management to identify areas for pollution and cost reduction and for profit improvement.

Following costs of poor quality, green costs can be categorized into four types: internal failure costs, external failure costs, appraisal costs, and prevention costs. These are generally considered waste costs because they do not add value to the product. Internal failure costs relate to expenses caused by a failed product, material, or process. The costs could be for testing, analyzing, correcting, reworking, repairing, or scrapping a failed item before a customer receives the product. External failure costs, on the other hand, relate to costs accrued for failures after the customer receives the product. These include costs relating to recall and repair, environmental fines, penalties, cleanups, liability, and goodwill. Prevention costs are those incurred to prevent the occurrence of product or process failures. Costs associated with waste minimization, pollution prevention, and product testing are some examples. Appraisal costs are associated with the inspection and testing of products and the measurement of emissions. The purpose of these activities is to ensure greenness in products, processes, and disposal. Figure 12.1 presents prevention and pollution costs for various levels of pollution. Based on these curves, it is assumed that there is an optimal level of pollution at which both costs are minimized and that it would not be profitable to improve pollution below this optimal level. However, this is not true as there are several alternatives that can reduce pollution without increasing costs using the existing technology.

FIGURE 12.1
Misconception about Green Costs

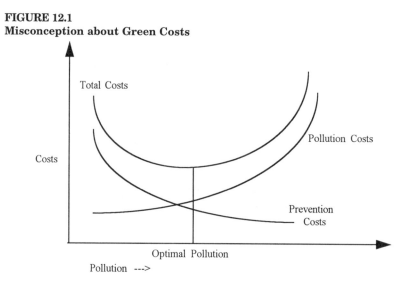

Accurate accounting systems are essential to make cost effective decisions about pollution prevention. Current accounting systems suffer from their failure to include all environmental costs and aggregation of accounting data can hide pollution costs. Two improvements that will provide a clearer picture of environmental costs can easily be implemented: full cost accounting[2] and green cost accounting.

A full cost accounting system identifies four types of costs for products, processes, or projects — direct costs, hidden costs, contingent liability costs, and intangible costs — and uses all these costs in decision making. Full cost accounting can also identify superior pollution-reduction projects. Financial measures such as net present value, internal rate of return, profitability index, and payback period are useless unless the right costs are included. Direct costs related to a project, product, or process include costs of buildings, equipment, equipment installation, and so on. Operating and maintenance costs include materials, labor, waste management, and utilities. Management accounting does a good job of capturing direct costs, but hidden costs are usually aggregated as overhead costs. Hidden costs include costs of compliance such as reporting, monitoring, legal support, testing, training, and waste management. The first step in the estimation of these costs is to determine the rules and regulations that affect the product, project, or process. The next step is to identify all costs related to the compliance of these laws and regulations. When these costs are used to select a pollution-prevention alternative, it is necessary to anticipate changes in regulations so future cost projections can be estimated. Costs related to cleaning, degraded or discharged materials, and materials lost during recycling are typically ignored. Contingent liability costs include those of inadvertent releases and remedial action, personal injury, property damage, and legal damages and settlement. These costs can be estimated by examining the past records of companies in the same industry. Less tangible costs include those related to goodwill, public relations, and so on.

Misallocation of costs to products is another drawback of traditional accounting.[3] Product costs are estimated by aggregating costs of direct materials, direct labor, and allocated indirect overhead. Production costs are those directly related to the product — costs of materials that become part of the product and costs of labor that is required to convert raw materials into finished products. All other costs such as salaries of managers, utilities, material-handling costs, and waste-management costs are aggregated into the category of overhead. These costs are allocated to different products using some rational cost-allocation method such as direct labor hours. Estimation of product costs using a traditional absorption costing method has several drawbacks. First, waste-management costs are hidden in the aggregation. For example, if two products are produced and only one product generates waste, then the cost-allocation method allocates waste-management costs to a

product that does not produce any waste. This results in a miscalcula-
tion of profitability. Second, because waste-management costs are
hidden within overhead costs, managers do not have an incentive to
reduce them. One way to overcome this problem is to identify wastes
generated by each product and allocate their waste-management costs
to individual products (see figures 12.2 and 12.3). Waste-management
costs should include all direct costs, hidden costs, contingent liability
costs, and less tangible costs. When the green cost accounting method
was used to compute total environmental costs at some DuPont and
Amoco Oil plants, these costs were found to constitute as much as 20
percent of the total operating costs.[4]

GREEN TOOLS FOR NUMERIC DATA

Data collection, histograms, Pareto charts, Ishikawa diagrams,
stratification, scatter plots, run charts, flow charts, matrix data
analysis, and control charts are some of the green tools that can be used
to develop strategies to reduce pollution. A unique feature of these tools
is that they can be used by teams.

Data collection is the first step in any program to reduce pollution.
Teams must use data to make effective pollution-reduction decisions.
Data collection involves asking what the pollution problem is and
identifying information that needs to be collected to answer the
problem.

Histograms are useful for analyzing large quantities of data. The
histogram is a frequency diagram displaying causes on the x-axis and
their frequency on the y-axis. They can show variations in product or
process characteristics. Histograms display data making it easy to
analyze data.

The Pareto chart, a bar chart drawn with causes on x-axis and frequency on y-axis, concentrates on the significant few rather than the
insignificant many. Causes are ranked by frequency. Often, however, it
is not the frequency of causes that determines the remedial actions; it
is the extent of consequences. In these instances, Pareto charts should
be drawn based on consequences rather than frequency.

The Ishikawa diagram, also known as a fishbone or a cause-and-
effect diagram, helps to identify the root causes of a problem. Causes
can fall into categories of management, labor, process, material,
machine, testing instrument, or operating environment. The first step
in the development of an Ishikawa diagram is to identify the problem.
The next step is to develop various causes. These causes are then categorized into groups such as management, labor, and so on. The
Ishikawa diagram is drawn showing various causes.

Stratification can help identify causes, particularly when data relate
to different sources. Some examples of stratification include classifying
materials by suppliers, machines by age and make, operators by

FIGURE 12.2
Traditional Cost Accounting System

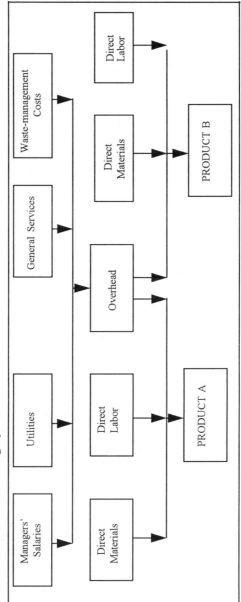

FIGURE 12.3
Green Cost Accounting System

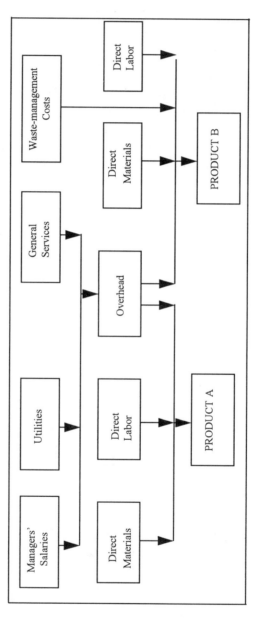

experience and shift, time by season and day or night, and operating environment by temperature.

If data stratified based on various causes are continuous, then the scatter plot is an excellent tool to identify causes.

Run charts display data over time or in the sequence in which they are generated. Run charts indicate variations in data over time.

Flow charts display how a process or system operates. Flow charts, along with material balance, are extremely useful for developing pollution-reduction strategies.

The matrix data analysis uses a statistical technique called "principal component analysis" to analyze data. It is particularly useful for analyzing vast quantities of data. Principal components are analyzed and the significant principal components are plotted on a graph.

Every process has variations and control charts keep track of them. However, if a process is going through random fluctuations, then the variations should lie between statistically determined upper and lower limits. If there are some assignable causes, then the process variations are likely to fall outside these limits. Therefore, intervening in the process whenever process variations fall outside the limits is an effective way to prevent waste generation. Often, waste discharges are monitored with control charts to ensure that the discharges do not deviate from normal levels.

Figure 12.4 summarizes green tools for numeric data.

GREEN TOOLS FOR NONNUMERIC DATA

Green tools for nonnumeric data include affinity diagrams, relation diagrams, matrix diagrams, process decision program charts, and arrow diagrams.

The affinity diagram is an excellent tool for organizing, grouping, and reducing large quantities of verbal data such as customer needs, ideas, and opinions based on their similarities. The emphasis of affinity diagrams is association rather than logical connections. The first step in the preparation of an affinity diagram is definition of subjects. The next step is to brainstorm to gather data regarding the subject matter. The next step is to organize data into groups in hierarchical order. Each higher order group should represent the sum of the members in the lower order groups.

The purpose of the relation diagram is to display the logical relationship between a proposal, idea, problem, question, and various data. The affinity diagram could be used to generate data. The relation diagram is useful when it is difficult to show relations between verbal ideas and when it is necessary to indicate steps sequentially.

Tree diagrams illustrate the categorization of problems, ideas, needs, and proposals in subgroups. The tree diagram is useful for

FIGURE 12.4
Green Tools for Numeric Data

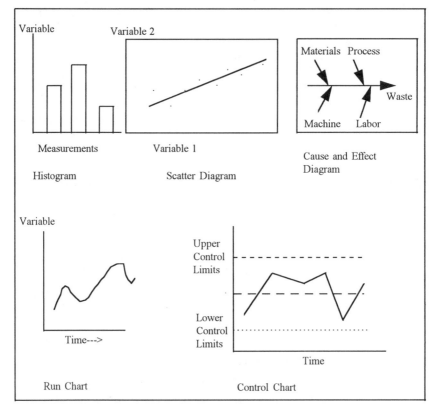

defining problems in terms of well-defined subproblems. Such a breakdown allows all components of a problem to be analyzed.

Matrix diagrams organize large quantities of data and display graphically logical connections between different attributes.

The process decision program chart is a flow chart that displays actions and decisions in sequential order to reach a desired outcome. It is useful for new plans and plans whose purpose is to avoid catastrophe.

The arrow diagram is a useful tool for planning. It can be used to display relationships among various activities. The Gantt chart and critical path methods are types of arrow diagrams.

RISK-MANAGEMENT TOOLS

Increasing safety and reducing costs are possible by appropriate allocation of resources based on risk criteria. The purpose of risk assessment is to estimate the probability of the occurrence of an adverse effect and the magnitude of consequences. Risk assessment can be financial risk analysis to estimate liability or property risk, safety hazard analysis to evaluate low probability–high consequence events, health risk assessment to examine human health risks, and environmental risk analysis to understand interactions between people and ecosystems. Risk assessment involves problem identification, probability estimation, analysis of consequences, and risk characterization. Typical outputs include number of deaths, injuries, health risks, and economic risks. Checklists, rough analysis, and "what if?" analysis are overview methods of risk analysis. Failure mode and effects analysis and fault tree analysis are two techniques commonly used to identify failures in a system.

The failure mode and effects analysis (FMEA) is a useful tool for identifying failures in a system. FMEA is a systematic analysis of a product or process, its functions, and failure causes and consequences. In FMEA, subsystem failures are identified and their effect on local as well as system level consequences are analyzed. A prerequisite for effective FMEA study is a thorough understanding of the functions of the subsystem components and their relationship to the function of the whole system. The goal of FMEA analysis is to identify potentials for failures and actions to avoid them. FMEA can be used in the design stage to develop products with the least potential for catastrophies and can also be used to analyze manufacturing systems and to develop suitable process control systems. FMEA can be used in the current operating systems to identify possibilities for failures and their consequences. FMEA analysis consists of system definition, depth of analysis, analyzing the function of the system, analyzing the function of the components, determining potential for failure, determining potential consequences of failures, developing methods for detecting failures, restricting failures from spreading, assessing the seriousness of failures, identifying failure causes, identifying relationships between various failures, and documentation. FMEA can be extended by quantifying likelihood of failure, seriousness of consequences of failures, and probability of detection.

The fault tree analysis displays connections between failures in a system and causes of these failures on lower system levels. Fault trees can lead to a better understanding of a system and its potential for failures. The drawing of a fault tree starts with the definition of a failure and identification of various causes. The relationships between causes and failures are identified using Boolean relationships such as or-gate, and-gate, and so on.

GREEN PROGRAMS

Most successful companies use a variety of techniques to encourage green programs. Written source-reduction policies, strong leadership, green goals, material tracking systems, materials balance audit, full cost accounting, and employee participation are some unique features of green programs.

Written Source Reduction Policies

Several companies publish explicit written policies promoting source reduction as the primary waste-reduction strategy. Others consider source reduction as one of several waste-reduction options including recycling, treatment, and disposal.

Leadership

Companies assign monitoring of waste-reduction activity to a top-level line manager or to an environmental or safety manager. Her level in the organizational structure reflects the impor-tance a company gives to the green programs.

Green Goals

Companies set goals for waste reduction. Goals can be set for specific chemicals or a group of chemicals defined by various statutes.

Material Tracking Systems

An effective material tracking system can easily uncover sources of material wastes. A good tracking system will record inputs and outputs of all processes. A full accounting system will keep track of both chemical specific and multimedia (solid, liquid, or gas) inputs and outputs. There are several inventory softwares for tracking materials.[5]

Materials Balance Audit

The materials balance audit is a simple yet underutilized tool for identifying sources of material wastes. The materials balance principle, which is based on the first law of thermodynamics, states that mass input should be equal to mass output plus mass accumulated. Frequently, the materials balance can provide more accurate estimates of wastes than direct measurements of wastes. The materials balance principle can also be used to develop estimates on past emissions.

Full Cost Accounting

A full cost accounting system records the pollution costs of each process rather than combining them in an overhead category. Companies with accounting systems that capture costs by processes can easily identify potential sources of wastes. Such an accounting system can also help companies come up with waste-reduction projects that reduce costs.

Employee Participation

There are a variety of ways to involve employees in total green management programs. Idea solicitation, suggestion programs, training programs, and reward systems are some of the ways to encourage employee participation. Green circles where a small group of employees discuss different problems and develop suggestions for waste reduction can also increase employee involvement.

Other Methods

State and federal government technical assistance programs, trade association and industry technical assistance programs, and vendor assistance are other sources of green programs.

Based on studies of 29 chemical plants, INFORM reported the effects of the first eight green programs on the number of source-reduction activities initiated by each plant.[6] Cost accounting, employee participation, a formal environmental program, leadership, and material accounting were all evident in the majority of companies. However, less than half of these companies had materials balance, environmental goals, and written source-reduction policies as a part of their green programs. Based on statistical analysis, INFORM reported that cost accounting, employee participation, and leadership from environmental as well as other departments can significantly increase source-reduction activities initiated by plants. Full cost accounting increases the number of source-reduction activities by as much as three times when compared with plants without full cost accounting. Plants with employee participation had, on average, twice as many source-reduction activities in place than those without it. It was found that having environmental leadership from both line and environmental departments better increased source-reduction activities.

The 1992 Toxics Release Inventory reported methods used to come up with a variety of source-reduction activities. Percentages of source reduction activities initiated by various methods are as follows:

Internal pollution prevention opportunity audit	21.6%
External pollution prevention opportunity audit	2.2%

Materials balance audit	7.1%
Participative team management	25.3%
Informal employee recommendations	10.3%
Formal employee recommendations	5.9%
Vendor assistance	12.9%
Trade/industry program	3.1%
Federal and state program	0.7%
Other	10.9%[7]

Participative team management generated more than one-fourth of all source-reduction activities initiated by 23,630 facilities in 1992.

INTERNATIONAL STANDARDIZATION ORGANIZATION CERTIFICATION OF ENVIRONMENTAL MANAGEMENT SYSTEMS

The International Standardization Organization (ISO) has historically dealt with international technical and safety standards. However, about ten years ago it decided to extend beyond these areas and announced the ISO 9000 series of quality standards. ISO 9000 describes the elements of an effective quality system. It is a generic system with universal application to any business. If an accredited independent third party vouches that an organization satisfies the requirements of the ISO, then the organization can be registered. Registration is recognized by customers worldwide and consequently it is becoming a competitive weapon. Fifty-three nations have adopted ISO 9000 and chemical-, electronic-, and machinery-exporting industries in the United States are aggressively pursuing registration. The success of the ISO 9000 system for quality has encouraged initiatives to develop standards for environmental management. These standards will have several advantages. A single set of efficient and simple international standards will eliminate the need for duplicate registrations, inspections, certifications, and product labels. Such standards will also avoid the need for command-and-control regulations in every country and will enhance credibility and allow organizations to maintain compliance with regulations all over the world. Excessive costs, potential trade barriers, and conflicts among national standards are some of the obstacles in developing and implementing these standards.

To make a system of international environmental management standards more desirable, the standards should advance green management, be consistent with existing systems, reduce trade barriers, be cost effective, incorporate best environmental management practices, be uniform in all countries, be a representation of an effective system, have no quantitative goals, describe criteria for management commitment, be optional, improve organizational effectiveness, be challenging, be adaptable, include guidance for communication, be compatible with other systems, and not mandate disclosure of information to third parties.[8] There are already several environmental management system standards in play. BS 7750, emerging ISO 14000 environmental management system, and Eco-Management and Audit Scheme are some popular standards for green management. Responsible Care® of the Chemical Manufacturers Association, Encouraging Environmental Excellence of the American Textile Manufacturers Institute, Strategies for Today's Environmental Partnership of the American Petroleum Institute, and Environmental Self-Assessment Program of the Global Environmental Management Initiative are other excellent guidelines companies can use to improve their environmental performance. Elements of these standards include environmental policy, objectives and targets, structure and responsibility, programs, management review, operational control, management audit, documentation and records, training, communication, and legal requirements. The *ISO 14001 Comparison Matrix* describes similarities and differences among these various standards.[9]

GOVERNMENT AWARDS

The President's Environment and Conservation Challenge Award represents the highest honor for greenness in the United States. This award, bestowed for excellence in the field of environmental conservation, is given for environmental quality management, partnership, innovation, and education and communications. Some of the companies that received medals and citations under this program in 1991 and 1992 are:

Corporation	*Basis for Award*
Pacific Gas and Electric Company	Environmental policy and program
Los Angeles Times	Environmentally conscious programs
McDonald's Corporation and the Environmental Defense Fund	Waste-reduction task force
New England Electric and the Energy Conservation Law Foundation Effort of New England	Conservation collaborative
IBM Corporation	Environmental management and conservation programs
Saunders Hotels Group, Inc. and Boston Park Plaza Hotel and Towers	Environmental action program
Northern Telecom, Inc.	CFC phaseout
Unocal Corporation	South Coast Recycled Auto Project (SCRAP)

Citations	
The Kroger Company	Marketing
3M	Quality environmental management
BankAmerica Corporation	Environmental policies
SC Johnson Wax	Innovative environmental technology

Corporation	Basis for Award
Hermen Miller, Inc.	Environmental-consciousness policies
AT&T	Global elimination of ozone-depleting CFCs
Reynolds Metals Company	Consumer aluminum recycling
Eaton Corporation	Dissolved air flotation system
Greenbay Packaging	Marketing ecologically responsible packaging
Procter & Gamble Company	Plastic recycling with innovation and technology; innovative source reduction
Southern California Edison	Customer technology application center
3COM Corporation	Corporate environmental policies
Chrysler Corporation	Jefferson North project
Hannaford Brothers Co.	Earth Matters program[10]

LAUNCHING TOTAL GREEN MANAGEMENT

Top Management Commitment

To launch a successful total green management, top management commitment is essential. In order to convert skeptical employees into doers, management must show commitment by appropriately recasting policies, goals, philosophies, and executive behavior. Management must allocate adequate resources. It must take a leadership role by learning about greenness and periodically evaluating progress. Management must make pollution reduction a part of the company's goals and strategies. Special attention must be paid to green aspects during recruitment, selection, and appraisal of employees. Training and education programs must emphasize pollution reduction. An appraisal and reward system should be instituted for green performance. Management should encourage team work because employee involvement is essential for a successful green program. Departmental heads should be given training in interpersonal skills to help employees adapt to change.

Communicating Benefits

The first step in launching a successful green program is to communicate benefits. Wastefulness typically reduces process yields and underutilizes raw materials. This increases product costs. Waste management, which includes storage, record keeping, transportation, and disposal, costs money. Improper disposal can result in third-party liability costs. Communicating costs associated with waste management is a strong motivator for total green management.

The development of corporate policies and goals to reduce waste provides the impetus for waste reduction on a continuous basis. Setting numeric goals to reduce waste can provide managers with a measurable performance indicator.

Waste minimization is a strong public relations strategy. It is no longer possible to keep hidden the quantities of waste generated. Various right-to-know regulations require facilities that store, process, or handle certain materials above threshold level to report to the regulatory agencies. Falling threshold levels and the increasing number of materials that are subject to reporting requirements are exposing companies to increased scrutiny. Therefore, reducing waste generation can significantly increase public goodwill toward the company.

While regulations are effective in compelling companies to reduce waste, many companies are developing strategies that go beyond compliance. Proactive companies with lower pollution levels than those required by law have a significant economic advantage over other competitors because their cost-effective foresight will find them already prepared when regulations are tightened up in the future. In addition, market-based pollution regulations such as those relating to power plants allow companies to sell their pollution rights to others at considerable prices. Bettering the environment for people living around the plant and improving the working conditions of employees are other incentives for implementing total green management.

Identifying Hurdles

Despite the advantages of total green management, its implementation can be difficult. A shortage of capital can cripple even a well-planned pollution-reduction program. A lack of understanding about pollution reduction and the intangible aspects of some of its benefits may cause top management to apportion inadequate amounts of capital for green programs. In addition, inaccurate cost-benefit estimates can hinder proper evaluations of green programs.

The lack of well-trained personnel is another hurdle for green programs. Downsizing and restructuring have reduced the number of competent people employed in waste management. Lack of management support can destroy a total green management program. Many managers find themselves complacent toward these programs once they are in compliance with regulations. Competing priorities like production goals and budgets typically distract management's attention from green programs. A lack of appreciation for waste reduction also hurts total green management. Downtime associated with implementing total green management is a strong disincentive for plants operating at full capacity. Uncertainties about future regulations and the lack of technology can also prevent companies from supporting total green management.

The Total Green Management
Approach for Pollution Prevention

There are several ways to implement total green management. The Quality Environmental Management Subcommittee of the President's Commission on Environmental Quality outlines an eight-step process for implementing a pollution-prevention program: establishing management commitment, forming crossfunctional teams, training, identifying environmental impacts, choosing improvement projects, implementing improvement projects, monitoring the progress, and repeating the whole process.

Establishing management commitment encourages the participation of stakeholders including employee unions, regulatory agencies, community members, and environmental groups. Employees should be encouraged to develop their own ideas for pollution reduction and to implement them. Top management should allocate adequate resources for implementing total green management.

Crossfunctional teams should be responsible for identifying and implementing pollution-reduction plans consistent with the overall strategic goals established by top management. Teams should consist of various department members who have demonstrated their strong dedication to improving the environment. The team members should have competence in total green management and plant operations. Using existing teams can considerably reduce difficulties in starting pollution-reduction projects. Periodic meetings between top management and green management teams are essential to avoid surprises and to encourage top management input.

Teams should be trained in waste-reduction techniques, introduction to environmental laws, typical wastes generated in the plant, total green management techniques, team building skills, conflict resolution skills, and so on.

For maximum impact, projects should be identified that respond to the needs of stakeholders and are consistent with corporate goals. They should be selected based on costs, resources, and technology. Teams are responsible for identifying criteria by which the success of the projects will be evaluated. Criteria such as waste volume, cost, regulations, potential liability, feasibility, toxicity, and health and safety concerns should be used for selecting projects.

All employees affected by the projects should be informed about their implementation. In addition, project teams should acquire additional resources needed to ensure successful implementation.

Projects must be evaluated in an ongoing manner in order to ensure successful execution. Any problems identified can help improve future green management efforts.

Finally, green management must be institutionalized. People involved in the project should be recognized and rewarded. The lessons learned during these eight steps should be incorporated into future endeavors. The results should be communicated to all stakeholders. In addition, the management cycle should begin again with renewed vigor.

Total green management typically takes a long time to implement. The Global Environmental Management Initiative suggests a systematic approach consisting of evaluating a company's current condition; identifying internal and external customers; and training in the planning, doing, checking, and acting cycles and green tools.[11] The crux of green management lies in its customer focus, systems approach, desire for continuous improvement, and belief in doing things right the first time.

GUIDELINES FOR IMPLEMENTING TOTAL GREEN MANAGEMENT

Crosby's 14 points and Deming's 14 points for total quality management provide an excellent foundation on which to implement total green management. Crosby's guidelines follow.

1. Top management commitment is essential for total green management.
2. There should be a green champion to implement total green management.
3. Full accounting and green cost accounting system should indicate current and potential environmental problems.
4. Pollution cost should account for costs to a company as well as to the society.
5. Green awareness should motivate employees to develop ideas to reduce pollution.
6. Total green management should indicate methods to reduce pollution.
7. Zero-emission planning should begin with management commitment for pollution reduction.
8. Employee training should include pollution elimination and reduction.
9. "Zero-emission Day" represents the company's and employees' commitment to a green corporation.
10. Goal setting translates individual actions into the reduction of pollution.
11. Error-cause removal helps employees to identify problems for achieving zero emission.
12. Recognition in appreciation of those who achieved their goals
13. Green councils are meetings of professional people to improve greenness of a corporation.
14. Doing it over represents the never-ending nature of total green management.[12]

Deming's 14-point guidelines include:

1. Management should define green goals and express its commitments.
2. Management should promote a new green philosophy.
3. The purpose of pollution reduction should be to reduce costs and remain competitive.
4. Purchasing decisions should be based on both price and environmental considerations.
5. Greenness should be improved during all stages of a product including design, process, distribution, and use.
6. Training people on pollution reduction is essential.
7. Supervision should motivate and encourage pollution reduction.
8. Keep an open communication channel.
9. An interdisciplinary functional approach to pollution reduction should be adopted.
10. Do not exhort employees on pollution reduction.
11. The pollution generated during each stage of production depends on the decisions made during other stages and also on equipment, materials, and processes. Therefore, setting numeric goals for pollution reduction for each employee is counterproductive.
12. Avoid pollution reduction by objectives.
13. Introduce on the job training programs for employees and supervisors on pollution reduction.
14. Introduce green circles to reduce pollution.[13]

There are several voluntary programs to reduce pollution with its guidelines and benefits. These include the following.

Program	Goals
33/50 program	To reduce emissions of 17 toxic chemicals by 33 percent by 1992 and by 50 percent by 1995
Climate Wise Recognition program	To reduce greenhouse gas emissions
Water Alliances for Voluntary Efficiency	To reduce water and energy consumption through the installation of water-efficient equipment at hotels and lodging establishments
Wastewise program	To reduce municipal solid waste through waste prevention, recycling, and the use of recycled products
Green Lights program	To encourage the use of energy-efficient lighting technologies
Energy Star Computers	To encourage computer manufacturers to develop computers that consume less energy when not in use
Building Air Quality Alliance	Improve air quality in commercial and public buildings[14]

CONCLUSION

Total green management is the cornerstone of pollution reduction. Total green management is focused on customers, which include employees, stockholders, consumers, and members of the public. Total green management is guided by a continuous improvement philosophy. The emphasis is on not only doing the right thing but also on doing it right the first time. Such an approach reflects a company's credo that the prevention is better than the cure. Total green management relies on a systems rather than departmental outlook whereby problems are analyzed from all perspectives and change is continuous.

NOTES

1. Philip B. Crosby, *Quality Is Free* (New York: McGraw-Hill, 1979); W. Edwards Deming, *Out of the Crisis* (Cambridge, Mass.: MIT, Center for Advanced Engineering Study, 1986).

2. Global Environmental Management Initiative, *Finding Cost-Effective Pollution Prevention Initiatives: Incorporating Environmental Costs into Business Decision Making* (Washington, D.C.: Global Environmental Management Initiative, 1994).

3. Rebecca Todd, "Zero-loss Environmental Accounting Systems," in *The Greening of Industrial Ecosystems*, ed. Braden R. Allenby and Deanna J. Richards (Washington, D.C.: National Academy Press, 1994), pp. 191–200.

4. Daryl Ditz, Janet Ranganathan, R. Darryl Banks, *Green Ledgers: Case Studies in Corporate Environmental Accounting* (Washington, D.C.: World Resources Institute, 1995), p. 15.

5. Elizabeth M. Donley, ed., *Environmental Software Directory* (Garrisonville, Va.: Donley Technology, 1992–1993).

6. Mark J. Dorfman, Warren R. Muir, and Catherine G. Miller, *Environmental Dividends: Cutting More Chemical Wastes* (New York: INFORM, 1992).

7. U.S. Environmental Protection Agency, *1992 Toxics Release Inventory: Public Data Release*, EPA 745-R-94-001 (Washington, D.C.: Government Printing Office, 1994), pp. 138–39.

8. Susan L. Jackson, "Certification of Environmental Management Systems — ISO 9000 and Competitive Advantage," in *Environmental TQM*, 2d ed., ed. John T. Willig (New York: McGraw-Hill, 1994), p. 38.

9. Global Environmental Management Initiative, *ISO 14001 Comparison Matrix* (Washington, D.C.: Global Environmental Management Initiative, 1995).

10. Council on Environmental Quality, *Environmental Quality* (Washington, D.C.: Government Printing Office, 1993).

11. Global Environmental Management Initiative, *Total Quality Environmental Management: The Primer* (Washington, D.C.: Global Environmental Management Initiative, 1993).

12. Crosby, *Quality is Free*, pp. 175–259.

13. Deming, *Out of the Crisis*, pp. 23–24.

14. Global Environmental Management Initiative, *GEMI Reference to EPA Voluntary Programs* (Washington, D.C.: Global Environmental Management Initiative, 1994).

13

Green Auditing

Green auditing is the tool used to evaluate green performance. According to the U.S. Environmental Protection Agency (EPA), "environmental auditing is a systematic, documented, periodic and objective review by regulated entities of facility operations and practices related to meeting environmental requirements." The purpose of green auditing is to improve management control of green practices and ensure compliance with environmental regulations and company policies. Green auditing essentially involves questioning current practices regarding compliance with external government laws and regulations; codes of practices; and internal guidelines, policies, and procedures. It also examines whether current practices can be improved in terms of cost effectiveness. To make green auditing successful, it must be integrated with the total green management system. Even though regulatory agencies encourage green auditing, it is typically initiated by companies. It is an objective and systematic self-evaluation procedure performed to uncover deficiencies and take corrective actions. Auditing does not develop internal controls. It only evaluates the effectiveness of internal control systems and ensures that the company complies with them. It is a diagnostic tool, not a substitute for environmental compliance activities.

The complexity and scope of environmental laws, and the stiff penalties for violating them, have encouraged top management to develop green auditing procedures in order to evaluate compliance with environmental regulations. To make green auditing effective, open communication between auditors and operating departments is essential. In addition, the audit must be appropriately documented. By identifying deficiencies, audits serve as a management tool for continuous improvement.

Green auditing has several benefits. It helps top management to anticipate rather than simply react to crises. By bringing to the attention of management current and impending regulatory requirements, a company can improve its environmental compliance record. Green auditing can also point to effective remedies to frequent environmental problems on a companywide basis. The U.S. Department of Justice considers audits to be a crucial factor in enforcing laws against environmental crimes. Green auditing promotes communication between plants and improves employee knowledge about green policies. Green auditing can uncover opportunities for waste and cost reduction and provide an objective rating of various internal functions and procedures. Audits must be conducted on a periodic basis to develop an environmental database and time series data on environmental performance. Auditing is an excellent basis for a reward system. Because of its objective evaluation system, an environmental audit can serve as an excellent public relations tool. It lowers insurance premiums by reducing liability risks and makes it easier to obtain insurance coverage.

The U.S. EPA, the British Standards Institution, and the European Union have all promulgated green auditing guidelines. The purpose of voluntary eco-management audit schemes is to encourage companies to institute environmental policies that contain commitments to continuous improvement and to disclose information, in the form of verified public statements, about the measures companies are taking to improve environmental performance. Costs, use of audit information by competitors and environmental groups, and fear of self-incrimination are some of the reasons cited by companies for not implementing environmental auditing. In the United Kingdom, British Standard (BS) 7750 describes green auditing criteria and objectives. The purpose of BS 7750 is to improve management performance and to enhance the competitiveness of a company. BS 7750 is a company-specific, not site-specific, guideline. It does not require publication of externally verified statements. The environmental auditing guidelines promulgated by the U.S. EPA are reproduced at the end of this chapter.

AUDIT PROCEDURES

Procedures for auditing should be well defined. Management should evaluate audit results and take action to reduce the deficiencies identified by the audit team. Audit procedures should indicate responsibilities of audit teams, performance standards, audit frequencies, auditor train-ing, reporting procedures, and follow-up actions. For the purpose of developing auditing plans, green auditing can be divided into three phases, namely preparation, auditing, and postaudit activities. Preparation includes establishing auditing goals, defining the scope of the audit, forming the audit team, selecting sites to be audited, and developing an audit plan. The audit should study internal control systems to identify their strengths and weaknesses, examine them for their effectiveness, and evaluate them. Postaudit activities involve preparing the audit report and conducting follow-up.

PREPARATION

Audit Goals

Green auditing objectives are typically internally driven. Green auditing ensures that a company is complying with environmental laws, regulations, policies, and procedures and also ensures that systems are in place to monitor continued compliance. Audits that focus on functions will examine permits, company policies, management control systems, training programs, and so on. Activity-oriented audits will examine air pollution, water pollution, solid waste disposal, occupational health, and so on. Compliance may involve both laws and corporate policies and procedures. The audit should strive to identify unsafe operating procedures. It should evaluate current waste disposal practices to identify cost-reduction opportunities. The green audit should also look for potential bombshells that may result in costly litigation or remedial actions. The purpose of green audit is not simply to assess and grade green performance but rather to evaluate the whole spectrum of activities that create and maintain safe and healthy working conditions. It should also identify performance shortfalls of various pollution-reduction projects in which a company has invested considerable capital.

Audit Scope

Every green audit should examine compliance with environmental regulations and company policies and procedures. In addition, auditing should analyze management; environmental functions; operating facilities; the pollution-control infrastructure; the impact on the surrounding areas including atmosphere, rivers, and groundwater; emergency preparedness; contractor selection and management; external communication; and management of regulated wastes.

Formation of Audit Teams

The audit team should comprise members who are independent of those who have responsibility for the environmental programs. The team members should only be responsible for auditing. The responsibility for auditing can be entrusted to an external organization or an internal group consisting of full-time employees of the organization. External audit teams are expensive and can create a hindrance to open communication. An internal team, however, may not have the knowledge required to perform an audit. The audit team may also consist of independent employees from an audit department, external consultants, and members from various departments who are not responsible for the function they are auditing. To ensure audit quality, there should be written protocols to guide the team through the audit. Furthermore, the audit itself should be continuously audited to ensure that protocols are followed. In addition, all audit reports should be reviewed by the legal department or an outside consultant to ensure their integrity.

Site Selection

A company should try to audit as many sites as possible. However, prohibitive costs and the scarcity of technical manpower make it necessary to have a selection system for auditing. Auditing frequency should depend on the risk factors of each site. New laws, size, toxicity of chemicals used, employee exposure, waste generated, and the population of the surrounding community are some of the factors to be considered for site selection. To schedule various sites, Union Carbide, for example, uses the Audit Timeliness Index, which takes into account such factors as potential hazard, performance in previous two audits, number of years since previous audit, number of employees and on-site contractors, and other special situations.[1]

Developing an Auditing Plan

Once the sites are selected, the next step is to inform the facility and collect background information. Previous audit reports; corporate files; plant layout diagrams; policies and procedures; operating manuals; and permits and regulations applicable to the facility should all be examined to determine the auditing plan.

AUDITING

Studying Control Systems

The first step in auditing is to conduct a survey of the plant and surroundings. All environmental records including permits, waste records, standing instructions, maintenance procedures, and reports submitted to regulatory agencies should be analyzed. In addition, auditors should conduct informal interviews so they will understand the internal control systems. A questionnaire relating to operations, processes, and management control can be used during these interviews.

Testing the Control Systems

Once information about the control systems has been collected, they must be tested. Testing can include visual observation, examination of discharge reports, reliability analysis of monitoring equipment, and so on. In addition, spot checks of sites with likely environmental problems should also be done.

Evaluating Control Systems

After testing various control systems, the next step is to develop conclusions about different elements of the system. Any deficiencies about operations, maintenance, equipment, or manpower should be discussed with site personnel and summarized.

POSTAUDIT ACTIVITIES

Preparing the Audit Report

Once the site has been visited and conclusions finalized, the next step is to prepare the audit report. The audit report should be objective and impersonal. It should be reviewed by and discussed with the site management; errors pointed out should be corrected. Audit reports generally consist of two sections. The first section includes an introduction to the facility — location, layout, operations, environmental considerations, and so on. The second section consists of findings of noncompliance with external federal, state, and local laws and internal policies and procedures in the areas of air emissions; water discharges; solid waste management; storage; noise; operating practices, procedures, and policies; and so on.

Preparing the Action Plan to Correct Deficiencies

The green audit does not end with the findings report. Based on the deficiencies identified in the audit report, facility personnel must prepare a corrective action plan in which they outline remedies, assign responsibilities, and determine a timeframe for implementation.

CONCLUSION

Green auditing is a powerful management tool for ensuring environmental protection and regulatory compliance. According to a 1993 *National Law Journal* survey, 65 percent of the corporate clients of survey lawyers performed environmental audits and another 18 percent were planning programs.[2] However, many companies avoid green auditing for fear of self-incrimination. The U.S. EPA can use environmental audit documentation as evidence in certain cases. According to a survey of Indiana manufacturers, 42 percent have never performed an audit and the reason cited by two out of three of them was fear of criminal or civil prosecution or "toxic tort."[3] The essential requirements for a successful green audit include management commitment, impartial and competent audit team, well-defined and comprehensive auditing procedures, written documentation of audit, audit quality assurance, and follow-up action plan and implementation.[4] The periodic review of facilities in the form of green auditing can ferret out potential problems. Management can take suitable actions to correct problems and improve environmental performance records. A continuous improvement program can be built around the green auditing program.

NOTES

1. Paul D. Coulter, "Auditing for Environmental Excellence at Union Carbide," in *Environmental TQM*, 2d ed., ed. John T. Willig (New York: McGraw-Hill, 1994), pp. 257–267.
2. Elizabeth M. Kirschner, "Self-incrimination Remains a Major Problem with Environmental Audits," *Chemical and Engineering News*, August 22, 1994, pp. 13–16.
3. Ibid.
4. United Nations Environment Programme, *Environmental Auditing*, Technical Report Series No. 2 (Paris: United Nations Environmental Programme, 1990).

APPENDIX: U.S. ENVIRONMENTAL PROTECTION AGENCY ENVIRONMENTAL AUDITING POLICY STATEMENT

SUMMARY

It is EPA policy to encourage the use of environmental auditing by regulated entities to help achieve and maintain compliance with environmental laws and regulations, as well as to help identify and correct unregulated environmental hazards. EPA first published this policy as interim guidance on November 8, 1985 (50 FR 46504). Based on comments received regarding the interim guidance, the Agency is issuing today's final policy statement with only minor changes.

This final policy statement specifically:

- encourages regulated entities to develop, implement and upgrade environmental auditing programs;
- discusses when the agency may or may not request audit reports;
- explains how EPA's inspection and enforcement activities may respond to regulated entities' efforts to assure compliance through auditing;
- endorses environmental auditing at federal facilities;
- encourages state and local environmental auditing initiatives; and
- outlines elements of effective audit programs.

Federal Register, 51(131) (July 9, 1986): pp. 25004–25010.

Environmental auditing includes a variety of compliance assessment techniques which go beyond those legally required and are used to identify actual and potential environmental problems. Effective environmental auditing can lead to higher levels of overall compliance and reduced risk to human health and the environment. EPA endorses the practice of environmental auditing and supports its accelerated use by regulated entities to help meet the goals of federal, state and local environmental requirements. However the existence of an auditing program does not create any defense to, or otherwise limit, the responsibility of any regulated entity to comply with applicable regulatory requirements.

States are encouraged to adopt these or similar and equally effective policies in order to advance the use of environmental auditing on a consistent nationwide basis.

Dates: This final policy statement is effective July 9, 1986.
For further information contact: Leonard Fleckenstein, Office of Policy Planning and Evaluation (202) 382-2726 or Cheryl Wasserman, Office of Enforcement and Compliance Monitoring (202) 382-7550.

SUPPLEMENTARY INFORMATION

I. PREAMBLE

On November 8, 1985 EPA published an Environmental Auditing Policy Statement, effective as interim guidance, and solicited written comments until January 7, 1986.

Thirteen commenters submitted written comments. Eight were from private industry. Two commenters represented industry trade associations. One federal agency, one consulting firm and one law firm also submitted comments.

Twelve commenters addressed EPA requests for audit reports. Three comments per subject were received regarding inspections enforcement response and elements of effective environmental auditing. One commenter addressed audit provisions as remedies in enforcement actions, one addressed environmental auditing at federal facilities, and one addressed the relationship of the policy statement to state or local regulatory agencies. Comments generally supported both the concept of a policy statement and the interim guidance, but raised specific concerns with respect to particular language and policy issued in sections of the guidance.

General Comments

Three commenters found the interim guidance to be constructive, balanced and effective at encouraging more and better environmental auditing.

Another commenter, while considering the policy on the whole to be constructive felt that new and identifiable auditing "incentives" should be offered by EPA. Based on earlier comments received from industry, EPA believes most companies would not support or participate in an "incentives-based" environmental auditing program with EPA. Moreover, general promises to forgo inspections or reduce enforcement responses in exchange for companies' adoption of environmental auditing programs — the "incentives" most frequently mentioned in this context — are fraught with legal and policy obstacles.

Several commenters expressed concern that states or localities might use the interim guidance to require auditing. The Agency disagrees that the policy statement opens the way for states and localities to require auditing. No EPA policy can grant states or localities any more (or less) authority than they already possess. EPA believes that the interim guidance effectively encourages voluntary auditing. In fact, Section II.B of the policy states: "because audit quality depends to a large degree on genuine management commitment to the program and its objectives, auditing should remain a voluntary program."

Another commenter suggested that EPA should not expect an audit to identify all potential problem areas or conclude that a problem identified in an audit reflects normal operations and procedures. EPA agrees that an audit report should clearly reflect these realities and should be written to point out the audit's limitations. However, since EPA will not routinely request audit reports, the Agency does not believe these concerns raise issues which need to be addressed in the policy statement.

A second concern expressed by the same commenter was that EPA should acknowledge that environmental audits are only part of a successful environmental management program and thus should not be expected to cover every environmental issue or solve all problems. EPA agrees and accordingly has amended the statement of purpose which appears at the end of the preamble.

Yet another commenter thought EPA should focus on environmental performance results (compliance or non-compliance), not on the processes or vehicles used to achieve those results. In general, EPA agreed with this statement and will continue to focus on environmental results. However, EPA also believes that such results can be improved through Agency efforts to identify and encourage effective environmental management practices and will continue to encourage such practices in non-regulatory ways.

A final general comment recommended that EPA should sponsor seminars for small businesses on how to start auditing programs. EPA agrees that such seminars would be useful. However, since audit seminars already are available from several private sector organizations, EPA does not believe it should intervene in that market with the possible exception of seminars for government agencies, especially federal agencies, for which EPA has a broad mandate under Executive Order 12068 to provide technical assistance for environmental compliance.

Requests for Reports

EPA received 12 comments regarding Agency requests for environmental audit reports, far more than on any other topic in the policy statement. One commenter felt that EPA struck an appropriate balance between respecting the need for self-evaluation with some measure of privacy, and allowing the Agency enough flexibility of inquiry to accomplish future statutory missions. However, most commenters expressed concern that the interim guidance did not go far enough to assuage corporate fears that EPA will use audit report for environmental compliance "witch hunts." Several commenters suggested additional specific assurances regarding the circumstances under which EPA will request such reports.

One commenter recommended that EPA request audit reports only "when the Agency can show the information it needs to perform its statutory mission cannot be obtained from the monitoring, compliance or other data that is otherwise reportable and/or accessible to EPA or where the Government deems an audit report material to a criminal investigation." EPA accepts this recommendation in part. The Agency believes it would not be in the best interest of human health and the environment to commit to making a "showing" of a compelling information need before ever requesting an audit report. While EPA may normally be willing to do so, the Agency cannot rule out in advance all circumstances in which such a showing may not be possible. However, it would be helpful to further clarify that a request for an audit report or a portion of a report normally will be made when needed information is not available by alternative means. Therefore, EPA has revised Section III.A, paragraph two and added the phrase: "and usually made where the information needed cannot be obtained from monitoring, reporting or other data otherwise available to the Agency."

Another commenter suggested that (except in the case of criminal investigations) EPA should limit requests for audit documents to specific questions. By including the phrase "or relevant portions of a report" in Section III.A, EPA meant to emphasize it would not request an entire audit document when only a relevant portion would suffice. Likewise, EPA fully intends not to request even a portion of a report if needed information or data can be otherwise obtained. To further clarify this point EPA has added the phrase "most likely focused on particular information need rather than the entire report" to the second sentence of paragraph two, Section III.A. Incorporating the two comments above, the first two sentences in paragraph two of final Section III.A now read: "EPA's authority to request an audit report, or relevant portions thereof, will be exercised on a case-by-case basis where the Agency determines it is needed to accomplish a statutory mission or the Government deems it to be material to a criminal investigation. EPA expects such requests to be limited, most likely focused on particular information needs rather than the entire report, and usually made where the information needed cannot be obtained from monitoring, reporting or other data otherwise available to the Agency."

Other commenters recommended that EPA not request audit reports under any circumstances, that requests be "restricted to only those legally required," that requests be limited to criminal investigations, or that requests be made only when EPA has reason to believe "that the audit programs or reports are being used to conceal evidence of environmental non-compliance or otherwise being used in bad faith." EPA appreciates concerns underlying all of these comments and has considered each carefully. However the Agency believes that these recommendations do not strike the appropriate balance between retaining the flexibility to accomplish EPA's statutory missions in future, unforeseen circumstances and acknowledging regulated entities' need to self-evaluate environmental performance with some measure of privacy. Indeed, based on prime informal comments, the small number of comments received and the even smaller number of adverse comments, EPA believes the final policy statement should remain largely unchanged from the interim version.

Elements of Effective Environmental Auditing

Three commenters expressed concerns regarding the seven general elements EPA outlined in the Appendix to the interim guidance.

One commenter noted that were EPA to further expand or more fully detail such elements, programs not specifically fulfilling each element would then be judged inadequate. EPA agrees that presenting highly specific and prescriptive auditing elements could be counter-productive by not taking into account numerous factors which vary extensively from one organization to another, but which may still result in effective auditing programs.

Accordingly, EPA does not plan to expand or more fully detail these auditing elements.

Another commenter asserted that states and localities should be cautioned not to consider EPA's auditing elements as mandatory steps. The Agency is fully aware of this concern and in the interim guidance noted its strong opinion that "regulatory agencies should not attempt to prescribe the precise form and structure of regulated entities' environmental management or auditing programs." While EPA cannot require state or local regulators to adopt this or similar policies, the Agency does strongly encourage them to do so, both in the interim and final policies.

A final commenter thought the Appendix too specifically prescribed what should and what should not be included in an auditing program. Other commenters, on the other hand, viewed the elements described as very general in nature. EPA agrees with these other commenters. The elements are in no way binding. Moreover, EPA believes that most mature, effective environmental auditing programs do incorporate each of these general elements in some form, and considers them useful yardsticks for those considering adopting or upgrading audit programs. For these reasons EPA has not revised the Appendix in today's final policy statement.

Other Comments

Other significant comments addressed EPA inspection priorities for, and enforcement responses to, organizations with environmental auditing programs.

One commenter, stressing that audit programs are internal management tools, took exception to the phrase in the second paragraph of Section III.B.1 of the interim guidance which states that environmental audits can "complement" regulatory oversight. By using the word "complement" in this context, EPA does not intend to imply that audit reports must be obtained by the agency in order to supplement regu-latory inspections. "Complement" is used in a broad sense of being in addition to inspections and providing something (i.e. self-assessment) which otherwise would be lacking. To clarify this point EPA has added the phrase "by providing self-assessment to assure compliance" after "environmental audits may complement inspections" in this paragraph.

The same commenter also expressed concern that, as EPA sets inspection priorities, a company having an audit program could appear to be a "poor performer" due to complete and accurate reporting when measured against a company which reports something less than required by law. EPA agrees that it is important to communicate this fact to Agency and state personnel, and will do so. However, the Agency does not believe a change in the policy statement is necessary.

A further comment suggested EPA should commit to take auditing programs into account when assessing all enforcement actions. However, in order to maintain enforcement flexibility under varied circumstances, the Agency cannot promise reduced enforcement responses to violations at all audited facilities when other factors may be overriding. Therefore the policy statement continues to state that EPA may exercise its discretion to consider auditing programs as evidence of honest and genuine efforts to assure compliance, which would then be taken into account in fashioning enforcement response to violations.

A final commenter suggested the phrase "expeditiously correct environmental problems" not be used in the enforcement context since it implied EPA would use an entity's record of correcting nonregulated matters when evaluating regulatory violations. EPA did not intend for such an inference to be made. EPA intended the term "environmental problems" to refer to the underlying circumstances which eventually lead up to the violations. To clarify this point, EPA is revising the first two sentences of the paragraph to which this comment refers by changing "environmental problems" to "violations and underlying environmental problems" in the first sentence and to "underlying environmental problems" in the second sentence.

In a separate development EPA is preparing an update of its January 1984 *Federal Facilities Compliance Strategy*, which is referenced in Section III.C of the auditing policy. The Strategy should be completed and available on request from EPA's Office of Federal Activities later this year.

EPA thanks all commenters for responding to the November 8, 1985 publication. Today's notice is being issued to inform regulated entities and the public of EPA's final policy toward environmental auditing. This policy was developed to help (a) encourage regulated entities to institutionalize effective audit practices as one means of improving compliance and sound environmental management, and (b) guide internal EPA actions directly related to regulated entities' environmental auditing programs.

EPA will evaluate implementation of this final policy to ensure it meets the above goals and continues to encourage better environmental management while strengthening the Agency's own efforts to monitor and enforce compliance with environmental requirements.

II. GENERAL EPA POLICY ON ENVIRONMENTAL AUDITING

A. Introduction

Environmental auditing is a systematic documented periodic and objective review by regulated entities[1] of facility operations and practices related to meeting environmental requirements. Audits can be designed to accomplish any or all of the following: verify compliance with environmental requirements; evaluate the effectiveness of environmental management systems already in place; or assess risk from regulated and unregulated materials and practices.

Auditing serves as a quality assurance check to help improve the effectiveness of basic environmental management by verifying that

---

[1]Regulated entities include private firms and public agencies with facilities subject to environmental regulations. Public agencies can include federal, state or local agencies as well as special purpose organizations such as regional sewage commissions.

management practices are in place, functioning and adequate. Environmental audits evaluate, and are not a substitute for, direct compliance activities such as obtaining permits, installing controls, monitoring compliance, reporting violations, and keeping records. Environmental auditing may verify but does not include activities required by law, regulation or permit (e.g. continuous emissions monitoring, composite correction plans at waste water treatment plants, etc.). Audits do not in any way replace regulatory agency inspections. However environmental audits can improve compliance by complementing conventional federal, state and local oversight.

The Appendix to this policy statement outlines some basic elements of environmental auditing (e.g. auditor independence and top management support) for use by those considering implementation of effective auditing programs to help achieve and maintain compliance. Additional information on environmental auditing practices can be found in various published materials.[2]

Environmental auditing has developed for sound business reasons, particularly as a means of helping regulated entities manage pollution control affirmatively over time instead of reacting to curses. Auditing can result in improved facility environmental performance, help communicate effective solutions to common environmental problems, focus facility managers' attention on current and upcoming regulatory requirements and generate protocols and checklists which help facilities better manage themselves. Auditing also can result in better-integrated management of environmental hazards, since auditors frequently identify environmental liabilities which go beyond regulatory compliance. Companies, public entities and federal facilities have employed a variety of environmental auditing practices in recent years. Several hundred major firms in diverse industries now have environmental auditing programs, although they often are known by other names such as assessment survey, surveillance, review or appraisal.

While auditing has demonstrated its usefulness to those with audit programs many others still do not audit. Clarification of EPA's position regarding auditing may help encourage regulated entities to establish audit programs or upgrade systems already in place.

B. EPA Encourages the Use of Environmental Auditing

EPA encourages regulated entities to adopt sound environmental management practices to improve environmental performance. In

---

[2]See, e.g., "Current Practices in Environmental Auditing," EPA Report No. EPA-230-09-83-006, February 1984; "Annotated Bibliography on Environmental Auditing," Fifth Edition, September 1985, both available from: Regulatory Reform Staff, PM-223, EPA, 401 M. Street SW, Washington, DC 20460.

particular, EPA encourages regulated entities subject to environmental regulations to institute environmental auditing programs to help ensure the adequacy of internal systems to achieve, maintain and monitor compliance. Implementation of environmental auditing programs can result in better identification, resolution and avoidance of environmental problems, as well as improvements to management practices. Audits can be conducted effectively by independent internal or third party auditors. Large organizations generally have greater resources to devote to an internal audit team, while smaller entities might be more likely to use outside auditors. Regulated entities are responsible for taking all necessary steps to ensure compliance with environmental requirements, whether or not they adopt audit programs. Although environmental laws do not require a regulated facility to have an auditing program, ultimate responsibility for the environmental performance of the facility lies with top management, which therefore has a strong incentive to use reasonable means, such as environmental auditing, to secure reliable information of facility compliance status.

EPA does not intend to dictate or interfere with the environmental management practices of private or public organizations. Nor does EPA intend to mandate auditing (though in certain instances EPA may seek to include provisions for environmental auditing as part of settlement agreements, as noted below). Because environmental auditing systems have been widely adopted on a voluntary basis in the past, and because audit quality depends to a large degree upon genuine management commitment to the program and its objectives, auditing should remain a voluntary activity.

III. EPA POLICY ON SPECIFIC ENVIRONMENTAL AUDITING ISSUES

A. Agency Requests for Audit Reports

EPA has broad statutory authority to request relevant information on the environmental compliance status of regulated entities. However, EPA believes routine Agency requests for audit reports[3] could inhibit auditing in the long run, decreasing both the quantity and quality of audits conducted. Therefore, as a matter of policy, EPA will not routinely request environmental audit reports.

---

[3]An "environmental audit report" is a written report which candidly and thoroughly presents findings from a review, conducted as part of an environmental audit as described in section II.A., of facility environmental performance and practices. An audit report is not a substitute for compliance monitoring reports or other reports or records which may be required by EPA or other regulatory agencies.

EPA's authority to request an audit report, or relevant portions thereof, will be exercised on a case-by-case basis where the Agency determines it is needed to accomplish a statutory mission, or where the Government deems it to be material to a criminal investigation. EPA expects such request to be limited, most likely focused on particular information needs rather than the entire report, and usually made where the information needed cannot be obtained from monitoring, reporting or other data otherwise available to the Agency. Examples would likely include situations where audits are conducted under consent decrees or other settlement agreements; a company has placed its management practices at issue by raising them as defence; or state of mind or intent are a relevant element of inquiry such as during a criminal investigation. This list is illustrative rather than exhaustive since there doubtless will be other situations, not subject to prediction, in which audit reports rather than information may be required.

EPA acknowledges regulated entities' need to self-evaluate environmental performance with some measure of privacy and encourages such activity. However, audit reports may not shield monitoring, compliance, or other information that would otherwise be reportable and/or accessible to EPA, even if there is no explicit "requirement" to generate that data.[4] Thus, this policy does not alter regulated entities' existing or future obligations to monitor, record or report information required under environmental statutes, regulations or permits, or to allow EPA access to that information. Nor does this policy alter EPA's authority to request and receive any relevant information — including that contained in audit reports — under various environmental statutes (e.g. Clean Water Act Section 308, Clean Air Act Sections 114 and 208) or in other administrative or judicial proceedings.

Regulated entities also should be aware that certain audit findings may by law have to be reported to government agencies. However, in addition to any such requirements, EPA encourages regulated entities to notify appropriate State or Federal Officials of findings which suggest significant environmental or public health risks, even when not specifically required to do so.

B. EPA Response to Environmental Auditing

1. General Policy

EPA will not promise to forgo inspections, reduce enforcement response, or offer other such incentives in exchange for implementation

---

[4]See, for example, "Duties to Report or Disclose Information on the Environmental Aspects of Business Activities," Environmental Law Institute report to EPA, final report, September 1985.

of environmental auditing or other sound environmental management practices. Indeed, a credible enforcement program provides a strong incentive for regulated entities to audit.

Regulatory agencies have an obligation to assess source compliance status independently and cannot eliminate inspections for particular firms or classes of firms. Although environmental audits may complement inspections by providing self-assessment to assure compliance, they are in no way a substitute for regulatory oversight. Moreover, certain statutes (e.g. RCRA) and Agency policies establish minimum facility inspection frequencies to which EPA will adhere.

However EPA will continue to address environmental problems on a priority basis and will consequently inspect facilities with poor environmental records and practices more frequently. Since effective environmental auditing helps management identify and promptly correct actual or potential problems, audited facilities, environmental performance should improve. Thus, while EPA inspections of self-audited facilities will continue, to the extent that compliance performance is considered in setting inspection priorities, facilities with a good compliance history may be subject to fewer inspections.

In fashioning enforcement responses to violations, EPA policy is to take into account, on a case-by-case basis, the honest and genuine efforts of regulated entities to avoid and promptly correct violations and underlying environmental problems. When regulated entities take reasonable precautions to avoid non-compliance, expeditiously correct underlying environmental problems discovered through audits or other means, and implement measures to prevent their recurrence. EPA may exercise its discretion to consider such actions as honest and genuine efforts to assure compliance. Such consideration applies particularly when a regulated entity promptly reports violations or compliance data which otherwise were not required to be recorded or reported to EPA.

2. Audit Provisions as Remedies in Enforcement Actions

EPA may propose environmental auditing provisions in consent decrees and in other settlement negotiations where auditing could provide a remedy for identified problems and reduce the likelihood of similar problems recurring in the future.[5] Environmental auditing provisions are most likely to be proposed in settlement negotiations where:

* a pattern of violations can be attributed at least in part, to the absence or poor functioning of an environmental management system; or

---

[5]EPA is developing guidance for use by Agency negotiators in structuring appropriate environmental audit provisions for consent decrees and other settlement negotiations.

- the type or nature of violations indicates a likelihood that similar non-compliance problems may exist or occur elsewhere in the facility or at other facilities operated by the regulated entity.

Through this consent decree approach and other means, EPA may consider how to encourage effective auditing by publicly owned sewage treatment works (POTWs). POTWs often have compliance problems related to operation and maintenance procedures which can be addressed effectively through the use of environmental auditing. Under its National Municipal Policy EPA already is requiring many POTWs to develop composite correction plans to identify and correct compliance problems.

C. Environmental Auditing of Federal Facilities

EPA encourages all federal agencies subject to environmental laws and regulations to institute environmental auditing systems to help ensure the adequacy of internal systems to achieve, maintain and monitor compliance. Environmental auditing at federal facilities can be an effective supplement to EPA and state inspections. Such federal facility environmental audit programs should be structured to promptly identify environmental problems and expeditiously develop schedules for remedial action.

To the extent feasible, EPA will provide technical assistance to help federal agencies design and initiate audit programs. Where appropriate, EPA will enter into agreements with other agencies to clarify the respective roles, responsibilities and commitments of each agency in conducting and responding to federal facility environmental audits.

With respect to inspections of self-audited facilities (see Section III.B.1 above) and requests for audit reports (see Section III.A above), EPA generally will respond to environmental audits by federal facilities in the same manner as it does for other regulated entities, in keeping with the spirit and intent of Executive Order 12088 and the EPA *Federal Facilities Compliance Strategy* (January 1984, update forthcoming in late 1986). Federal agencies should, however, be aware that the Freedom of Information Act will govern any disclosure of audits reports or audit-generated information requested from federal agencies by the public.

When federal agencies discover significant violations through an environmental audit, EPA encourages them to submit the related audit finding and remedial action plans expeditiously to the applicable EPA regional office (and responsible state agencies, where appropriate) even when not specifically required to do so. EPA will review the auditing findings and action plans and either provide written approval or negotiate a Federal Facilities Compliance Agreement. EPA will utilize the escalation procedures provided in Executive Order 12088 and the

EPA *Federal Facilities Compliance Strategy* only when agreement between agencies cannot be reached. In any event, federal agencies are expected to report pollution abatement projects involving costs (necessary to correct problems discovered through the audit) to EPA in accordance with OMB Circular A-106. Upon request and in appropriate circumstances, EPA will assist affected federal agencies through coordination of any public release of audit findings with approved action plans once agreement has been reached.

IV. RELATIONSHIP TO STATE OR LOCAL REGULATORY AGENCIES

State and local regulatory agencies have independent jurisdiction over regulated entities. EPA encourages them to adopt these or similar policies, in order to advance the use of effective environmental auditing in a consistent manner.

EPA recognizes that some states have already undertaken environmental auditing initiatives which differ somewhat from this policy. Other states also may want to develop auditing policies which accommodate their particular needs or circumstances. Nothing in this policy statement is intended to preempt or preclude states from developing other approaches to environmental auditing. EPA encourages state and local authorities to consider the basic principles which guided the Agency in developing this policy:

- Regulated entities must continue to report or record compliance information required under existing statutes or regulations, regardless of whether such information is generated by an environmental audit or contained in an audit report. Required information cannot be withheld merely because it is generated by an audit rather than by some other means.

- Regulatory agencies cannot make promises to forgo or limit enforcement action against a particular facility or class of facilities in exchange for the use of environmental auditing systems. However, such agencies may use their discretion to adjust enforcement actions on a case-by-case basis in response to honest and genuine efforts by regulated entities to assure environmental compliance.

- When setting inspection priorities regulatory agencies should focus to the extent possible on compliance performance and environmental results.

- Regulatory agencies must continue to meet minimum program requirements (e.g., minimum inspection requirements, etc.).

- Regulatory agencies should not attempt to prescribe the precise form and structure of regulated entities' environmental management or auditing programs.

An effective state/federal partnership is needed to accomplish the mutual goal of achieving and maintaining high levels of compliance with environmental laws and regulations. The greater the consistency between state or local policies and this federal response to environmental auditing, the greater the degree to which sound auditing practices might be adopted and compliance levels improve.

Dated: June 28, 1986
Lee M. Thomas
Administrator

APPENDIX — ELEMENTS OF EFFECTIVE ENVIRONMENTAL AUDITING PROGRAMS

INTRODUCTION

Environmental auditing is a systematic, documented, periodic and objective review by a regulated entity of facility operations and practices related to meeting environmental requirements.

Private sector environmental audits of facilities have been conducted for several years and have taken a variety of forms, in part to accommodate unique organizational structures and circumstances. Nevertheless, effective environmental audits appear to have certain discernible elements in common with other kinds of audits. Standards for internal audits have been documented extensively. The elements outlined below draw heavily on two of these documents: "Compendium of Audit Standards" (©1983, Walter Willborn, American Society for Quality Control) and "Standards for the Professional Practice of Internal Auditing" (©1981, The Institute of Internal Auditors, Inc.). They also reflect Agency analyses conducted over the last several years.

Performance-oriented auditing elements are outlined here to help accomplish several objectives. A general description of features of effective, mature audit programs can help those starting audit programs, especially federal agencies and smaller businesses. These elements also indicate the attributes of auditing EPA generally considers important to ensure program effectiveness. Regulatory agencies may use these elements in negotiating environmental auditing provisions for consent decrees. Finally, these elements can help guide states and localities considering auditing initiatives.

An effective environmental auditing system will likely include the following general elements:

I. *Explicit top management support for environmental auditing and commitment to follow-up on audit findings.* Management support may be demonstrated by a written policy articulating upper management support for the auditing program, and for compliance with all pertinent requirements, including corporate policies and permit requirements as well as federal, state and local statutes and regulations.

Management support for the auditing program also should be demonstrated by an explicit written commitment to follow up on audit findings to correct identified problems and prevent their recurrence.

II. *An environmental auditing function independent of audited activities.* The status or organizational locus of environmental auditors should be sufficient to ensure objective and unobstructed inquiry, observation and testing. Auditor objectivity should not be impaired by personal relationships, financial or other conflicts of interest, interference with free inquiry or judgement or fear of potential retribution.

III. *Adequate team staffing and auditor training.* Environmental auditors should possess or have ready access to the knowledge, skills and disciplines needed to accomplish audit objectives. Each individual auditor should comply with the company's professional standards of conduct. Auditors, whether full-time or part-time, should maintain their technical and analytical competence through continuing education and training.

IV. *Explicit audit program objectives, scope, resources and frequency.* At a minimum, audit objectives should include assessing compliance with applicable environmental laws and evaluating the adequacy of internal compliance policies, procedures and personnel training programs to ensure continued compliance.

Audits should be based on a process which provides auditors: all corporate policies, permits, and federal, state and local regulations pertinent to the facility; and checklists or protocols addressing specific features that should be evaluated by auditors.

Explicit written audit procedures generally should be used for planning audits, establishing audit scope, examining and evaluating audit findings, communicating audit results, and following up.

V. *A process which collects, analyzes, interprets and documents information sufficient to achieve audit objectives.* Information should be collected before and during an on-site visit regarding environmental compliance (1), environmental management effectiveness (2), and other matters (3) related to audit objectives and scope. This information should be sufficient, reliable, relevant and useful to provide a sound basis for audit findings and recommendations.

a. *Sufficient* information is factual, adequate and convincing so that a prudent, informed person would be likely to reach the same conclusions as the auditor.

b. *Reliable* information is the best attainable through use of appropriate audit techniques.

c. *Relevant* information supports audit findings and recommendations and is consistent with the objectives for the audit.

d. *Useful* information helps the organization meet its goals.

The audit process should include a periodic review of the reliability and integrity of this information and the means used to identify, measure, classify and report it. Audit procedures, including the testing and sampling techniques employed, should be selected in advance, to the extent practical, and expanded or altered if circumstances warrant. The process of collecting, analyzing, interpreting and documenting information should provide reasonable assurance that audit objectivity is maintained and audit goals are met.

VI. *A process which includes specific procedures to promptly prepare candid, clear and appropriate written reports on audit findings, corrective actions, and schedules for implementation.* Procedures should be in place to ensure that such information is communicated to managers, including facility and corporate management, who can evaluate the information and ensure correction of identified problems.

Procedures also should be in place for determining what internal findings are reportable to state or federal agencies.

VII. *A process which includes quality assurance procedures to assure the accuracy and thoroughness of environmental audits.* Quality assurance may be accomplished through supervision, independent internal reviews, external reviews or a combination of these approaches.

FOOTNOTES TO APPENDIX

(1) A comprehensive assessment of compliance with federal environmental regulations requires an analysis of facility performance against numerous environmental statutes and implementing regulations. These statutes include:

> Resource Conservation and Recovery Act
> Federal Water Pollution Control Act
> Clean Air Act
> Hazardous Materials Transportation Act
> Toxic Substances Control Act
> Comprehensive Environmental Response, Compensation and Liability Act
> Safe Drinking Water Act
> Federal Insecticide, Fungicide and Rodenticide Act
> Marine Protection, Research and Sanctuaries Act
> Uranium Mill Tailings Radiation Control Act

In addition, state and local governments are likely to have their own environmental laws. Many states have been delegated authority to administer federal programs. Many local governments' building fire safety and health codes also have environmental requirements relevant to an audit evaluation.

(2) An environmental audit could go well beyond the type of compliance assessment normally conducted during regulatory inspections, for example, by evaluating policies and practices, regardless of whether they are part of the environmental systems or the operating and

maintenance procedures. Specifically, audits can evaluate the extent to which systems or procedures:

1. Develop organizational environmental policies which: a. implement regulatory requirements; b. provide management guidance for environmental hazards not specifically addressed in regulations;

2. Train and motivate facility personnel to work in an environmentally acceptable manner and to understand and comply with government regulations and the entity's environmental policy;

3. Communicate relevant environmental developments expeditiously to facility and other personnel;

4. Communicate effectively with government and the public regarding serious environmental incidents;

5. Require third parties working for, with or on behalf of the organization to follow its environmental procedures;

6. Make proficient personnel available at all times to carry out environmental (especially emergency) procedures;

7. Incorporate environmental protection into written operating procedures;

8. Apply best management practices and operating procedures, including "good housekeeping" techniques;

9. Institute preventive and corrective maintenance systems to minimize actual and potential environmental harm;

10. Utilize best available process and control technologies;

11. Use most-effective sampling and monitoring techniques, test methods, recordkeeping systems or reporting protocols (beyond minimum legal requirements);

12. Evaluate causes behind any serious environmental incidents and establish procedures to avoid recurrence;

13. Exploit source reduction, recycle and reuse potential wherever practical; and

14. Substitute materials or processes to allow use of the least-hazardous substances feasible.

(3) Auditors could also assess environmental risks and uncertainties.

14

Benchmarking for
Green Excellence

American corporations are constantly facing changing competitive challenges. Cost reduction was the major competitive challenge during the 1960s. Demonstrating flexibility in responding to changing customer demands and specifications became the competitive weapon of the 1970s. Quality was the watchword of the 1980s. The world has now entered an era of environmentalism, the tools of which are zero discharge and total pollution management. Increasing public pressures, skyrocketing cleanup costs, rising criminal and civil liabilities, and stringent laws and regulations are making environmental excellence the top priority of corporate management. Not only are corporations spending billions of dollars to clean up the wastes they have generated, they are also paying for materials, labor, equipment, and other resources that generate these wastes. As was noted in Chapter 5, Robert Ayres conservatively estimated that only 6 percent of the 20,000 pounds of material extracted per person each year in the United States can be found in durable products; the remaining 94 percent are discarded as waste within a few months following their extraction.[1] Pollution reduction can not only eliminate waste-disposal costs but also substantially reduce the labor, material, and equipment costs that pay for the production of these gargantuan amounts of waste. According to recent data, the United States generates almost 230 times as much hazardous waste per capita as Japan and 23 times as much as Germany.[2] Therefore, if U.S. industries are to remain internationally competitive they must significantly reduce the pollutants they generate. Benchmarking is one of the techniques that can help industries to reduce pollution.

BENCHMARKING

The purpose of benchmarking is to inspire performance improvement by comparing a company's performance in terms of products, processes, methods, organization, and practices with companies that excel in these areas. Competitive intelligence gathering focuses on competitors. The goal of benchmarking is to identify performance shortfalls in comparison with companies that excel in a particular function and to take corrective actions to outperform them. Benchmarking achieves this by comparing and copying operations, products, and services both within and outside the company's primary industry.

Benchmarking helps companies to develop performance goals. It exposes companies to different operations, products, and services and provides ways to improve their own performance. The steps in the benchmarking process are as follows:

Obtain top management commitment for benchmarking.

Form a top management committee for benchmarking.

Identify functions to benchmark.

Form a mini-team to benchmark that function.

Train team members in benchmarking methodology.

Identify the best-in-the-class company in that function.

Select key performance measures for that function and establish current levels of performance.

Collect data.

Compare the performances and set goals to achieve.

Discuss the findings with the top management committee.

Develop and implement action plans.

Audit the implementation.

IDENTIFYING FUNCTIONS TO BENCHMARK

Scarce resources make identifying functions for benchmarking a critical step. The increasing variety of available materials, efficient processes, and the plethora of laws and regulations have made the selection of areas for environmental benchmarking a long and expensive process. Such regulatory requirements as fuel efficiency, building codes, tamper-proof packaging, and safety guidelines are already putting considerable restraints on the design, processes, and practices in a company. Some factors that need to be considered when deciding which functions should be benchmarked include the need to comply with the existing and future environmental laws, regulations, and licenses; waste treatment and disposal costs; potential environmental and safety liability; quantity of waste generated; properties such as toxicity, corrosivity, reactivity, and flammability of the wastes generated; effect of the waste on the employees and surrounding communities; cost-reduction potential of the waste elimination; recyclability of expensive material; low-yield process; and bottleneck process, which restricts the total output. Any function of business including products, processes, and strategies can be selected for benchmarking. Some specific areas for benchmarking include waste reduction, waste accounting, legal compliance, training, green information system, green performance measurement and reporting system, recycling, auditing, employee policies, injury and illness minimization, energy consumption, elimination of a hazardous chemical, the transporting of waste, public relations, communication, capital expenditure analysis, investor relations, and emergency planning.

TRAINING

To be successful, the benchmarking process requires well trained personnel. The type and nature of training will depend on the qualifications and experience of the individuals. However, everyone must at least have a rudimentary understanding of benchmarking methodology. In addition, team members should be knowledgeable about waste-reduction strategies, they should be technically trained, and they should have the ability to conduct interviews with personnel who come from a variety of technical and employment backgrounds. A solid benchmarking training program should encompass the outlined topics that follow.

Benchmarking methodology[3]
Company policies and standards
Introduction to federal, state, and local laws and regulations (see
    Chapter 3)
Waste-reduction strategies (see Chapter 6)
    Improving operating practices
    Redesigning products
    Substituting materials
    Changing processes
    Installing new equipment
    Separating wastes
    Concentrating wastes
    On-plant recovery
    Off-plant recovery
    Treatment and disposal
Pollution-reduction technologies
Data collection and analysis tools (see Chapter 12)
    Process flow diagrams
    Energy and material balance
    Brainstorming
    Flow chart
    Scatter diagrams
    Cause-and-effect diagrams

Run sheet
Pareto analysis
Histograms
Green circles
Typical wastes generated in the company and their properties
Community relations and emergency planning

SELECTING A PARTNER FOR BENCHMARKING

A benchmarking partner need not always be an outside organization. A department can benchmark against the same department of a company at another location. 3M, Dow Chemical, Procter & Gamble, Colgate Palmolive, AT&T, Browning-Ferris Industries, Boeing, DuPont, Texaco, Xerox, Alcoa, Polaroid, and Eli Lilly are some companies considered to be an excellent choice for benchmarking. However, these companies might not be willing to be partners for benchmarking for all organizations. Therefore, companies must perform extensive investigations to identify potential partners by which to evaluate their own performance. Criteria for selection may include company culture, sales volume, profitability, industry type, company location, process characteristics, green accomplishments, and waste complexity. The first step in identifying a potential partner is to determine what information resources are available. Several databases can provide information on pollution indicators. A database maintained by the EPA provides plant-level information about hazardous waste generated by various companies. However, special care should be taken not to be misled by quantities of waste generated by these companies. The chemical industry, for example, generates significant quantities of waste. Consequently, companies like DuPont, Monsanto, and American Cyanamid are among the top industrial waste generators in the United States. However, these companies have also demonstrated superb environmental practices. Companies that have received awards and citations are potential partners. Information resources are numerous and include consultants, sales forces, customers, annual reports, trade journals, industry associations, on-line databases (e.g., the Dow-Jones News Retrieval Service or the Toxic Release Inventory Data Base), government sources (e.g., *U.S. Industrial Outlook*, National Technical Information Service, U.S. Annual Survey of Manufacturers, congressional hearings, court reports, EPA and OECD reports, Council on Environmental Quality annual reports, state and local emergency planning reports, *The Citizen's Fund Report*, and *The State's Round Table*), analysts' reports, and directories (e.g., *Business Rankings, Findex: The Directory of Market Research Reports, Studies and Surveys, IRRC's Corporate Environmental Profiles Directory, Chemical Week*, and *Kline Guide to the Chemical Industry*). In addition, data on the environmental performance of various companies are available from several sources. Government agencies report on the hazardous waste cleanup responsibilities of the Superfund national priority list corrective actions, whether a company has been denied an RCRA permit, and whether a company is a potentially responsible party for a site under the Site Enforcement Tracking System. Other data that can be obtained from these agencies are contained in air permit files and inspection and litigation reports, the National Pollution Discharge Elimination Systems file, water quality data files, and sewage treatment plant surveys. Information on the number of minerals management service facility shut-ins, TRI chemical emissions, chemical spills reported, company compliance with various environmental statutes, and the penalties under those statutes is all readily available. Company reports are also a good source of information on environmental programs, policies, achievements, goals, and proxy activity. Form 10-K filings are particularly relevant. Newspapers, too, can supply useful information.

COLLECTING AND ANALYZING DATA

Collecting data involves time and should be well planned. Amounts of waste generated, processes responsible for these wastes, physical properties of the wastes, efficiency of each of the processes, and so on are some of the data that need to be collected. Specific data that are useful in benchmarking include

design information (e.g., process flow diagrams),

environmental information (e.g., hazardous wastes generated, environmental audit reports, spill prevention plans),

material information (e.g., health effects, whether material is carcinogenic, ozone depleting, etc.),

economic information (e.g., treatment and disposal costs, product costs, product yields, maintenance costs),

organizational information (e.g., environmental policy, standard operating procedures, organizational charts, accounting systems, reward and recognition processes, training programs).

When it is possible to generate data using material and energy balance principles, then it is not necessary to resort to benchmarking. However, companies may need to benchmark unstructured activities such as reduction of spills, avoidance of accidents, and so on. Talking with employees involved in the operations can provide valuable information. If the benchmarking partner is agreeable, photographs of the plant should be taken. Particular attention should be paid to housekeeping aspects of the operation. Administrative controls such as accounting and organizational structure of the plant should also be studied.

The data collected must be analyzed, the purpose of which is to generate goals and options. Every time a company is studied, practices followed by that company should be critically reviewed. Benefits gained by copying a particular practice should be reviewed in terms of costs, compliance, reduction in liability, and workplace safety. Analysis should focus on every stage of a product's life cycle rather than on a particular phase of its development.

ENVIRONMENTAL PERFORMANCE MEASUREMENTS

If performance cannot be measured, it cannot be improved. Performance should be measured over a period of time so that trends can be monitored. Measurements should be simple so that they can be easily understood by everyone. Performance measurement should be done for each functional area by first collecting information about activities carried out by each department and then estimating the costs of providing various services by each department. Customer needs and their reaction to the services rendered by various departments must then be determined so that standards can be set for each department. Measuring performance will not only identify problem areas; it will also highlight successes that should be rewarded.

The IRRC measures corporate environmental performance in terms of Superfund NPL sites, RCRA corrective actions requirements, the number of RCRA permit denials, the frequency of Minerals Management Service Facility shut-ins, number of TRI releases and transfers, number of oil spills, penalties under various environmental statutes, and so on.[4] In order to provide comparisons among companies of varying sizes, performance measures are expressed in terms of revenue dollars. TRI chemical releases reported to the EPA under section 313 of EPCRA are other measures of corporate performance. However, only manufacturing facilities belonging to Standard Industrial Classification codes 20 to 39 with ten or more employees are required to report. Because reports do not include production quantities, year-to-year or company-to-company comparisons of waste generation is not possible. All wastes, irrespective of their impact on humans or the environment, are added together. Because even a small quantity of certain chemicals could be highly damaging, considering quantities of waste generated without also factoring in differences in toxicity is of limited use. In addition, the reporting requirements of section 313 of EPCRA are only applicable to over 300 chemicals and few industries. In order to account for differences in toxicity, risk-weighted releases could be used to measure performance. However, toxicity data are uncertain and therefore estimates are subject to bias. Energy consumption, solid waste generation, waste-per-unit production, use of toxics regulated under various environmental statutes, and lost time and workday accident rates are other measures of corporate environmental performance.

Corporate-level performance measures could also be used at the plant level. Accident rates per employee hour, lost workday rate, energy consumption, water consumption, and amounts of waste discharged to the environment are some plant-level performance measures. Material balances can provide exact amounts of wastes that will be produced by different processes. Therefore, exploring the gap between actual waste produced and theoretical waste that should have been produced is a good starting point for improving efficiency. Material balances can provide precise measurements about inefficiencies in an organization. Typically, there may not exist a linear or nonlinear relationship between performance measures and volume of production. Therefore, converting performance measures to unit production can be misleading.

ESSENTIAL COMPONENTS FOR SUCCESSFUL BENCHMARKING

Successful benchmarking requires a champion to initiate and follow through with the program. Wastes that need to be reduced should be well defined. People of whom changes are required must be involved in the program. A company that is planning to implement benchmarking should be willing to share information. A good accounting system is essential for evaluating objectives and performance. To encourage benchmarking, top management should organize the benchmarking team, provide adequate resources and authority, provide leadership for employee training, set goals for the benchmarking study, help the team contact the partner for benchmarking, continue to monitor the performance of benchmarking process, and recognize and reward good performance.

CONCLUSION

Top management commitment is essential for successful benchmarking. The fact that benchmarking is essential to winning a Malcolm Baldridge National Quality Award for excellence has made benchmarking extremely popular among large companies. Competitive pressures are forcing companies to improve their environmental track record. Eliminating pollution is becoming synonymous with reducing costs and staying competitive. Benchmarking provides an effective method to improve environmental excellence.

NOTES

This chapter is revised from Vasanthakumar N. Bhat, "Benchmarking for Environmental Excellence," *Industrial Management*, January/February 1995, pp. 9–11. Reprinted from IIE Magazine, 25 Technology Park/Atlanta, Norcross, GA 30092 (404)449-0460. Copyright © 1995.

    1.   Robert U. Ayres, "Industrial Metabolism," in *Technology and Environment*, ed. Jesse H. Ausubel and Hedy E. Sladovich (Washington, D.C.: National Academy Press, 1989), p. 26.

    2.   Allen L. Hammond, *World Resources, 1990–91*, (Oxford: Oxford University Press, 1990), p. 325.

    3.   For information on benchmarking methodology, see Robert Camp, *Benchmarking: The Search for Industry Best Practices That Lead to Superior Performance* (Milwaukee, Wis.: ASQC Quality Press, 1989); Michael J. Spendolini, *The Benchmarking Book* (New York: American Management Association, 1992).

    4.   Investor Responsibility Research Center, *Corporate Environmental Profiles Directory* (Washington, D.C.: Investor Responsibility Research Center, 1993).

15

Green Business and Careers

The environmental industry is diverse, producing a variety of products and services. Most companies in the field deal in equipment, supplies, and services to help customers to comply with environmental regulations. According to the Organization for Economic Cooperation and Development, the world market for environmental goods and services is estimated to be $200 billion in 1990 and is likely to grow to $300 billion by the year 2000.[1] The United States accounts for about 40 percent of the world market with about 62,000 companies involved in environmental business. Between 1981 and 1992, abatement and control expenditures to combat air pollution increased from $26.3 billion to $28.6 billion. Expenditures for water pollution rose from $20.8 billion to $38.2 billion and for solid waste pollution from $10.2 billion to $36.1 billion.[2] Even though spending for pollution abatement has almost remained the same for air, expenditures on water pollution abatement have nearly doubled and on solid waste almost quadrupled during the 1981-1992 period. Total pollution abatement and control expenditures rose from $16.59 billion in 1972 to $101.95 billion in 1992.[3] Demand for a cleaner environment and stringent regulations are the major forces behind the spectacular growth of environmental industry. The global market for environmental products and services is likely to grow as more countries enact tough new laws. Therefore, significant opportunities exist around the world for environmental products and services.

DOMESTIC MARKETS

Growth rates and market sizes vary depending on how the environmental industry is defined and what segments are included. The U.S. Commerce Department presents the outlook for environmental technologies and services industry under pollution abatement equipment for media such as air, water, and solid waste. The exponential growth in environmental regulations during the last 25 years has been the major driving force behind the growth in the environmental industry. The Clean Air Act Amendments of 1990 will force the chemical, paper, petroleum, and electric power industries to make massive investments in air pollution abatement equipment. The demand for air pollution control equipment is likely to grow at the rate of $4.2 to $5.8 billion a year between 1995 and 2000.[4] The U.S. industries spent about $4 billion on air pollution control equipment and services in 1993. The market for control equipment for volatile organic compounds and nitrous oxides is estimated to grow at the rate of 46 percent from 1995 through 1997.

The Clean Water Act, Safe Drinking Water Act, Comprehensive Environmental Response, Compensation, and Liability Act, and Resource Conservation and Recovery Act are the driving forces behind the demand for water pollution abatement equipment. According to the Census Bureau, U.S. manufacturers spent $2.8 billion on water pollution equipment and $6.8 billion on water pollution operating costs in 1991.

Investments in solid waste and recycling are also rising fast. In 1991, U.S. manufacturers spent about $869 million on new solid waste equipment and $6 billion on cleanup operations. The tough regulatory constraints on landfills will reduce the number of landfills available and increase the size of individual landfills. As a result, demand for precompaction devices and transport equipment is likely to rise in coming years. This will also increase the demand for waste-to-energy plants.

Hazardous waste management provides a niche market for several small and large firms. Innovative technologies and the complexity of laws make hazardous waste management a sophisticated business. Companies are fast expanding through vertical and horizontal acquisitions. Spending for hazardous waste management services is estimated to be $17 billion in 1995, up from $14.2 billion in 1991. About 40 percent of the market for hazardous waste management services is likely to be found in federal and state governments.

Joan Berkowitz classifies the environmental industry into seven sectors, namely solid waste management, wastewater treatment, environmental engineering and consulting, hazardous waste management, remediation, lab services, and air pollution control.[5] The total revenues of these sectors are likely to grow from $56 billion in 1991 to $204 billion in 2001. The air pollution control sector is likely to grow fourteenfold and remediation eightfold during the 1991–2001 period. Environmental engineering and consulting businesses are likely to increase sixfold from a revenue of a mere $8 billion in 1991 to $49 billion in 2001.

The *Environmental Business Journal* divides environmental industry into services, equipment, and resources.[6] Services are then broken down into analytical services, water treatment works, solid waste management, and so on; equipment is subcategorized into water equipment, air pollution control equipment, and so on; and resources are divided into categories of water utilities, resources recovery, and so on. The environmental industry will grow from $170 billion in 1994 to $208 billion in 1999. Figure 15.1 presents revenues in 1994 and Figure 15.2 projects growth rates during the 1994–1999 period for the major environmental industry segments. Water treatment works, solid waste management, consulting and engineering, water equipment and chemicals, air pollution control equipment, waste management equipment, water utilities, and resource recovery are segments with revenue of more than $10 billion. Water treatment works is likely to grow by 30 percent during the next five years. However, 70 percent of the revenue in the water treatment works segment comes from public sector and budget cuts can affect growth in this segment. Solid waste management is expected to grow nearly 26 percent during the 1994–1999 period.

FIGURE 15.1
Revenues by U.S. Environmental Industry Segments in 1994
(total 1994 revenues = $170.4 billion)

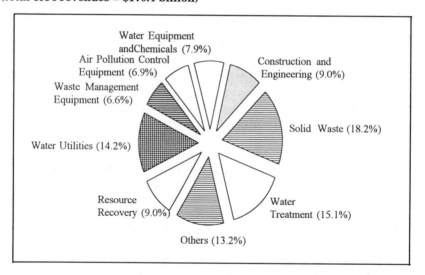

Source: *Environmental Business Journal*, April–May 1995, a publication of Environmental Business International, Inc., 4452 Park Blvd., Suite 306, San Diego, California 92116.

Environmental industry is undergoing significant changes. The regulations of the last 25 years have taught the industry how best to achieve compliance. Therefore, environmental expenditures are currently less driven by regulations and more by the need to prevent pollution. The integration of environmental industry with the economy has resulted in the former no longer being a recession-resistant industry. In

FIGURE 15.2
U.S. Environmental Industry Growth Rates by
Environmental Industry Segments, 1994–99

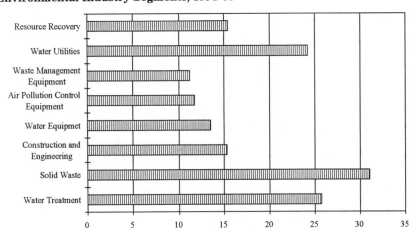

Source: Environmental Business Journal, April–May 1995, a publication of
Environmental Business International, Inc., 4452 Park Blvd., Suite 306, San Diego,
California 92116.

addition, pollution prevention and resource recovery will soon be
replacing pollution control, waste management, and cleanup as growth
areas of the future. Since recycling is displacing landfilling as a solid
waste disposal option, the demand for sorting, processing, and baling
equipment for recycling is increasing. The demand for consulting services in regulations, pollution prevention, and strategic green management is increasing while the demand for legal compliance consulting
services is wilting.

As companies become proficient in environmental technologies they
will rapidly diversify into environmental business activities. Many
chemical companies have started their own environmental businesses.
DuPont, for example, has at least ten businesses related to the environment, and its remediation services businesses are expected to grow to
$4 billion by the end of this decade. Dow Chemical has moved into the
area of polystyrene recycling, Air Products into waste-to-energy joint
venture with Browning-Ferris, Nalco into wastewater treatment
chemicals, Union Carbide into plastics recycling, and so on.[7]

INTERNATIONAL MARKETS

Public opinion polls in various countries indicate overwhelming
priority for environmental protection over economic growth. As more
environmental laws are enacted and as more countries demonstrate a

preference for cleaner technologies, worldwide demand for environmental products and services will increase. The United States, Canada, Western Europe, Japan, Australia, and New Zealand will account for about 80 percent of global demand for environmental goods and services. Developing countries and eastern European countries will become the fastest growing markets for environmental goods although they start with a low demand. The demand in these countries is for traditional technologies such as water and sewer services, solid waste disposal, and air pollution control equipment. Focus in these countries is on reducing environmental degradation rather than the cleanup of old contaminations. As the economies of Taiwan, Hong Kong, and Korea continue to grow, so do the market opportunities they offer. Public pressure to reduce pollution is strong in these regions. In addition, their environmental laws have strong roots and governments that are committed to environmental protection and remediation. Environmental spending is growing rapidly in Latin America. Mexico, Brazil, and Argentina will become major Latin American export countries for environmental goods and services. According to the Organization for Economic Cooperation and Development, the demand for environmental goods and services in the year 2000 will be $113 billion in the United States, $78 billion in Western Europe, $39 billion in Japan, and $300 billion in the world.[8] However, Environmental Business International has a more optimistic forecast. It forecasts the demand for environmental goods and services in 1997 to be $180 billion in the United States, $132 billion in Western Europe, $31 billion in Japan, and $426 billion in the world.[9] Although markets for environmental goods and services are large, most environmental projects involve construction and use of local labor. However, the substantial demand for sophisticated equipment and services cannot be met locally.

Germany, the United States, and Japan are major exporters of environmental technologies and services, having exported $11 billion, $7 billion, and $5 billion, respectively, of environmental products in 1992.[10] Global competition in environmental technologies is fierce. The United States does not have a dominant position in the field of environmental technologies. Because the United States has the largest market in the world, most U.S. companies are concentrating their efforts in the domestic market. However, U.S. firms face strong competition even in their domestic markets. Foreign firms have built strong networks in the United States through the licensing of technologies, joint ventures, and acquisitions. Five of the top ten wastewater treatment equipment manufacturers in the United States are foreign owned.[11] Several U.S. companies are dependent on foreign technologies, particularly those technologies that deal with air pollution control and incineration. U.S. environmental companies come in various sizes. Small companies find it hard to expand abroad. Innovations in environmental industry are driven by regulations. However, inflexible regulations can impede the development and use of new technologies. To help companies sell new technologies, the Environmental Protection Agency (EPA) has recently started a certification program that evaluates new technologies. The U.S. environmental industry has several strengths including a large domestic market providing economies of scale advantages, some of the most stringent environmental standards in several areas, outstanding technical expertise, technical information available from the EPA, excellent R&D capabilities, a large number of small companies, and leadership positions in several areas. However, the industry also suffers from several weaknesses including a large domestic market that discourages export, a perception that U.S. technology is expensive and inappropriate for other countries, inadequate export promotion, a slow pace of technology transfer, the inability of small firms to exploit resources, and regulatory impediments to adoption of new technologies.[12]

The United States is a major exporter of environmental equipment. Imports supplied only 21 percent of the domestic demand for air pollution control equipment in 1991. U.S. trade in environmental protection equipment in 1991 is shown in Table 15.1.[13]

TABLE 15.1
U.S. Trade in Environmental Protection Equipment, 1991
(in thousands of dollars)

Item	Exports	Imports	Balance
Air	885,620	127,995	757,625
Water	449,798	216,060	233,738
Other	344,603	222,866	121,737
Total	1,680,021	566,921	1,113,100

The United States had a trade surplus of about $1.1 billion in pollution control equipment trade in 1991, a surplus that has been increasing since 1989. In addition, during the 1989–91 period, U.S. exports increased by nearly 70 percent and imports by 45 percent. U.S. trade by country in environmental equipment in 1991 is presented in Table 15.2. It is evident that the United States has a trade balance with all countries in environmental protection equipment. However, in 1989 the United States had a trade deficit with Germany and in 1990 with both Germany and the United Kingdom.

TABLE 15.2
U.S. Trade in Environmental Protection Equipment, by Country, 1991
(in thousands of dollars)

Country	Exports	Imports	Balance
Canada	420,399	102,901	317,498
France	71,104	24,253	46,851
Germany	97,161	88,057	9,104
Japan	319,789	118,102	201,687
Mexico	94,720	18,561	76,159
Korea	57,959	4,680	53,279
China	72,427	18,863	45,726
United Kingdom	92,282	45,532	52,750
Total	1,680,021	566,921	1,113,100

GREEN BUSINESS OPPORTUNITIES

According to a 1991 *Money* magazine survey, three environmentally related businesses — Environmental Services, Recycling Center, and Asbestos Removal — fell among three of the eight fastest growing categories of yellow pages listings. Other environmental listings found in the yellow pages include air cleaning and purifying, air pollution measuring equipment, indoor air quality, pollution control and measuring, and water treatment. It is obvious from these listings that tremendous opportunities exist in green business. Paper, plastics, glass, and aluminum recycling; measuring indoor pollution and taking corrective actions; air filtration; radon testing; energy conservation products (e.g., energy-saving lightbulbs and appliances); green lawn care services; green groceries; used auto parts; and rebuilt furniture are all examples of environmental businesses.

ENVIRONMENTAL CAREERS

According to the *Environmental Business Journal*, 971,000 employees work for various segments of the environmental industry (Figure 15.3). The figure presents the distribution of employees in these various segments. Employment in three segments — solid waste, resource recovery and recycling, and engineering and consulting — accounts for more than half of environmental industry employment. In addition, several thousand employees work for federal, state, and local governments; international organizations; environmental and legal departments of companies; and nonprofit organizations.

According to Figure 15.3 one-fourth of those employed in the environmental industry are found in areas relating to solid waste management. Almost every municipality has someone working to ensure that municipal solid waste is either landfilled or incinerated. New regulations regarding landfills have created a demand for people with expertise in landfill designs. Dwindling landfills have created a demand for waste-to-energy plants. Mandatory recycling laws require implementation of recycling programs. Together, these have created a demand for well-trained civil engineers, environmental engineers, hydrologists, mechanical engineers, recycling coordinators, and logistic experts. About 40 percent of environmental jobs are in the public sector in federal, state, and local governments. Regulations are driving out smaller companies which are then acquired by larger companies. As a result, the solid waste market is dominated by a handful of large waste management companies. Private companies and consulting firms account for about 45 percent of solid waste management jobs. Nonprofit jobs in solid waste management predominantly are in recycling. A background in engineering, urban planning, business administration, and environmental science is extremely useful for a career in solid waste management.

FIGURE 15.3

**Employment in Environmental Industry, by Industry Segment, 1991
(1991 total employment = 971,000)**

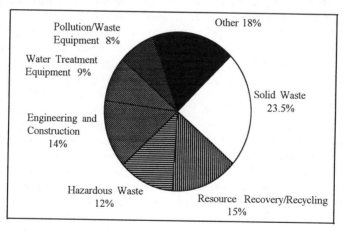

Source: *Environmental Business Journal*, April–May 1995, a publication of Environmental Business International, Inc., 4452 Park Blvd., Suite 306, San Diego, California 92116.

The Comprehensive Environmental Response, Compensation, and Liability Act, Resource Conservation and Recovery Act, and community right-to-know laws have created an unprecedented number of jobs in hazardous waste management. Seventy-five percent of these jobs are in the private sector. Hazardous waste management involves identifying hazardous wastes, meeting regulatory requirements, tracking wastes, disposing of wastes, cleaning up existing wastes, and communicating with the public. Chemists, civil engineers, environmental engineers, hazardous materials specialists, lawyers, and process engineers are some of the jobs found in the field. A number of universities offer undergraduate and graduate degree programs in hazardous waste management. Some offer hazardous waste courses in their engineering programs. A background in environmental engineering, toxicology, industrial hygiene, and remediation is extremely useful for a career in hazardous waste management.

Air quality engineers, analytical chemists, risk assessment specialists, and toxicologists are required to perform air quality management jobs. Amendments to the Clean Air Act have increased compliance requirements significantly. Federal, state, and local governments require engineers and environmental scientists to perform basic research, assess risks, and evaluate crop and environmental damages. About 80 percent of jobs in air quality management are in the private sector. Chemical and paper industries and electric power companies require air quality managers to ensure that they are in compliance with the Clean Air Act.

Water quality management involves drinking water supply and treatment, wastewater treatment, groundwater protection, and so on. Most towns have water supply companies. The Safe Drinking Water Act and the Clean Water Act have created a demand for aquatic toxicologists, civil engineers, water quality technicians, and environmental engineers. Professionals in land and water conservation produce databases of flora, fauna, ecosystems, and watershed systems; protect habitat in a watershed; and defend ecosystems against unnecessary development. Most land and water conservation jobs are found in the public sector, particularly in the Department of the Interior. Utilities and timber companies also hire land and water conservation professionals. Some job titles in land and water conservation include geographic information systems specialist, land acquisition professional, natural resources manager, and soil conservation specialist.

Most jobs in fishery and wildlife management are in the public sector. Endangered species, habitat protection, and wetlands protection programs require wildlife biologists and fishery biologists. In addition, there is a demand for botanists, data management specialists, naturalists, and wetlands ecologists.

Park rangers, park administrators, and natural resource managers are some of the job titles in the parks and outdoor recreation field. Park administrators manage parks and other outside areas, park rangers educate the public, enforce laws, and manage recreational programs. About 75,000 full-time and 40,000 part-time and seasonal employees work in the parks and outdoor recreation field. Foresters in the public sector primarily preserve forests and make them available for exploration. The federal government employs about 25 percent of all foresters. In the private sector forests are viewed as a source of wood products and are managed accordingly. Job titles in forestry include forest entomologist, forest pathologist, and land manager. Forty thousand foresters and 15,000 forestry technicians manage forests that cover approximately one-third of the United States.

Planners are required in almost all fields. Planners are required by federal, state, and city governments. Typically, a planner will need an undergraduate degree in science and a graduate degree in planning.

Communication specialists and trainers are required by governments, private companies, and nonprofit organizations. Excellent writing, speaking, and teaching skills are prerequisites for a career in this area. Education is another area in which environmental jobs are found. Even though a doctoral degree is required to teach in graduate schools, teaching jobs that do not require a doctoral degree can be found in high schools, community colleges, and nonprofit organizations.

Even though technical and specialized education can help to advance a career in the environmental field, several jobs are also available for people with a background in business administration, public administration, and liberal arts. People with skills in accounting, economics, planning, communication, and marketing are welcome in environmental fields. Approximate employment in various fields along with percentages of people working in the public, private, and nonprofit sectors is shown in Table 15.3.

TABLE 15.3
Environmental Employment, by Sector, 1993
(in thousands)

Segment	Employees	Public	Private	Nonprofit
Solid Waste	300	40	45	15
Hazardous Waste	90–120	24	75	1
Air Quality	60	13	83	4
Water Quality	143	45	50	5
Land and Water Conservation	356	75	6	19
Fisheries	18	70	15	15
Wildlife	15	50	16	34
Parks and Recreation	95	80	10	10
Forestry	55	43	45	12

Source: Environmental Careers Organization, *The New Complete Guide to Environmental Careers* (Washington, D.C.: Island Press, 1993).

Most public sector jobs in the environmental field are found in the federal government, particularly in the EPA and the Department of

Interior and its agencies, including the Bureau of Land Management, Fish and Wildlife Service, National Park Service, Bureau of Reclamation, and Geological Survey. Almost all states have environmental departments. In addition, environmental jobs can be found in state planning and transportation departments.

There are a variety of environmental jobs available in the private sector. Private sector jobs involve compliance, litigation, maintenance of pollution control equipment, coordination with consultants, laboratory work, and so on. Consulting is also an attractive area.

There are several thousand nonprofit environmental organizations. Many of them stand out in environmental fields through their research, publications, and legal actions. The work is challenging. Nonprofits hire only a few environmental professionals, but they do require people with skills in communication, writing, fund raising, lobbying, and community relations.

Education

Law schools offer courses on environmental laws and regulations. Engineering schools, which traditionally taught courses in chemical, industrial, civil, and materials engineering, now offer interdisciplinary programs in environmental engineering that integrate disciplines from biology, chemistry, and ecology. A number of universities have set up centers, institutes, and programs. Business schools have typically lagged in environmental education although courses on business ethics and business, government, and society incorporate environmental concerns. A number of business schools have recently started offering graduate business courses in environmental management.

Planning for a Career in the Environmental Field

Planning for a career in the environmental field begins with an assessment of one's interests, goals, and aptitude. While many environmental jobs do not require special skills, they tend to pay low wages. Those jobs that pay high salaries, found primarily in consulting firms and private companies, require a strong background in environmental engineering, planning, or forestry. Additional degrees in business administration, nonprofit management, or law are extremely useful. Individuals planning an environmental career must match their skills, interests, talents, and values with the jobs available. The next step is to seek out organizations. Attending job fairs and conferences, sending résumés, and networking are some ways to approach the job market. Getting in touch with the organization through alumni is another approach. Internships and temporary or seasonal employment with an organization is a good way for job seekers to get a foot in the door.

CONCLUSION

The environmental industry offers many opportunities for domestic production, exports, and careers. As environmental awareness spreads, the demand for environmental goods and services will grow. Industries are beginning to focus on pollution prevention and are selecting non-polluting rather than polluting technologies. The growth market of the future will be found in green technologies.

NOTES

1. Organization for Economic Cooperation and Development, *The OECD Environment Industry, Situation, Prospects, and Government Policies* (Paris: Organization for Economic Cooperation and Development, 1992).

2. Council on Environmental Quality, *Environmental Quality, Twenty-fourth Annual Report* (Washington, D.C.: Government Printing Office, 1995), p. 391.

3. Ibid., p. 390.

4. U.S. Department of Commerce, *U.S. Industrial Outlook 1994*, 35th Annual Edition (Washington, D.C.: Government Printing Office, 1994), p. 19-2.

5. Joan B. Berkowitz, "Outlook for the Industry," *Environmental Forum*, 9 (January–February 1992): 19–27.

6. *Environmental Business Journal* (April–May 1995), a publication of Environmental Business International, Inc., 4452 Park Blvd., Suite 306, San Diego, California 92116.

7. Karen Heller, "Environmental Services," *ChemicalWeek*, May 2, 1990, p. 26.

8. Organization for Economic Cooperation and Development, *The OECD Environment Industry, Situation, Prospects, and Government Policies* (Paris: Organization for Economic Cooperation and Development, 1992).

9. U.S. Congress, Office of Technology Assessment, *Industry, Technology and the Environment: Competitive Challenges and Business Opportunities* (Washington, D.C.: Government Printing Office, 1994), p. 17.

10. Wendell Fletcher and Rodney Sobin, "The Environmental Market for Environmental Goods and Services," *EPA Journal*, 20 (Fall 1994): 34–36.

11. U.S. Congress, Office of Technology Assessment, *Industry, Technology and the Environment*, p. 5.

12. Ibid., pp. 17–18.

13. Council on Environmental Quality, *Environmental Quality, Twenty-fourth Annual Report*, p. 337.

Appendix I:
Environmental Expenditures and Profit Margins

This appendix analyzes the link between profit margins and environmental capital expenditures. Environmental regulations are often blamed for reduced competitiveness of U.S. firms. In 1992, U.S. businesses spent about $63 billion on pollution abatement. Since it is very hard to define what environmental expenditure is, costs are likely to be estimated incorrectly. Costs associated with design, paperwork, and time spent by top management responding to environmental regulations are not likely to be included in environmental expenditures and therefore tend to be underestimated. According to a study of chemical plants by INFORM, the most frequently quoted reason for supporting waste-reduction measures during the 1985–90 period was the cost of waste disposal.[1] Other reasons cited were environmental regulations, product output, and liability concerns. Since reasons other than cost of waste disposal account for the motivation for 70 percent of waste-reduction activities undertaken by these plants, most waste-reduction activities may not result in cost reduction. However, according to the same study, nearly two-thirds of the source-reduction activities had a payback period of less than six months. The reasons for such high returns might again stem from underestimated costs.

According to Michael Porter, "national prosperity is created, not inherited."[2] Pressures from government competitors, suppliers, and customers are more likely than the availability of natural resources to make companies competitive. Consistent with this hypothesis, the countries with the most stringent environmental laws are likely to prosper. According to a survey conducted by Ann Rappaport and Margaret Flaherty, 55 percent of those surveyed disagreed with the statement that "stronger environmental regulation causes decreased productivity."[3]

Several studies have been published on the impact of environmental regulations on productivity. Based on econometric analysis of plant-level data, J. Anthony Barbera and Virginia McConnell concluded that more regulated plants and industries were likely to have lower productivity levels and slower productivity growth.[4] A recent study by Wayne Gray and Ronald Shadbegian examined plants in the paper, oil, and steel industries and concluded that those plants with higher abatement costs had lower productivity.[5]

This appendix relates companywide performance to environmental expenditures. Data on environmental expenditures have been collected for about 70 large companies belonging to the Standard and Poor Index for the years 1987, 1988, and 1989.[6] The goal is to identify the effects of environmental capital expenditures on profit margins, defined as sales minus the cost of goods sold. Regression analysis is used to determine the relationship.

EMPIRICAL FRAMEWORK

It is assumed that the production functions of businesses can be represented by a Cobb-Douglas function. The inputs consist of labor (L) and assets (K). The production function can be written as:

$$Q = AK^{\alpha}L^{\beta}.$$

Taking the logarithm of both sides of the equation, we get:

$$\log Q = \log A + \alpha \log K + \beta \log L + \varepsilon.$$

To remove fixed effects, we use the differences in variables in two consecutive years.

$$\log Q_t - \log Q_{t-1} = \alpha (\log K_t - \log K_{t-1}) + \beta (\log L_t - \log L_{t-1}) \tag{1}$$

The effects of research and development (T), advertisement expenditures (D), newness of the plant represented by age (N), and size of the plant by assets and environmental expenditures of the previous year (V) are incorporated by rewriting Equation 1 as:

$$\log Q_t - \log Q_{t-1} = \text{intercept} + \alpha (\log K_t - \log K_{t-1}) + \beta (\log L_t - \log L_{t-1}) + \gamma \log (T) + \delta \log (D) + \zeta \log (N) + \Theta \log (K_t) + \eta \log (V) + \text{dummies for the year} \tag{2}$$

Q is measured in terms of profit margin, defined as sales minus the cost of goods sold. When inputs are increased, the sales margin should also increase. Therefore α and β should be positive. R&D spending should result in increased sales margins and therefore γ should also be positive. The sign for advertisement expenditure should be positive. The sign for

N should be negative since older plants should have lower sales margins. The sign for assets should be positive because of the economies of scale effects.

RESULTS

The profit margin is regressed against assets, labor, R&D spending, advertisement spending, age of the plant, and environmental capital expenditure of the preceding year as given in Equation 1. Most of the data are from the Computstat database for the years 1987 to 1990. The environmental capital expenditure data is for the years 1987 to 1989. The regression results are as follows:

Variables	Coefficients	$Pr > t$	Coefficients	$Pr > t$
Constant	−0.148	0.419	−0.053	0.357
Assets K (diff)	0.380	0.000	0.382	0.000
Labor L (diff)	0.291	0.028	0.330	0.081
R&D T	0.004	0.206		
Advertisement Expenditures D	0.000	0.986		
Age N	−0.096	0.000		
Assets K	0.040	0.080		
Environmental Expenditures V	−0.018	0.236	−0.006	0.604
Observations	207		207	
Prob > F	0.0001		0.0001	
R^2	0.7019		0.6484	

Regressions include dummy variables for the years. The signs of the coefficients are according to the expectations. Variance inflation indicates that there is no multicolinearity. From the F-statistics, it can be concluded that the probability that all coefficients are zero is less than .05. The R^2 of .70 suggests that independent variables can explain 70 percent of the variations in the profit margin. The sign for environmental expenditure in both specifications are negative, indicating a negative relationship between environmental expenditure and profit margin. However, our confidence in this conclusion is low as the level of confidence is about .24 and .6 based on two regression specifications.

Profit margins are calculated by subtracting the cost of goods from sales. When companies make capital expenditures to comply with environmental law and they cannot pass on the extra costs to consumers, their profit margins are likely to fall. In addition, most environmental capital expenditures may be to retrofit existing equipment for the purpose of cleaning up waste. Because these additional expenses do not contribute to improvement in productivity, profit margins are likely to fall. Therefore, the relationship between environmental expenditure and the sales margin is negative.

CONCLUSION

An analysis of 207 observations relating to environmental capital expenditures over the 1987–89 period indicates a negative relationship between environmental capital expenditures and profit margin of the succeeding years. However, our confidence in this conclusion is low.

NOTES

1.   Mark H. Dorfman, Warren R. Muir, and Catherine G. Miller, *Environmental Dividends* (New York: INFORM, 1992), p. 44.

2.   Michael Porter, *The Competitive Advantage of Nations* (New York: Free Press, 1990).

3.   Ann Rappaport and Margaret Fresher Flaherty, *Corporate Responses to Environmental Challenges* (Westport, Conn.: Quorum Books, 1993), p. 153.

4.   J. Anthony Barbera and Virginia D. McConnell, "Effects of Pollution Control on Industry Productivity: A Factor Demand Approach," *Journal of Industrial Economics*, 35(2) (1986): 161–172.

5.   Wayne B. Gray and Ronald J. Shadbegian, "Pollution Abatement Costs, Regulation, and Plant-level Productivity," NBER working paper #4994, National Bureau of Economic Research, Cambridge, Massachusetts, January 1995.

6.   Investor Responsibility Research Center, *Corporate Environmental Profiles Directory* (Washington, D.C.: Investor Responsibility Research Center, 1993).

Appendix II:
Emissions, Profit Margins, and Market Values

This appendix examines whether emissions have any influence on the market value and profit margins of a company. There are several yardsticks with which to measure the performance of a company. Return on assets, return on equity, and sales growth are considered benchmarks for evaluating a company's performance. However, from the shareholders' point of view, it is the market value of the company that determines its performance. Investors consider, for example, advertisement, R&D, and capital expenditures to determine the value of a company. These expenditures are considered investments that have effects on the future cash flows of the company.

The United States spends more on environmental protection as a percentage of gross national product than any other country. Several studies have shown that environmental regulations inhibit productivity growth. According to these studies the average decline in the annual productivity growth rate ranges from zero to 0.28 percent.[1] The opponents of the environmental regulations argue that these regulations are putting Americans out of jobs and U.S. companies out of business. This appendix analyzes whether Wall Street, the most astute appraiser of companies in the world, imparts higher valuation for companies with superior emission records than for companies with inferior emission records. Using a model similar to the one presented in Appendix I, the effect of emissions is also verified.

METHODOLOGY

The objective of this study is to analyze the impact of emissions as a determinant of the current market value of a company. Cash flow, growth, risk, market share, advertising expenditures, and R&D spendings are factors that influence the market value of a company.[2] The effect of these variables must be considered to isolate the effects of emissions on the market value. Current cash flow is an important variable that determines future cash flow. Growth has a positive effect on the market value if growth has positive effects on future returns. Growth is computed by dividing current sales by sales from the previous five years. Risk is estimated using a logarithm of the ratio of 52-week high and low stock prices for each company. This is an indirect measure for volatility. Instead of market share, we use a logarithm of the sales revenue. This accounts for the effect of the size on the stock price. The R&D spendings, advertisement expenditures, and market values are normalized by dividing them by sales. Emissions are measured by summing toxic emissions into air, water, and land as reported under the Toxics Release Inventory. Emissions are normalized by dividing them by domestic sales revenue expressed in thousands of dollars. Financial data is obtained from the Compustat database; emission data is from the Investor Responsibility Research Center Corporate Environmental Profiles Directory. Financial data for 1990 and emissions data for the 1988–90 period are used.

To evaluate the effects of emissions on the market value, market values are regressed against cash flow, growth, risk, logarithms of the sales, advertisement expenses, R&D expenditures, and emissions. Market values, cash flow, advertisement expenses, and R&D expenditures are normalized using sales revenue.

To examine the effects of emissions on the profit margin, we assume that the production functions of the businesses can be represented by a Cobb-Douglas function. The inputs consist of labor (L), and assets (K). The production function can be written as:

$$Q = AK^{\alpha}L^{\beta}.$$

Taking the logarithm of both sides of the equation produces:

$$\log Q = \log A + \alpha \log K + \beta \log L + \varepsilon.$$

To account for the effects of size and emissions, the equation is rewritten as:

$$\log Q = \log A + \alpha \log K + \beta \log L + \tau \log (\text{sales}) + \delta \log (\text{emission/sales}) + \varepsilon.$$

The logarithm of profit margin (sales minus cost of goods sold) is regressed against logarithm of labor, logarithm of assets, logarithm of sales, and logarithm of emissions (emissions in pounds normalized by the sales in thousands of dollars). The mean of the data for years 1988 to 1990 and the emission data of the years 1988 to 1990 are used.

RESULTS

The regression output in which the dependent variable is market value is given below:

Variable	Parameter Estimate	$Pr > t$
Intercept	1.816	0.000
Growth	0.000	0.506
Cash Flow	14.169	0.001
Risk	−0.153	0.568
R&D	3.988	0.033
Advertisement Expenditures	2.033	0.232
Log (sales)	−0.288	0.000
Emissions	−0.015	0.120
$Pr > F$	0.0001	
R^2	0.5055	
Observations	250	

The F-value suggests that the probability of all parameters being zero is very low. The R^2 value of 0.51 indicates that the independent variables explain about 51 percent of the variations in the market value. The signs are as expected. The sign for the emission parameter is negative, suggesting a negative relationship between emissions and market value. In other words, companies with low emissions are likely to have higher market values and vice versa. However, the t-probability suggests that our confidence in this conclusion is low. In other words, the probability that companies with low emissions have higher market values and vice versa is about .88 and we could be wrong with a probability of 0.12. A recent study sponsored by the World Resources Institute indicates that firms with superior environmental performance are not likely to be less profitable than firms with inferior environmental performance.[3] This study is limited to large heterogenous companies for one year.

The results of the regression analysis in which the dependent variable is profit margin and the independent variables are labor, assets, log of sales, and emissions are given below:

Variable	Parameter	$Pr > t$
Intercept	−0.119	.702
Labor	0.108	.081
Assets	0.325	.000
Log (sales)	0.513	.000
Log (emission)	−0.050	.012
$Pr > F$	.000	
R^2	.867	
Observations	231	

The signs are as expected. The emission parameter has a negative sign, indicating companies with lower emissions have higher profit margins. We have high confidence in our results as the t-test indicates statistical significance of less than .05.

CONCLUSION

The analysis presented in Chapter 3 indicated that companies with high emissions per revenue dollar were likely to have higher penalties per revenue dollar, more spills per revenue dollar, more national priorities list sites per revenue dollar and more RCRA corrective actions per revenue dollar. This analysis indicates that, other things being equal, investors are likely to attribute higher valuation to companies with lower emissions. The second regression indicates that there is a negative relationship between emissions and profit margin. Higher-emission companies have lower profit margins. As the database consists of only 231 heterogenous companies and only mean values for the years 1988 to 1990 were tested, the results must be considered preliminary. Still, this is a significant result for companies thinking of going green.

NOTES

1.   Congressional Budget Office, *Environmental Regulation and Economic Efficiency* (Washington, D.C.: Congressional Budget Office, 1985), p. xvii.

2.   Keith W. Chauvin and Mark Hirschey, "Advertising, R&D Expenditures and the Market Value of the Firm," *Financial Management*, 22 (Winter 1993): 140.

3.   Robert Repetto, *Jobs, Competitiveness, and Environmental Regulation: What Are the Real Issues?* (Washington, D.C.: World Resources Institute, 1995), p. 20.

Selected Bibliography

Allenby, Braden R., and Deanna J. Richards, eds. *The Greening of Industrial Ecosystems*. Washington, D.C.: National Academy Press, 1994.

Ausubel, Jesse H., and Hedy E. Sladovich, eds. *Technology and Environment*. Washington, D.C.: National Academy Press, 1989.

Avila, Joseph A., and Bradley W. Whitehead. "What Is Environmental Strategy?" *McKinsey Quarterly*, 4 (1993): 53–68.

Caincross, Frances. *Costing the Earth: The Challenge for Governments, the Opportunities for Business*. Cambridge, Mass.: Harvard Business School Press, 1992.

"The Challenge of Going Green." *Harvard Business Review*, 72 (July–August 1994): 37–50.

Cohn, Susan. *Green at Work*. Washington, D.C.: Island Press, 1992.

CRS Report for Congress. *Summaries of Environmental Laws Administered by the EPA*. Congressional Research Service, Library of Congress, January 13, 1993.

Coddingon, Walter. *Environmental Marketing*. New York: McGraw-Hill, 1993.

Ditz, Daryl, Janet Ranganathan, and R. Darryl Banks. *Green Ledgers: Case Studies in Corporate Environmental Accounting*. Washington, D.C.: World Resources Institute, May 1995.

Environmental Business Journal. Environmental Business International, Inc., San Diego, California.

Environmental Career Organization. *The New Complete Guide to Environmental Careers*. Washington, D.C.: Island Press, 1993.

Fischer, Kurt, and Johan Schot, eds. *Environmental Strategies for Industry*. Washington, D.C.: Island Press, 1993.

Freeman, Harry M. *Industrial Pollution Prevention Handbook*. New York: McGraw-Hill, 1995.

Global Environmental Management Initiative. *Benchmarking: The Primer*. Washington, D.C.: Global Environmental Management Initiative, 1994.

Global Environmental Management Initiative. *Total Quality Environmental Management: The Primer*. Washington, D.C.: Global Environmental Management Initiative, 1993.

Gore, A. *Earth in the Balance*. Boston: Houghton Mifflin, 1992.

Harrison, Bruce E. *Going Green: How to Communicate Your Company's Environmental Commitment*. Homewood, Ill: Business One Irwin, 1993.

Kolluru, Rao V., ed. *Environmental Strategies Handbook*. New York: McGraw-Hill, 1994.

Levy, Geoffrey M., ed. *Packaging in the Environment*. London: Blackie Academic & Professional, 1993.

Meadows, Donella H., Dennis L. Meadows, and Jorgen Randers. *Beyond the Limits: Confronting the Global Collapse, Envisioning a Sustainable Future*. Post Mills, Vt.: Chelsea Green, 1992.

National Research Council. *Prudent Practices for Disposal of Chemicals from Laboratories*. Washington, D.C.: National Academy Press, 1983.

North, Klaus. *Environmental Business Management*. Geneva: International Labor Office, 1992.

Ottman, Jacquelyn A. *Green Marketing*. Lincolnwood, Ill.: NTC Business Books, 1994.

Powelson, David R., and Melinda A. Powelson. *The Recycler's Manual for Business, Government, and the Environmental Community*. New York: Van Nostrand Reinhold, 1992.

President's Commission on Environmental Quality, Quality Environmental Management Subcommittee. *Total Quality Management: A Framework for Pollution Prevention*. Washington, D.C.: Government Printing Office, January 1993.

Repetto, Robert. *Jobs, Competitiveness, and Environmental Regulation: What Are the Real Issues?* Washington, D.C.: World Resources Institute, 1995.

Ryding, Sven-Olof. *Environmental Management Book*. Amsterdam: IOS Press, 1992.

Schmidheiny, Stephan. *Changing Course: A Global Business Perspective on Development and the Environment*. Cambridge, Mass.: MIT Press, 1992.

Stilwell, Joseph E., R. Claire Canty, Peter W. Kopf, and Anthony M. Montrone. *Packaging for the Environment: A Partnership for Progress*. New York: American Management Association, 1991.

United Nations Environmental Programme. *Environmental Auditing*. Technical Report Series No. 2. Paris: United Nations Environmental Programme, 1990.

U.S. Congress, Office of Technology Assessment. *Green Products by Design: Choices for a Cleaner Environment*, OTA-E-541. Washington, D.C.: Government Printing Office, 1992.

U.S. Environmental Protection Agency. *Guides to Pollution Prevention: Research and Educational Institutions*, EPA 625-7-90-010, Cincinnati, Ohio: Center for Environmental Research Information, Risk Reduction Engineering Laboratory, June 1990.

U.S. Environmental Protection Agency. *Life-cycle Assessment: Investor Guidelines and Principles*, NTIS PB 93-139681. Washington, D.C.: Government Printing Office, 1993.

U.S. Environmental Protection Agency. *Life-cycle Assessment: Public Data Sources for the LCA Practitioner*. Report prepared by Battelle for the Office of Solid Waste, Washington, D.C., September 1993.

U.S. Environmental Protection Agency. *Life-cycle Design Guidance Manual: Environmental Requirements and the Product System*, EPA 600-R-92-226. Washington, D.C.: National Technical Information Service.

Walley, Noah, and Bradley W. Whitehead. "It's Not Easy Being Green." *Harvard Business Review*, May–June 1994, pp. 46–52.

Willig, John T. *Environmental TQM*. New York: Executive Enterprises Publications, 1994.

World Commission on Environment and Development. *Our Common Future*. Oxford: Oxford University Press, 1987.

Name Index

Subject Index

ABOUT THE AUTHOR

VASANTHAKUMAR N. BHAT is Associate Professor of Management
Science and Operations Management at the Lubin Graduate School of
Business, Pace University. Dr. Bhat is interested in applying his
management training and training in industrial and mechanical
engineering to promote green management.